The PIANIST'S GUIDE
to STANDARD TEACHING and PERFORMANCE CONCERTOS

Karen Beres and Christopher Hahn

*An Invaluable Resource of **Keyboard Concertos** from Baroque Through Contemporary Periods for Teachers, Students, and Performers*

Alfred Music

Los Angeles

Copyright © 2017 by Alfred Music
P.O. Box 10003, Van Nuys, CA 91410-0003

ISBN-10: 1-4706-3810-X
ISBN-13: 978-1-4706-3810-8

Library of Congress Cataloging-in-Publication Data

Names: Beres, Karen, 1969- author. | Hahn, Christopher, 1973- author.
Title: The pianist's guide to standard teaching and performance concertos :
    an invaluable resource of keyboard concertos from baroque through
    contemporary periods for teachers, students, and performers / Karen Beres
    and Christopher Hahn.
Description: Van Nuys, CA : Alfred Music, [2017] | Includes bibliographical
    references and index.
Identifiers: LCCN 2017019955| ISBN 9781470638108 (pbk. : alk. paper) | ISBN
    147063810X (pbk. : alk. paper)
Subjects: LCSH: Concertos (Piano)--Bibliography. | Concertos (Keyboard
    instrument)--Bibliography.
Classification: LCC ML128.P3 B47 2017 | DDC 016.7842/62186--dc23 LC record available at https://lccn.loc.gov/2017019955

Table of Contents

Preface

The purpose of this book is to provide a resource that promotes interest in and awareness of the available body of concerto literature written for the intermediate-level pianist. The study of piano concertos is sometimes considered a landmark goal for piano students. It is a musical genre often reserved for the most advanced students, as many of the most well-known works in the concerto genre are very challenging, beyond the skill set of intermediate-level pianists. However, numerous composers, from the early Baroque masters through contemporary composers, have created captivating works at the intermediate level. These engaging and musically satisfying compositions are the focus of this volume.

At the end of our research, we studied over 270 complete pieces, most of which contain multiple movements. We reviewed concertos that are currently in print as well as a number of out-of-print items that were procured through interlibrary loan holdings. All works annotated in this volume were personally examined, and every effort was taken to ensure the accuracy of the information provided. We chose not to identify individual works as "in print" or "out of print," as the market for in-print materials is constantly in flux.

Our desire was to create a straightforward resource. Throughout the book, composers are arranged alphabetically by last name. An index is also included listing all composers alphabetically by last name. Appendix A lists composers by historical period. For the purposes of this book, musical periods are defined as follows: Baroque (1600–1750), Classical (1750–1825), Romantic (1825–1900), and 20th Century/Contemporary (1900–present day).

The descriptions include information about publishers, tempo, key, instrumentation, and technical and musical content. Annotations highlight the challenges and inspirations of each movement, as well as pertinent stylistic features.

The compositions were written for a variety of keyboard instruments, including the harpsichord, organ, clavichord, and piano; this is specified under the title of each entry. Additionally, each entry identifies the collaborating ensemble, whether it is an original part for a second piano, an orchestral reduction for piano, or an original part for string orchestra, orchestra, band, rhythm ensemble, or even a "humming audience." Listings with the designation of "full score" do not have an available piano reduction.

The tempos provided have been taken directly from the printed edition whenever possible. For editorial markings, suggested tempos appear in this bracketed format: [♩ = ca. 120]. Tempos in parentheses, such as (♩ = ca. 120), are given by the composer.

The commentary, while intended to be objective, also naturally reflects the experiences of the reviewers. All comments are meant to guide the teacher's selection process in a positive manner, without bias or personal influence.

Jane Magrath's 10-level grading system from *The Pianist's Guide to Standard Teaching and Performance Literature* served as our model. We added a Level 10+ to accommodate upper-level concertos that contain some Level 8, 9, or 10 movements along with movements of greater difficulty. Length, technical requirements, and tempo were all considered when determining the level of a piece. As in any subjective system, some readers may hold a differing opinion of the levels assigned. Grading allows a point of comparison between the works included in this book and is not an absolute determination.

Writing this book has been a labor of love for both of us. We continue to be amazed by the vast body of literature available to students and teachers under the umbrella of "intermediate piano concertos." We hope that this volume encourages more frequent and diverse use of this wonderful genre of music.

Karen Beres, Winston-Salem, North Carolina
Christopher Hahn, Missoula, Montana

Using This Resource

Arrangement of Entries

Composers are listed alphabetically rather than by style period. For composers with more than one compositional entry, pieces are ordered by catalogue number (Op., Hob., etc.) or alphabetically by title for works without catalogue numbers. All movements have been annotated individually, with tempo, key, and level indications provided for each. In some instances, composer biographical information has been included to familiarize the reader with lesser-known composers or to summarize a composer's style and contributions to the concerto genre.

Appendices

Two appendices provide additional ways to sort the repertoire. Appendix A, *Composers by Historical Period*, presents a quick view of composers included in this book sorted by compositional period. Appendix B, *Concertos by Level*, is a comprehensive list of each movement sorted from level 1 to level 10+.

Descriptions

Descriptions are generally limited to style characteristics, technical demands, and pedagogical uses of the work. Additional comments have been included to convey benefits or drawbacks of a particular piece. When there are multiple publishers of a composition, the indication "many standard editions" is often used rather than a citation for each individual publisher.

SAMPLE ENTRY

COMPOSER (LAST, First) (Birth Year–Death Year) Country of Birth/Nationality

Background information about composer's works and/or compositional style.

Title

General background information about the specific piece (occasionally included).

(Original Instrumentation, Score Format, Publisher(s))

1. *Movement title* (metronome marking)

Description, including musical characteristics, technical challenges, and reasons for recommendation. (Key/tonality, suggested level)

Acknowledgements

In a project as large as this, there are many people to thank. First, deep gratitude is expressed to E. L. Lancaster, Senior Vice President and Keyboard-Editor-in-Chief at Alfred Music, whose vision identified the need for this particular book and whose counsel brought it to print. We are indebted to Albert Mendoza, Senior Keyboard Editor at Alfred Music, for lending his inimitable eye for detail and keen editorial skill to our manuscript. Thanks must also be expressed to Dr. Jane Magrath, Professor of Music at the University of Oklahoma. Her guidance and wisdom during our doctoral studies have allowed us to become the teachers that we are today. Her leveling system for intermediate piano music is a foundation for this book, and we are grateful for the path that she has forged.

We are indebted to the music library staff members at the University of North Carolina School of the Arts and the University of Montana for their help in obtaining concertos through interlibrary loan. Leslie Kamtman at UNCSA was a particularly invaluable resource in finding compositions that were difficult to locate.

Anna Asch, Dianne Goolkasian Rahbee, Stephen Halloran, Alexander Peskanov, and Tanya Shevtsova provided us with self-published copies of their concertos. In addition, we want to offer our appreciation to the publishers who provided us with scores, including Alfred Music, A-R Editions, The FJH Music Company, Hal Leonard Corporation, The Lorenz Corporation, and Willis Music.

Most importantly, we want to express our deep appreciation and love for our spouses and families, who have supported and encouraged us throughout this process and in every adventure we undertake.

Leveling of Literature

Based on Jane Magrath's leveling system in *The Pianist's Guide to Standard Teaching and Performance Literature.**

Reference Chart for Grading

Level   1   Walter and Carol Noona, *Little Concertino in C Major*

Level   2   George Anson, *Kid Koncerto*; Albert Rozin, *Little Concerto*

Level   3   Franz Joseph Haydn, *Concertino in C Major (Divertimento), Hob. XIV:3* (movements 1 and 3); John Thompson, *Concerto Americana*

Level   4   Isaak Berkovich, *Piano Concerto, Op. 44, for Student and Teacher* (movements 2 and 3); Matthew Edwards, *Concerto for Young Pianists* (movements 1 and 2)

Level   5   Helen Boykin, *Concerto in F Major* (movements 1 and 3); Alexander Peskanov, *Concerto No. 8, "Spring Concerto"*

Level   6   Dennis Alexander, *Concertino in D Major*; Joseph Frederick Wagner, *Concertino in G Minor* (movements 1 and 3)

Level   7   Anna Asch, *Concertino No. 1 in C Major*; Giovanni Paisiello, *Concerto No. 2 in F Major* (movements 1 and 2)

Level   8   Johann Nepomuk Hummel, *Concertino for Piano and Orchestra, Op. 73, in G Major* (movement 3); Jean Williams, *Concerto in A Minor*

Level   9   Franz Anton Hoffmeister, *Concerto in D Major, Op. 24* (movements 1 and 3); Alexander Peskanov, *Concerto No. 7*

Level   10   Johann Christian Bach, *Keyboard Concerto in E-flat Major, Op. 7, No. 5* (movement 1); Dmitri Shostakovich, *Concerto No. 2 in F Major, Op. 102* (movement 1)

Level   10+   Ludwig van Beethoven, *Piano Concerto No. 2 in B-flat Major, Op. 19* (movements 1 and 3)

---

* Jane Magrath, *The Pianist's Guide to Standard Teaching and Performance Literature* (Van Nuys, CA: Alfred Music, 1995).

Abbreviations

BWV   *Bach-Werke-Verzeichnis* or *Bach Catalogue of Works*, the numbering system for
J. S. Bach's works

ca.   circa

F.   numbering as given by Martin **F**alck, who published a catalogue of Wilhelm
Friedemann Bach's works in 1913

H.   E. Eugene **H**elm, *Thematic Catalogue of the Works of Carl Philipp Emanuel Bach*
(New Haven: Yale University Press, 1989), a thematic catalogue for the works of
C. P. E. Bach

Hob.   Anthony van **Hob**oken *Joseph Haydn: Thematisch-bibliographisches werkverzeichnis*,
the thematic catalogue of Haydn's works

IMSLP   **I**nternational **M**usic **S**core **L**ibrary **P**roject (https://imslp.org)

K.   Ludwig Ritter von **K**öchel, *Chronologisch-thematisches Verzeichnis sämtlicher
Tonwerke Wolfgang Amadeus Mozarts*, the chronological catalogue of Mozart's works

No.   number

Op.   Opus

Vol.   Volume

WoO   **W**erke **o**hne **O**puszah (works without opus number), referring to works by Beethoven
in George Kinsky and Hans Halm's *Das Werk Beethovens: Thematisch-Bibliographisches
Verzeichnis seiner sämtlichen vollendeten Kompositionen*

Wq.   Alfred **W**ot**q**uenne, *Thematisches Verzeichnis der Werke von Carl Philipp Emanuel Bach*,
a thematic catalogue for the works of C. P. E. Bach

ABEL, Carl Friedrich (1723–1787) Germany

Abel wrote six piano concertos in Op. 11, each of which is performed with seven instrumentalists: two each of Violin I, Violin II, and Viola, and one Cello. These works are musical and technical predecessors of Wolfgang Amadeus Mozart's piano concertos, but in a more concentrated, two-movement form.

Concerto in F Major, Op. 11, No. 1

(Piano and string orchestra, full score, handwritten manuscript, IMSLP)

1. *Allegro ma non troppo* [♩ = ca. 132–138]

Written in an accessible two-part texture, this movement features a right-hand melody over left-hand accompaniment patterns. Abel utilizes many Classical compositional techniques, including sequential progressions, duple versus triple subdivisions of the beat, and straightforward yet engaging themes. A short cadenza allows the student to experiment with thematic ideas in an improvisatory manner. (F major, level 7)

2. *Menuetto* [♩ = ca. 136]

The movement opens with an orchestral statement of the theme followed by the keyboard solo entrance in a two-part form with repeats. Opportunities for elaboration exist in the repetitions of the introduction as well as in the second half of the D minor section of the piece. A few cadential passages foreshadow keyboard figurations of well-known Classical compositions. (F major, level 7)

Concerto in B-flat Major, Op. 11, No. 2

(Piano and string orchestra, full score, handwritten manuscript, IMSLP)

1. *Allegro* [♩ = ca. 132]

An orchestral statement of the main theme precedes the initial solo piano entrance. The pianist serves as both a soloist and a member of the ensemble, with the keyboard part fluctuating between presentations of the themes and harmonic outlining. This movement contains an abundance of scales and arpeggios, and provides multiple opportunities to include cadenzas. (B-flat major, level 7)

2. *Rondo allegro* [♩ = ca. 92–96]

Beautiful, lyrical lines contrast with sprightly, playful moments in this rondo. The mood is stately and joyous. Keyboard solo statements are followed by a repetition of these statements supported by the orchestra. The recurrent rondo theme (of the ABACA form) facilitates solid memorization throughout the movement. (B-flat major, level 7)

Concerto in E-flat Major, Op. 11, No. 3

This delightful work would be an effective substitute for an early Mozart or Haydn concerto.

(Piano and string orchestra, full score, C. F. Peters)

1. *Allegro maestoso* [♩ = ca. 132]

Incorporating more chromatic alterations, this *Allegro maestoso* is harmonically and technically more involved than *Concerto No. 1* or *No. 2*. Duple and triple subdivisions of the beat are found in frequent alternation in this movement. Musically dramatic, it offers opportunities for nuance in performance, even into the movement's cadenza. (E-flat major, level 9)

2. *Tempo di menuetto* [♩ = ca. 132]

A regal minuet opens the second movement with a highly decorated theme and incorporates more complex rhythmic gestures and technical demands than Abel's earlier concertos. The keyboard solo and orchestral lines reflect an aristocratic air. The work moves through a number of tonal centers. (E-flat major, level 8)

Concerto in D Major, Op. 11, No. 4

These animated movements require quick fingers and balance control.

(Piano and string orchestra, full score, IMSLP)

1. *Allegro di molto* [♩ = ca. 108]

A vivacious, brisk movement presents expanded harmonic and technical involvement. Technical focus is on scale and arpeggio passages, with stepwise motion and minimal chromatic alteration. A cadenza is indicated. (D major, level 8)

2. *Allegro* [♩. = ca. 92–96]

The main theme, presented in an eight-bar phrase, is passed between the orchestra and the soloist throughout the movement. Harmonic 3rds are featured in the keyboard part. (D major, level 8)

Concerto in G Major, Op. 11, No. 5

(Piano and string orchestra, full score, IMSLP)

1. *Allegro* [♩ = ca. 132–136]

A lengthy orchestral introduction of 32 measures opens this movement. The movement is constructed in sonata form with a cadenza, and the style and technical demands of the music are reminiscent of early Mozart writing. The recapitulation of the main theme is accompanied by broken-chord triplets in place of the eighth-note motion presented in the first thematic statement of the theme. (G major, level 9)

2. *Allegretto* [♩ = ca. 80]

In ritornello form (ABACADA), this regal, dance-like sonata-rondo movement vacillates between the tonalities of G major, E minor, and G minor. A graceful touch and refined sense of musicality are required for an effective performance. (G major, level 8)

Concerto in C Major, Op. 11, No. 6

(Piano and string orchestra, full score, IMSLP)

1. *Allegro maestoso* [♩ = ca. 76]

The final concerto of Abel's Op. 11 is, appropriately, more forward-looking into the Classical period. This first movement is perhaps less musically captivating than *Concertos 3, 4,* and *5,* with the keyboard outlining harmonic structures and sequences and generally serving an accompanimental role throughout much of the movement. An opportunity for a cadenza is provided. (C major, level 8)

2. *Tempo di menuetto* [♩. = ca. 50]

A reflective movement, this minuet has less energy but is no less stunning than the other works of Abel's Op. 11. A successful performance requires a thorough understanding of the graceful minuet style. (C major, level 8)

ALEXANDER, Dennis (b. 1947) USA

Dennis Alexander's three concertos are written for solo piano with piano accompaniment. The level of the accompaniment is slightly less demanding than that of the solo part.

Concertante in G Major

(Solo piano with piano accompaniment, two pianos, Alfred Music)

1. *Maestoso/Allegro gioioso/Andantino/Presto* (♩ = 60, 120–126, 92, 132)

A grand introduction is followed by a jovial, energetic theme with sparkling figuration that demands adept fingerwork. A fully notated cadenza showcases the soloist's technical mastery. (G major, level 8)

2. *Andante amorevole* (♪ = 80)

The slow movement opens with a solo that consists of a rhythmically sophisticated theme accompanied by 7th-chord harmonies. Following the solo introduction, the theme shifts into the accompanying piano supported by arpeggiated fingerwork in the solo piano line. (D major, level 7)

3. *Rondo (Allegro giocoso/Moderato/Allegro risoluto)* (♩ = 138, [♪ = ca. 176,] ♪ = ca. 184)

Alexander's tuneful melody requires careful attention to capture its rhythmic complexity and mixed meters. Glissandos add an exciting element to the solo part. The *Allegro risoluto* may be particularly challenging, with its combination of a rapid tempo and quick choreographic shifts. (G major, level 9)

Concertino in D Major

(Solo piano with piano accompaniment, two pianos, Alfred Music)

Allegro giocoso/Andante cantabile (♩ = 120, 60)

Written in one continuous movement, this piece winds its way through a number of key changes to a driving finish. Piano I involves chromaticism, with arpeggios divided thoughtfully between the hands. The work demands quick, clean fingerwork and clear articulation. According to the publication's introduction, Alexander wrote this composition to include "brisk passagework designed to fit neatly in the hand, seamless harmonic shifts, thrilling meter changes, and built-in technical fireworks." (D major, level 6)

Imperial Concertante

(Solo piano with piano accompaniment, two pianos, Alfred Music)

1. *Allegro molto* (♩ = 108)

Traversing four octaves of the piano in its first 24 measures, this work combines a quick pulse with offbeat harmonic punctuations supporting a catchy theme. Alexander creates a seamless transition into a lyrical middle section, with the solo piano taking the melodic lead. Cross-hand arpeggiations support the second piano's following statement of the theme. Note distributions between the hands are carefully marked, and chords are written in positions that should be familiar to the intermediate pianist. Sixteenth-note flourishes in the second piano add to the solo piano's dazzling ending. (C major, level 5)

2. *Andante cantabile* (♩ = 84)

Following traditional bass-line motion, this movement's theme is attractive and technically accessible. Challenges for the pianist include syncopated pedaling and shaping of long melodic lines. The short duration of the work, along with its limited hand span demands and slower tempo, make this middle movement slightly less difficult than the preceding one. (G major, level 4)

3. *Presto brilliante* (♩ = 120–126)

Sprightly and bright, this concluding movement grabs the listener with its syncopations, staccato articulation, and straightforward themes. Some quick passagework will require special attention, although its patterned construction will ease the learning process. Lush harmonies replete with 7th chords, many in the piano accompaniment, make for a lovely contrasting B section. Restatements of the original theme, moving rapidly through more remote keys, usher in the final section, which builds to a brilliant close. (C major, level 4)

ANDERSON, Garland (1933–2001) USA

Concertino for Piano and Orchestra in F Major

The orchestral reduction (level 7) for this work is more demanding than the solo line. Pairing of a more experienced student as the orchestra with a less skilled pianist as the soloist may be effective.

(Piano and orchestra, two piano reduction, American Music Edition)

1. *Allegro* [♩ = ca. 120]

This movement, which uses an unexpected harmonic palette, is not technically demanding for the soloist. A study in broken chords, the solo is ideal for a student who has done technical work with root-position and inverted triads. (F major, level 5)

2. *Andante* [♩ = ca. 76–80]

A four-part chorale texture contrasts with outlined arpeggios in this slow movement. Unanticipated chord resolutions can be challenging for the soloist to memorize. Pedal indications in the score may defy what the ear suggests to be most clear. (F major, level 4)

3. *Allegro vivace* [♩ = ca. 126]

Perhaps the most attractive movement of this *Concertino*, the *Allegro vivace* presents a quirky melody in limited hand ranges. The lack of large intervals in the hand make this movement accessible to students with smaller hand spans. The B section utilizes steadily moving 16th notes at the same quick tempo. (F major, level 5)

ANDERSON, Leroy (1908–1975) USA

Concerto in C Major

While the first and third movements of this concerto are beyond the technical scope of the intermediate pianist, the second movement can stand alone as a marvelous concerto option for the intermediate-level performer. A little-known work, Anderson's concerto was performed only three times before he withdrew it from his list of works in 1970. After his death, his family agreed to publish the piece.

(Piano and orchestra, two piano reduction, Woodbury Music Co.)

2. *Andante/Allegretto* (♩ = 96, 138)

A wide-reaching arpeggio figure introduces the movement and sets the tone for the lush main theme. The melody displays characteristics of a love song from a classic musical. The contrasting middle section is in a quicker *Allegretto* with a rousing mood. This energetic theme combines with a closing arpeggio to end the work. (E major, level 9)

ANSON, George (1903–1985) USA

George Anson composed two intermediate concertos for two pianos. In his *Kid Koncerto*, the pianos are equally matched in difficulty. In the *Miniature Concerto*, Piano II is more challenging than Piano I.

Kid Koncerto

This concerto is a great choice for a student who is exploring how to portray divergent moods.

(Two pianos, Willis Music Co.)

1. *I'm Mad—fast and furious* [♩ = ca. 148–160]

This work incorporates some parallel scales and contrary scales, mostly within a one-octave range. Chords in clusters, as well as triads in root position, combine with quick hand-position shifts at the octave. Students should have an easy time capturing the mood of this movement. (C major, level 2)

2. *I'm Sad—slowly and sadly* [♩ = ca. 80–86]

Piano I features a mostly homophonic, two-note texture that provides an opportunity for working on sustaining a long melodic line. The middle section uses three- and four-voice chords to create a thicker texture. (F major, level 2)

3. *I'm Bad—quite lively—mischievous* [♩ = ca. 160]

The musical motion in this movement shifts between the hands in highly chromatic patterns. To achieve the appropriate range of sound, dramatic dynamic changes are required. (C major, level 2)

4. *I'm Glad—with plenty of vim and vigor* [♩ = ca. 120–126]

The texture of this movement is simple, with hands playing in unison or in imitation. Piano I presents a jaunty theme accompanied by rhythmic chords in Piano II. A white-key glissando adds sparkle to the solo keyboard line. (C major, level 2)

Miniature Concerto in C Major

(Two pianos, Sam Fox Publishing Co.)

1. *Swing Along—brisk march tempo* [♩ = ca. 156]

The soloist's hands are in unison at the octave throughout this opening movement. Syncopated rhythms and the execution of occasional pedal indications are the main challenges. (C major, level 2)

2. *Short and Sweet—slow and singing* [♩ = ca. 88]

A lyrical melody is traded between the hands of Piano I. Limited cross-hand work and pedaling are required by the soloist. (F major, level 2)

3. *A Laughing Matter—quickly—lightly* [♩ = ca. 120]

Technical requirements for Piano I include left-hand imitation of right-hand gestures and hands-together root-position triads. (A minor, level 2)

4. *A Bit Jazzy—not too fast—very rhythmic* [♩ = ca. 120–126]

The syncopated melody of Piano I is played between the hands, mostly in a unison statement at the octave, but sometimes punctuated by a few moments where the hands are separated by a 10th. (C major, level 2)

ARNE, Thomas Augustine (1710–1778) Great Britain

Arne is known as one of the most important English composers of the 18th century. Charles Burney, the author of *A General History of Music,* wrote, "The melody of Arne at this time forms an era in English Music; it was so easy, natural, and agreeable to the whole kingdom, that it had an effect upon our national taste."[1]

Concerto No. 4 in B-flat Major

Written for Arne's precocious son Michael, this concerto may be performed as an ensemble for keyboard, two oboes, and strings, or for keyboard alone with orchestral cues played by the soloist.

(Keyboard and string orchestra, full score, Oxford University Press)

1. *Con spirito* [♩ = ca. 66–70]

A galant opening movement features idiomatic keyboard writing. Challenges include trills and tricky fingering patterns in the right hand. Pianists should be exact in distinguishing between the ♫ rhythms and the triplet figures that occur frequently in close proximity. A fully notated cadenza remains within the scope of the rest of the movement in difficulty, yet offers a showcase moment for the pianist through its use of sequences and diminished-7th chords. (B-flat major, level 6)

2. *Minuetto* [♩ = ca. 116]

Opening with a large orchestral introduction that includes keyboard continuo, this dance movement highlights the keyboard in the second half of the work. The soloist uses the main theme, previously stated in the strings and oboes, by varying it rhythmically and adding figurative decoration without any orchestral presence until the final five measures of the movement. This is an atypical concerto in its construction, with very limited interaction between the soloist and orchestra other than the final cadential gesture. (B-flat major, level 6)

3. *Giga: Moderato* [♩. = ca. 104]

A fun frolic with imitation throughout, this movement contains *tutti* and keyboard solo sections that alternate, testing the performer's ability to easily shift roles from continuo to soloist. The patterns fit the hand well, as no large chords or intervals are involved, making this work an excellent choice for a student with small hands. It maintains an exciting drive from the first orchestral statement to the ending cadence. (B-flat major, level 7)

ASCH, Anna (b. 1933) USA

Anna Asch taught for 41 years at the University of Wisconsin-Washington County. Her interest in concerto performance, and the inspiration of her students, led her to focus her creative abilities on the composition of 12 single-movement concertinos for intermediate and early advanced students. The orchestrations for these compositions were written by her late husband, Albert. Many of her concertos are self-published by her company AJA Arts.

Concertino No. 1 in C Major

(Two pianos or solo piano with orchestra, Hal Leonard)

Allegro—Molto legato e espressivo (♩ = 120, 54)

Written in one continuous movement, this first concertino has a tonal shift to the parallel minor in the midst of frequent chromatic alterations. The contrasting middle section is modal. Many root-position chords are present in this work. Large contrasts exist between the bigger moments of non-legato playing and the *Molto legato e espressivo* section. The solo piano plays octaves in both hands, requiring solid octave expansion. An energetic, compelling coda brings the piece to a gratifying end. (C major, level 7)

---

[1] Charles Burney, *A General History of Music, from the Earliest Ages to the Present Period* (1789), Vol. II (New York: Dover Publications, 1957), 1004.

Concertino No. 2 in C Major

(Two pianos or solo piano with orchestra, Hal Leonard)

Gently flowing, espressively—More lively (♩ = 80, 138, 160)

One of Asch's easier concertos, this piece contains broken triads and patterns in open 5ths and octaves which constitute the majority of the soloist's left-hand work. Repetition of the opening theme occurs a number of times, varying the tonal center, with the last statement doubled between the hands at the octave. The most challenging section involves harmonic 3rds in the right hand over a left-hand accompaniment. The number of musical ideas is relatively small, but the elements present are well developed. They include a variety of articulations, dynamic shaping, and tempo indications, requiring an intense focus on musicality. (C major, level 4)

Concertino No. 3

(Two pianos or solo piano with orchestra, AJA Arts)

Lively/Moderato/Adagio/Legato espressivo (♩ = 120, ♩. = 100, ♩ = 60, 50)

A study in chords, this *Concertino* uses three main contrasting ideas: a march-like opening, a theme in 2nds, and a lyrical middle section. An introspective mood is introduced in the *Adagio* section. A theme with flowing forward motion, presented at the *Legato espressivo* section in the second piano/orchestra, is accompanied by rich, arpeggiated figuration in the solo line. The writing is patterned and falls within a limited range of the keyboard; this limitation is balanced by a wide musical palette, juxtaposing energy with cantabile playing, staccato with expressive legato, and a broad range of tempo indications. (C minor, level 5)

Concertino No. 4

(Two pianos or solo piano with orchestra, AJA Arts)

Allegro—Flowing and expressive (♩ = 126, 80)

This single-movement work is written in three distinct sections with excellent opportunities to focus on artistic playing. In each of the three sections, the soloist performs both the melody and the accompaniment. The first theme is a sprightly, diatonic melody. In the second theme, the solo piano plays a sonorous accompaniment with arpeggiated harmonic figuration, supporting an enchanting melody that is assumed by the soloist midway through the section. The third theme is built on energetic open 5ths traded between the pianos or between the piano and the orchestra. It is then combined with the opening theme in a transition leading to the finale. (D major, level 6)

Concertino No. 5, Festive March

(Two pianos or solo piano with orchestra, AJA Arts)

[♩. = ca. 82–86]

More challenging than Asch's other works, this *Concertino* possesses a distinct march-like style that may be particularly attractive to an intermediate student. Modal and quartal (4th) harmonies are abundant. The secondary theme in a major key is based on a rhythmic motive introduced in the solo piano and later picked up by the second piano/orchestra. A short cadenza leads to a final iteration of the opening theme. No tempo indication is provided by the composer. (C modal, level 7)

Concertino No. 6, Aquila Variations

(Two pianos or solo piano with orchestra, AJA Arts)

Intro—Allegro; theme (♩ = 132, 140)

A unique concerto in Asch's output, the *Aquila Variations* was originally composed as a piano solo. Aquila, a constellation in the northern sky, is the inspiration for this set of variations based on the well-known

"Twinkle, Twinkle, Little Star." Arranged as a concerto, the piece consists of an introduction, theme, and nine variations. Instructions from the composer indicate that students may play the variations of their choice, personalizing both the length and difficulty of the concerto based on these decisions. (C major, levels 5–6)

- *Variation 1*—Piano II/orchestra has the melody with Piano I playing a broken-chord accompaniment. (♩ = 132)
- *Variation 2*—The Piano I melody is juxtaposed with D-flat and A-flat scale patterns. (♩ = 132)
- *Variation 3*—The distinctive motive suggests a horn call. (♩. = 80)
- *Variation 4*—No clear melody is present; focus is on harmonic elements. (♩ = 112)
- *Variation 5*—The jaunty theme is full of chromatic neighbor notes. (♩. = 140)
- *Variation 6*—A straightforward presentation of the theme is accompanied by lush 7th-chord harmonies. (♩ = 120)
- *Variation 7*—This variation is a chromatic study, with the theme present only in only bits and pieces. (♩ = 44)
- *Variation 8*—The solo piano plays the theme in the left hand, juxtaposed with the children's tune "White Coral Bells" in Piano II/orchestra. (♩ = 120)
- *Variation 9*—The theme played by the piano is paired with the orchestra playing the melodies "Amazing Grace" and "How Brightly Shines the Morning Star." (♩. = 80)
- *Finale*—Titled "Atar—Brightest Star in Aquila," this piece concludes with a rushing flurry of 16th notes leading to a triumphant end. (♩ = 140)

Concertino No. 7, Taratina

(Two pianos or solo piano with orchestra, AJA Arts)

Allegro Brilliante; slower and expressive (♩ = 132, 76)

Less melodic than some other Asch concertos, this work contains sections based on whole-tone and modal constructs. Rhythmic and technical emphasis is on two versus three subdivisions of the beat between the hands of Piano I, as well as between the two parts (Piano I and Piano II/orchestra). The contrasting middle section paints a dreamy picture, though still with two versus three at the heart of the solo statement. Ensemble challenges exist. The main challenge of this work lies in reading the music, and once the student has established the feel of each gesture, the technical difficulties are minimal. (C-sharp whole-tone/pentatonic, level 8)

Concertino No. 8, Jubilation!

(Two pianos or solo piano with orchestra, Hal Leonard)

Exuberant—Freely (♩. = 108, ♩ = 52)

More substantial in length than many of the other Asch concertos, this composition requires aggressive playing. Driving, energetic rhythms and frequent tenutos for melodic projection are characteristic of this piece. Octaves are required in both hands of Piano I, in addition to four- and five-note chords. Though the piece sounds difficult, its highly patterned construction makes it easy to read. (D modal, level 8)

Concertino No. 9, Dana's Delight

(Two pianos, AJA Arts)

Flowing and expressive [♩ = ca. 108–120]

A good introduction to Asch's concerto writing, this piece is one of her most accessible concertos. Both parts are equally matched in difficulty. The work is comprised of a few repeated sections:

- A reiterated arpeggio progression divided between the hands.
- A single-note melody, doubled in octaves.
- A section containing root-position and first-inversion triads in a repeated pattern.

All sections are unified under one overall tempo. (A minor, level 4)

Concertino No. 10

(Two pianos or solo piano with orchestra, AJA Arts)

Andante/Adagio/Scherzando (♩ = 66, 50, ♩. = 100)

This concerto has an expansive sound, with frequent use of open intervals. The melody of the opening section begins in 5ths. This theme is repeated by the orchestra and combined with arpeggiated patterns by the soloist. A secondary theme continues the open 5ths, allowing for an introspective, thoughtful sound. The required speed of fingerwork in the *Scherzando* may challenge the student, but figures are written very pianistically. Repeated ideas and new themes are presented with increasing difficulty through more intricate rhythms or increased coordination demands. Both parts are equal in difficulty. (F minor, level 8)

Concertino No. 11

(Two pianos or solo piano with orchestra, AJA Arts)

Expressively/Detached and lively (♪ = 80, ♩ = 76)

A tuneful, artfully woven piece, this *Concertino* begins with a brief introduction followed by a melody in the solo piano. A secondary theme based on open 5ths has a toccata-like feel and an edgier, more energetic sound. A familiar chord progression (I–vi–ii–V) provides the foundation for the main theme. Fluctuations between $\frac{4}{4}$ time and $\frac{5}{4}$ time abound, although they are not always clearly indicated. The piece has a poignant feel and would be an excellent concerto for a thoughtful, expressive student. The second piano part (level 8) is slightly more technically advanced than Piano I. (F major, level 7)

Concertino No. 12

(Two pianos or solo piano with orchestra, AJA Arts)

Moderato/Più mosso (♩ = 65, 110)

A touching, emotional work, this final *Concertino* opens with a rising and falling bass line and requires careful voicing of tenutos in the upper left-hand line. The tender melodic line grows and develops with support from chordal textures, combining in canon with a statement of the theme in Piano II/orchestra. The piece moves into a contrasting section, incorporating the tune "I Wonder As I Wander" with a sentimental waltz. As the Piano II/orchestra continues with the "I Wonder As I Wander" theme, the solo piano expands into 6ths and scales in an accompanimental role. A few cadenza-like moments in Piano I lead to a return of the opening melody. Teachers and students may consider this piece as an effective holiday recital selection, based on its inclusion of the familiar Christmas melody. (C major, level 8)

AVERY, Stanley (1897–1967) USA

An American composer who embraced a light, natural writing style, Avery is best known for his vocal music, church music, and energetic patriotic or civic music.

Concertino on Familiar Tunes for Young Players in F Major

Piano II is written at a more demanding technical level (levels 6–8) than the Piano I part.

(Piano and school orchestra, two piano reduction, Theodore Presser)

1. *Allegro moderato* (♩ = 104–126)

Based on the tunes "Twinkle, Twinkle, Little Star," "All Through the Night," and "London Bridge," this opening movement showcases writing with both hands in unison at the octave, sprinkled with a few doubled 3rds. A passage with an improvisatory feel includes figuration and trill terminations that could serve as an introduction to the concept of a cadenza. (F major, level 4)

2. *Andante* (♩ = 100–108)

Based on the tune "Drink to Me Only with Thine Eyes," a simple melodic statement, supported by rich harmonies in Piano II, provides the foundation for this movement. Perhaps the most appealing of the three movements, the *Andante* would also be effective as a stand-alone piece for performance. (B-flat major, level 3)

3. *Allegro con brio* (♩. = 132–152)

Based on the tunes "Pop Goes the Weasel" and "Three Blind Mice," this playful movement includes interwoven lines. (F major, level 3)

BACH, Carl Philipp Emanuel (1714–1788) Germany

Carl Philipp Emanuel Bach, the second son of Johann Sebastian Bach, was one of the most influential and productive composers of the 18th century. As Wolfgang Amadeus Mozart remarked to the important Viennese aristocrat and patron Gottfried van Swieten, "Bach is the father. We are the children."[2] C. P. E. Bach became one of the leading representatives of the *Empfindsamer Stil* or "sentimental style." Most of his concertos were written for advanced keyboardists, while Wq. 23 and the six Wq. 43 "Hamburg Concertos" stand as exceptions, having been written instead for amateur players. Freedom in the choice of solo keyboard instrument is suggested by Bach's designations *für das Clavier* or *per il cembalo*.

Keyboard Concerto in D Minor, Wq. 23 (H. 427)

(Piano and orchestra, full score, Boosey & Hawkes)

1. *Allegro* [♩ = ca. 132–136]

Operatic in nature, this movement features dramatic statements and recitative-like interruptions. Technical requirements encompass scales and arpeggios, occasional stationary chordal flourishes using 32nd notes, and various ornaments including trills, turns, and mordents. Some patterned sections are easier to play than they appear in the score. (D minor, level 9)

2. *Poco andante* [♪ = ca. 76–80]

Phrasing and shaping captures the character of this refined movement. It is more musically mature than it is technically demanding. Before the last phrase, the pianist has an opportunity to include a short improvisatory statement. (F major, level 7)

---

[2] Hans-Günter Ottenberg, C. P. E. Bach, translated by Philip J. Whitmore (New York: Oxford University Press, 1987), 191.

3. *Allegro assai* [♩ = ca. 144]

This movement reflects the unstable mood characteristic of the *Sturm und Drang* style. Long strains of *arpeggio* fragments decorated with lower neighbor-note gestures present one of the most formidable tasks for the pianist. The quick tempo, coupled with more advanced technical requirements, moves this *Allegro assai* beyond level 10. (D minor, level 10+)

Keyboard Concerto in D Major, Wq. 27, (H. 433)

(Harpsichord and Orchestra, full score, A-R Editions)

1. *Allegro* [♩ = ca. 108]

A triumphant orchestral introduction, replete with trumpets, horns, winds, and timpani, ushers in the first keyboard statement, appearing in a much more reserved style. Bach writes very idiomatically for the keyboard, using sequential passages typical of the period. Little interaction between the soloist and takes place; rather, the two entities trade statements, with sparse orchestral support added at times to the keyboard lines. A short cadenza, restatement of the opening keyboard theme, and final orchestral flourish round out the *Allegro*. This sprightly concerto movement poses challenges in speed and figuration within a harmonic framework typical of the period. (D major, level 9)

2. *Siciliana* [♪ = ca. 86–90]

A master study in ornamentation, this slow, languid movement displays only a few moments where the melody winds its way without a detour of a turn, trill, mordent, or other embellishment. In a melancholic mood, the work embraces frequent chromatic notes which tug at the line in a state of longing. The tempo and contrapuntal texture, combined with a full complement of ornamental symbols, elevate the movement to a more advanced level. (D major, level 9)

3. *Allegro* [♩ = 116–124]

Brushing off the mood of the preceding movement, the *Allegro* sparkles with a driving pulse. Requiring crystal-clear finger control, the keyboard writing ventures through long-winding technical passages constructed on scalar and arpeggiated figures. Several statements of the opening keyboard theme serve as guideposts on the journey through the movement, supported by pulsing eighth notes in the bass. Unison orchestral statements begin and end this upbeat work. (D major, level 9)

Keyboard Concerto in F Major, Wq. 43, No. 1 (H. 471)

(Piano and orchestra, full score, handwritten manuscript, Sächsische Landesbibliothek)

1. *Allegro molto* [♩ = ca. 132]

Bach opens this first movement in rousing fashion with an energetic orchestral introduction and a theme that recurs numerous times throughout the *Allegro*. The piece is musically accessible with expected figurations and a left hand relegated almost exclusively to a single-note texture. A cadenza lends a moment of fantasy to this exciting movement, whose final thematic statement leads abruptly and unexpectedly into the contrasting *Andante*. (F major, level 9)

2. *Andante* [♪ = ca. 66]

A highly decorated work, rife with longing, the *Andante* is musically demanding in its use of non-harmonic embellishment. Its complexity lies in stylistic nuance rather than technical demands. A winding chromatic line in the right hand weaves questioningly into the *attacca tutti* of the concluding *Prestissimo*. The short length of the movement, in which the solo statements are combined with several orchestral interludes, limits soloistic demands. (F minor, level 8)

3. *Prestissimo* [♩ = ca. 108]

A delightful and occasionally frenetic romp in **⁶⁄₈**, this final movement feels toccata-like in the hands. The writing is angular with arpeggiated outlines carving wide, quickly moving swaths over several octaves of the keyboard. Running lines build to exciting climaxes that are greeted with surprising silences before diving headlong into the unanticipated harmony of the next passage. Soloist and orchestra spur each other on through the *Prestissimo*, incessantly driving ahead toward the final notes. Stamina in rapid passagework is a major challenge of this energetic finale. (F major, level 10+)

Keyboard Concerto in D Major, Wq. 43, No. 2 (H. 472)

(Piano and orchestra, full score, Edition Heinrichshofen)

1. Allegro di molto/Andante [♩ = ca. 132, 90]

A brilliant orchestral statement in triple meter opens this unpredictable movement. The statement is interrupted by the piano's first solo declaration, a lyrical section in duple meter that stands calmly against the exciting surrounding sections. Bach's writing is punctuated by dramatic dynamic effects and shifts in tempo and key. This work is a graceful vehicle for a sparkling technique. (D major, level 10+)

2. Andante (sostenuto) [♩ = ca. 42]

A somber orchestral *tutti* introduction, anchored by a weighty bass line, opens this slow movement in E minor. In an unforeseen twist, the solo piano appears in E major with an elegant, easy feel. The mournful E minor center returns after a 16-measure interlude, followed by a second solo keyboard piano appearance in G major that transcends the darkness of the minor introduction. This is a touching, emotional movement that demands mature shaping of lines free from a strict metronomic feel. (E minor, level 10)

3. Allegretto [♩. = ca. 50]

Accessible to the intermediate pianist, this movement includes a piano solo line that teems with arpeggios and scalar passages in lilting ⅜ time. The frequent exchange of ideas between soloist and orchestra creates an engaging musical interplay. A sense of drama is cultivated through the surprise appearance of the opening theme in D minor, while measures of rest in both parts build heightened expectations for the listener. (D major, level 9)

Keyboard Concerto in E-flat Major, Wq. 43, No. 3 (H. 473)

(Piano and orchestra, full score, Edward Schuberth & Co.)

1. Allegro [♩ = ca. 92–96]

The orchestra is featured in lengthy *tuttis*, including a 32-measure opening and a substantial interlude. Piano writing is straightforward, with repeated left-hand chords, scalar passages, and limited ornamentation. A brilliant sequential section beginning at measure 101 is an exciting vehicle for the pianist without being overly demanding technically. The crisp, "clean" writing resembles that of Mozart, though without the technical requirements found in his concertos. (E-flat major, level 8)

2. Larghetto [♩ = ca. 60]

A controlled lyricism filled with typical cadential gestures characterizes this movement. Only 59 measures long, the movement is rather terse. It does not effectively stand on its own, since the movement's non-resolution on the dominant moves immediately into the third movement. (C major, level 6)

3. Presto [♩ = ca. 124]

Long, sustained scalar runs are interrupted by momentary arpeggiated chord structures, demanding a high level of technical control and focus. This animated movement puts clarity, a characteristic of the Classical era, on full display, but is just beyond the skill level of intermediate concerto literature. (E-flat major, level 10+)

Keyboard Concerto in C Minor, Wq. 43, No. 4 (H. 474)

(Piano and orchestra, two piano reduction, Boosey & Hawkes)

1. *Allegro assai* [♩ = ca. 132]

Elegant writing is accentuated with dotted rhythms in the orchestra. Being a short movement with minimal ensemble difficulty between the piano and orchestra makes this an appropriate choice for a less-experienced intermediate pianist. Both the soloist and the orchestra have featured sections, although the keyboard often takes a lead role. The first movement leads directly into the second movement through a transition full of chromatic drama. (C minor, level 7)

2. *Poco adagio* [♪ = ca. 52]

This beautifully simple and concise slow movement provides a lovely contrast to the first movement during a full concerto performance. (G minor, level 6)

3. *Tempo di menuetto/Allegro assai* [♩. = ca. 60]

This great work achieves a characteristic minuet feel, with opportunities to explore ornamentation on sectional repeats and in a short improvisatory section before the return of the *Allegro assai*. A written-out cadenza for the keyboard occurs prior to the final orchestral declaration. It is attractive as a stand-alone movement. (E-flat major, level 9)

Keyboard Concerto in G Major, Wq. 43, No. 5 (H. 475)

(Piano and orchestra, full score, Edward Schuberth & Co.)

1. *Adagio/Presto* [♪ = ca. 70, ♩. = ca. 80]

The *Adagio* section is brief and only present in the orchestral introduction. The first keyboard entrance announces the *Presto* section with continuous runs and arpeggiated figures. Technical demands of this movement push it above the level of intermediate repertoire. (G major, level 10+)

2. *Adagio* [♪ = ca. 70]

This brief movement dissipates the energy of the preceding one and builds anticipation for the upcoming final movement. It is pleasant but less effective without its companion movements. (G major, level 7)

3. *Allegro* [♩ = ca. 126]

This stately movement, in an easily flowing ¾ meter, frequently uses triplet subdivisions. The keyboard part is presented in short phrases juxtaposed with orchestral answers. With an appropriate foundation of scales in a student's technique, many of the passages will be immediately accessible. Remaining challenges include broken arpeggios and limited ornamentation found mainly at cadence points. A stunning moment occurs when the pulse moves into 16th-note subdivisions. It is a great choice as a Classical concerto movement. (G major, level 10)

Keyboard Concerto in C Major, Wq. 43, No. 6 (H. 476)

(Piano and orchestra, full score, handwritten manuscript, Sächsische Landesbibliothek)

1. *Allegro di molto* [♩ = ca. 132]

Regal in nature, the highly decorated opening theme of this movement does little to foreshadow the technical demands of the running 16th-note passagework in the development section. In the middle of the work, a key center of E minor lends a serious tone to the previously sunny theme. The cadenza section is less challenging, simply offering the opportunity for the soloist to restate themes without orchestral support. Hints of the following movement appear in some striking harmonies and key shifts, with the *Allegro* ending on a half cadence in D minor. (C major, level 9)

2. *Larghetto* [♩ = ca. 60]

While juxtaposing theme statements in minor with immediate iterations in the relative major, this movement maintains its regality throughout. Pianistic demands are limited, focusing mainly on ornamentation. Interesting key twists end this movement on a C Major harmony, ushering in the final movement without delay. (D minor, level 8)

3. *Allegro* [♩ = ca. 108]

A lively, simple theme is presented in double exposition in the final movement. The solo statement is shared with the orchestra, with the two entities trading short phrases of the theme. Interesting pointillistic textures contrast with singable lines in the keyboard writing, while similar iterations in various keys may present memorization challenges. This movement fits well in the hands and provides for a very satisfying conclusion to the entire concerto, although it could also stand on its own. (C major, level 9)

BACH, Johann Christian (1735–1782) Germany

Johann Christian Bach was the 11th and youngest of J. S. Bach's sons. His Op. 7 concertos helped to establish the Classical concerto form, with more limited ritornellos and a simpler keyboard style. Opus 7, numbers 1–4 have two movements, while numbers 5–6 expand into the three-movement form. J. C. Bach partnered with Carl Friedrich Abel (1723–1787) in a series of subscription concerts in London, the first of their kind and forerunners of the modern classical concert series.[3] J. C. Bach's music served as an important influence on young Mozart.

Keyboard Concerto in D Major, Op. 7, No. 3

(Piano and orchestra, two piano reduction, Summy-Birchard)

1. *Allegro con spirito* [♩ = ca. 132]

With high energy, this movement contains a broad harmonic range and multiple sequences in the development section. The left hand often plays broken octaves and repeated two-note chords, simplifying the coordination challenges for the pianist. (D major, level 9)

2. *Allegretto/Rondeau* [♩ = ca. 66]

A dainty *Rondeau* section with an elegant dance theme, this movement is composed in ABACA form with refined decoration of the main theme through trills. Rhythmic complexities include duple versus triple subdivision of the beat, as well as some tricky coordination aligning the hands in the ornamentation. (D major, level 8)

Keyboard Concerto in E-flat Major, Op. 7, No. 5

This concerto is a "miniature masterpiece," according to Maurice Hinson's *Music for Piano and Orchestra*.[4]

(Piano and orchestra, full score, Edizioni De Santis)

1. *Allegro di molto* [♩ = ca. 126–132]

The first movement, regal in nature, is anchored by a captivating theme. Harmonic twists and turns are frequent, as the movement follows an adventurous harmonic path. Bright figuration forecasts the style and vivacity of Mozart's early music. A cadenza is included. (E-flat major, level 10)

2. *Andante* [♪ = ca. 82]

Cantabile writing is featured, displaying the influence of Italian opera. Attention is required to shape its long, lyrical lines and to project its deep emotional sense. (C minor, level 9)

[3] *Grove Music Online*, s.v. "Bach, Johann Christian," by Christoph Wolff et al., accessed September 21, 2016, http://www.oxfordmusiconline.com/subscriber/article/grove/music/40023pg15.

[4] Maurice Hinson, *Music for Piano and Orchestra* (Bloomington, IN: Indiana University Press, 1981), 14.

3. *Allegro* [♩. = ca. 100]

The final movement is a vivacious romp with a highly playful spirit. Swift 16th-note passages combine chord outlines with a melodic presence, requiring careful voicing. The energy and drive continue throughout the movement to its very last cadence. (E-flat major, level 10+)

Keyboard Concerto in D Major, Op. 13, No. 2

(Piano and orchestra, two piano reduction, C. F. Peters)

1. *Allegro con spirito* [♩ = ca. 132]

Mozartian in sound, this movement's technical challenges include broken 3rds and a left-hand melody involving trills in the development section. It is an excellent choice for an advancing student who wants to play a Classical concerto, possibly a substitute for Haydn's popular *D Major Concerto, Hob. XVIII:11.* (D major, level 10)

2. *Andante* [♩ = ca. 62]

This charming theme-and-variations movement is an excellent vehicle to display technical facility and musical maturity. The variation treatments include trills, a left-hand Alberti bass pattern with melodic elaboration, 16th-note triplet arpeggios and scales in the right hand, and a pairing of the melody with a left-hand, broken-chord accompaniment. (G major, level 10)

3. *Allegro non tanto* [♩ = ca. 80–86]

This third movement is not as challenging as the previous two movements. Short statements in the keyboard alternate with the orchestra and offer moments of rest for the soloist. An interesting section in D minor/F major requires greater musical expression in timing and color than the lighthearted D major thematic statements. (D major, level 8)

Keyboard Concerto in B-flat Major, Op. 13, No. 4

(Piano and Orchestra, full score, C. F. Peters)

1. *Allegro* [♩ = ca. 132]

This movement in sonata form includes a double exposition. Classical-style elements include left-hand Alberti bass, arpeggio figurations, scalar passages, and sequential harmonic motion. Possessing a more attractive main theme than the first movement of Op. 13, No. 2, this work could be played as a separate Classical concerto movement. (B-flat major, level 9)

2. *Andante* [♪ = ca. 96]

This movement's focus is on double-3rd melodic right-hand motion. Its style is refined, with an included cadenza, but less effective if performed on its own. (E-flat major, level 9)

3. *Andante con moto* [♩ = ca. 126]

A lovely, regal texture is a prominent characteristic of this highly decorated movement. Accurately executing the dotted rhythms is a potential challenge, particularly with the addition of a left-hand Alberti bass support. Variations of the theme in 3rds and 6ths become highly chromatic, with rapid figuration in repeated triplets. It is a charming, brief movement that lasts approximately three minutes. (B-flat major, level 10+)

BACH, Johann Sebastian (1685–1750) Germany

Johann Sebastian Bach's harpsichord concertos were the first works written for solo keyboard and orchestra. It is likely that these keyboard concertos were composed for performance by the Collegium Musicum that Bach directed in Leipzig. All of the solo keyboard concertos appear to have been arranged from cantatas or concertos previously written by Bach for other instruments.

Keyboard Concerto No. 2 in E Major, BWV 1053

Historians speculate that this concerto was arranged in the 1730s and is based on cantatas that Bach had written in 1726.

(Harpsichord and string orchestra, full score, Dover Publications)

1. *Allegro* [♩ = ca. 92]

This regal movement is energetic but not overly challenging due to the tempo. The quickest motions are flourishes or ornaments. The enchanting dance feel requires delicate musical nuance for full effect. In limited three-part *da capo form*, the piece is technically a level 10, but the scope and length of the movement project it to a higher level. (E major, level 10+)

2. *Siciliano* [♪ = ca. 90]

This musically mature work is evocative of Bach's great aria "Erbarme Dich" from the *St. Matthew Passion.* Sparse string accompaniment—mostly eighth notes on the strong beats—make the piece accessible for a younger orchestra. The keyboard left hand is never more active than eighth notes or quarter notes pulsed in octaves, below an intricate right-hand line weaving melodic figuration. It is a short movement of only four pages. (C-sharp minor, level 10)

3. *Allegro* [♩. = ca. 69]

A highly energetic movement, this *Allegro* constantly demands clarity and control at a brisk tempo. Features include brilliant keyboard writing with faster figures often arpeggiated or in short scalar bursts. The piece moves along in an incessant 16th-note flow. The minor-key middle section provides a contrasting mood to this otherwise sunny, animated movement. (E major, level 10+)

Keyboard Concerto No. 4 in A Major, BWV 1055

Scholars believe that this concerto is likely based on a lost concerto for oboe d'amore.

(Harpsichord and string orchestra, full score, Dover Publications)

1. *Allegro* [♩ = ca. 108–112]

This *Allegro* is shorter than many other Bach movements. The main melodic theme, comprised of descending arpeggiated figures, is followed by a lilting continuation. Sequences and frequent recurrences of the main theme ease the pianist's technical challenges and theoretical demands of the movement. This appealing piece is a worthy choice for a student who has a predilection for Bach's keyboard writing. (A major, level 10)

2. *Larghetto* [♪ = ca. 92]

A strikingly melodic work, this movement is filled with stunning beauty and glimpses of deep passion. The relatively short length makes it accessible for the intermediate student. Effective performance requires a developed sense of musical shaping and nuance. (F-sharp minor, level 9)

3. *Allegro ma non tanto* [♪ = ca. 136]

Written in *da capo form*, the sprightly opening section shifts to a contrasting minor before returning to the stately opening theme in A major. It features idiomatic Baroque writing complete with sequential passages and running scale work, but with less incessant movement for the pianist than in many of Bach's faster movements. (A major, level 10)

Keyboard Concerto No. 5 in F Minor, BWV 1056

This concerto is often performed by solo violin or oboe with orchestra. The outer movements are written in ritornello form, alternating sections of *tutti* with solo sections.

(Harpsichord and string orchestra, full score, Dover Publications)

1. *Allegro* [♩ = ca. 76–80]

The basis of the main theme involves cascading triplets and recurrences of the F minor arpeggio, which give this movement a sense of perpetual forward motion, continuously pulsing with a sense of drama and pathos. The left hand alternates between a repeated rhythmic motive and even eighth notes. The limited hand span and florid linear writing are great for a student who is not ready for the thicker textures characteristic of concertos from later musical periods. The movement demands a solid sense of pulse, an appropriate awareness of forward motion, and diligent attention to articulation. (F minor, level 10)

2. *Largo (Arioso)* [♩ = ca. 66]

This aria also appears as the opening sinfonia in Bach's *Cantata, BWV 156*. The pianist's right hand winds its way over a foundation of steady eighth notes in the left hand and pizzicato eighths in the strings. The sustaining quality of the violin or oboe melody does not translate well to the harpsichord; consequently, the melody uses elaborate embellishment. Although only 21 measures long, this is one of Bach's most enduring melodies. (A-flat major, level 8)

3. *Presto* [♩. = ca. 66]

A dialogue between the hands in the keyboard differs from the usual continuo role of the left hand in Bach's concerto writing, leading to increased coordination challenges. The perpetual motion creates a movement that is exciting and technically demanding. A short opportunity for a cadenza flourish appears before the final thematic statement. (F minor, level 10+)

Keyboard Concerto No. 7 in G Minor, BWV 1058

This work is an adaptation of the *Violin Concerto in A Minor, BWV 1041*.

(Harpsichord and string orchestra, full score, Dover Publications)

1. *Allegro* [♩ = ca. 92]

Written in ritornello form, this movement combines a somber mood with rigorous rhythmic drive. The keyboardist plays continually for the relatively short duration of the work. Involved left-hand lines create a thick texture and powerful drive and are skillfully interwoven with the right hand. Keyboard gestures are intricately designed, with more frequent turns and changes of direction, and without the clear scalar and arpeggiated patterns seen in the earlier concertos. (G minor, level 10+)

2. *Andante* [♩ = ca. 60]

A serene, lyrical theme is built on a four-measure ostinato bass figure and interspersed solo episodes. The movement's dignified spirit is propelled by the buoyant feel of the pulsing keyboard bass along with support from the strings. The juxtaposition of textures suggests the use of terraced dynamics for clarity. (B-flat major, level 9)

3. *Allegro assai* [♩. = ca. 116–120]

The opening statement of the fugue in the orchestra is later reiterated by the keyboard. A grand spirit encompasses a thick texture in both the keyboard and orchestra. A cadenza-like flourish is provided during a fermata. Sections of 16th-note figures present the challenges of speed, dexterity, and clarity to the performer. (G minor, level 10+)

BACH, Wilhelm Friedemann (1710–1784) Germany

Wilhelm Friedemann Bach, the eldest of J. S. Bach's sons, was renowned for his improvisatory skills at the keyboard. He utilized more of his father's contrapuntal style in his writing than did his three musical brothers, but also combined counterpoint with an improvisatory sense of his own, as reflected in his *Keyboard Concerto, F. 41*.

Keyboard Concerto in D Major, F. 41

(Piano and orchestra, two piano reduction, Edition Steingräber)

1. *Allegro* [♩ = ca. 86]

The opening movement is elegant and highly decorated. Intricate embellishments may be a deterrent to teaching or studying this movement. Maintaining a steady pulse throughout the flourishes can be daunting. The straightforward main theme incorporates a dancing, syncopated element and returns a number of times, providing a helpful foundation. Ornaments occur in both hands but fall within the scope of a relatively small hand span. A cadenza is included. (D major, level 10)

2. *Andante* [♪ = ca. 86]

Short solo statements, supported by sparse orchestral outlines, alternate with full orchestral declarations of the melody. Fairly straightforward in a rhythm free from decoration, this work is emotionally reflective movement with two-note slurs throughout. (B minor, level 8)

3. *Presto* [♩. = ca. 69]

Energetic without hurrying, this final *Presto* easily slips into the feeling of one pulse per measure. Showy arpeggio outlines in stationary chord positions sound more impressive than they are technically demanding. There is a flashy nature to the keyboard lines, due to their speed and variety of technical patterns, including cross-hand work, single lines quickly flowing between the hands in close choreography, and numerous flourishes. With its attractive improvisatory edge, this concerto movement is a potential showcase piece for the late intermediate student. (D major, level 9)

BAUER, Marion Eugénie (1882–1955) USA

American Youth Concerto in G Minor

Originally written for piano and orchestra in 1943, the *American Youth Concerto* was arranged for two pianos in 1946. The second piano part is more difficult than the first.

(Piano and orchestra, two piano reduction, G. Schirmer, Inc.)

1. *Majestic—Light and crisp—Very brilliant* (♩ = 108, ♪ = 176 / ♩ = 88, [♩ = 120])

This movement evokes a Russian spirit with rich sonorities and stately rhythms. The form, which includes a cadenza and extended orchestral interludes, provides a satisfying concerto experience. This movement can be effectively programmed and performed without the other two. (G minor, level 8)

2. *Dignified, yet lyric* (♩. = ca. 69)

The work begins with an orchestral statement full of extended harmonies. Piano I has thinner textures, but a few six-voice chords contribute to a lush jazz feel. (C major, level 7)

3. *Humorous—Quiet—Vivacious* (♩ = 100, ♩ = 100, ♩ = 120)

A rhythmically syncopated theme with limited technical demands propels the opening forward into a more reverent, calmer section. An extended trill in Piano I builds to a driving and dramatic final resolution. (G major, level 8)

BEARD, Katherine (1926–1990) USA

Concerto in D Minor

(Piano and orchestra, two piano reduction, Wynn Music)

Allegro moderato (♩ = ca. 126)

In one continuous movement, this short concerto showcases uncomplicated writing with few surprises. Clear articulation and dynamic directions as well as efficient fingering suggestions are provided, and the work is well designed for the player with small hands. With imitation used as the main compositional device in the development section, the technical demands are thoughtfully controlled in the solo. The Piano II part (level 4) is slightly less difficult. This is a solid choice as a straightforward intermediate concerto. (D minor, level 5)

BEETHOVEN, Ludwig van (1770–1827) Germany

The five standard piano concertos of Ludwig van Beethoven are well-known works, presenting formidable challenges that place most of them outside of the limits of this volume's grading system. Only three of his works for piano and orchestra fall within the technical and artistic range of this book and are annotated here.

Concerto in E-flat Major, WoO 4

This concerto appears to be Beethoven's earliest existing work to incorporate the orchestra and is assumed to have been composed at the young age of 14.

(Piano and orchestra, full score, A-R Editions)

1. *Allegro moderato* [♩ = ca. 96–116]

Opening with a galant orchestral theme, this movement showcases the pianist in flurrying passages of scalar and arpeggiated figures, double 3rds, and broken octaves, among other technical demands. The opportunity to craft a cadenza opens up possibilities for greater personal expression. The relatively unknown status of this work, combined with the charming themes and stately feel of the movement, make this an attractive option for a pianist venturing beyond the scope of intermediate repertoire. (E-flat major, level 10+)

2. *Larghetto* [♪ = ca. 50]

An intimate work with an emphasis on expressive and rhythmic demands, this slow movement showcases a number of passages that contain decorated 64th-note runs. The occasional embellishment in triplets adds interest to the delicate line. In binary form, the work contains a middle section of technical display over slowly punctuated orchestral harmonies. Emotional depth is necessary to communicate the beauty of this *Larghetto* amid the dense notation. (B-flat major, level 10)

3. *Rondo [Allegretto]* [♩ = ca. 66–72]

The opening rondo theme, with its infectious youthful spirit, permeates an intricately designed final movement in ABACADAEA form. Alternating with the "childlike" melody are sections of arpeggiated figurations with a Hungarian-style theme in E-flat minor that inserts a few moments of gravitas into an altogether exuberant work. (E-flat major, level 10+)

Rondo in B-flat Major, WoO 6

Originally intended as the final movement of Beethoven's *Piano Concerto No. 2 in B-flat Major*, this rondo displays attributes of Mozart's writing style.

(Piano and orchestra, full score, Breitkopf & Härtel)

Allegro/Andante [♩. = ca. 100, ♪ = ca. 50]

Beethoven's *Rondo* is a vivacious, innocent work published posthumously. The *Andante* section inserted into this one-movement work lends an effortless feel to the piece. Some rapid Alberti bass patterns cover a 10th, challenging the left-hand span of the player. A cadenza is included. A brief but thrilling *Presto* section concludes the work. Editions vary in the presence of octaves versus single notes, as well as the inclusion of improvisational gestures at transition points in the solo part. A more recent Henle edition based on the musical text in the *Beethoven Complete Edition* simplifies the second piano (orchestral reduction) part. (B-flat major, level 10)

Piano Concerto No. 2 in B-flat Major, Op. 19

Beethoven's *Piano Concerto No. 2* was actually written first, but it was published after *Piano Concerto No. 1*. The shortest of Beethoven's five concertos, this one is similar to Mozart's style, particularly in the first and third movements.

(Piano and orchestra, two piano reduction, many standard editions)

1. *Allegro con brio* [♩ = ca. 132]

A distinct military style is first heard in the lengthy orchestral introduction. A sparkling keyboard sound is necessary. Technical requirements include Alberti bass figuration, extended scale work, and some challenging chromatic passages. The interspersed statements of a lyrical theme offer technical rest to the pianist. The indicated cadenza was written almost nine years after Beethoven completed the concerto. A truly great work, it is more appropriate for the inspired advanced pianist. (B-flat major, level 10+)

2. *Adagio* [♩ = ca. 80]

An introspective, cantabile movement, the *Adagio* is known more for its stunning musical line than its technical fireworks. The main challenge for the pianist is to maintain the relaxed pulse throughout the movement despite the numerous subdivisions of the beat. (E-flat major, level 10)

3. *Rondo—Molto allegro* [♩ = ca. 108]

In this seven-part rondo (ABACABA), Beethoven utilizes shifting accents to purposefully skew the pulse of the ⁶⁄₈ meter and create a persistently angular sound. Technical control is essential in quick broken octaves, scales, and arpeggiated right-hand gestures. The C section of the rondo contrasts with a Hungarian gypsy spirit in G minor to create a lighthearted and sparkling gem. (B-flat major, level 10+)

BENNETT, Richard Rodney (1936–2012) Great Britain

Party Piece for Young Players

(Piano and orchestra, full score, Universal Edition)

Allegro giocoso—Andante, alla 'blues' (♩ = 96, ♩ = 76)

Based on jazz and blues, this one-movement work combines energetic, rhythmic playing with more improvisational-style sections. The opening jazz segment features a theme doubled at the octave between the hands. This theme moves into the winds, accompanied by arpeggiated figures that utilize neighbor tones. Occasional improvisatory flourishes and piano solos fit easily into the hand yet sound impressive. A 13-measure piano solo introduces the *Andante, alla 'blues.'* This middle section incorporates triplets into the rhythmic framework, which was previously based on duple figures.

Lengthy orchestral rests and intricate rhythms with syncopation, triplets, and grace notes require careful counting and keen attention to properly execute all piano entrances. The opening key of G major is embellished with numerous chromatic alterations, as is the blues section in four flats. This attractive piece sounds more complicated than it is to play due to its orchestration and rhythmic construction. (D modal, level 5)

BERKOVICH, Isaak (1902–1972) Ukraine

Piano Concerto, Op. 44

(Two pianos, Associated Music Publishers)

1. *Allegro* [♩ = ca. 96]

Berkovich's spirited opening movement has limited technical demands but many stylistic considerations. A contrasting B section requires performers to shape a lyrical line, and a short cadenza leads to a brisk but grand conclusion. (C major, level 5)

2. *Andante con moto* [♩ = ca. 60]

A beautifully wistful melody, with harmonic support from Piano II, makes the work sound more mature than it is challenging. It is an excellent study in trading roles between being soloist and providing chordal support as the accompaniment. (A minor, level 4)

3. *Allegro assai* [♩ = ca. 80]

This playful last movement has a solo line that requires mostly single-note playing in each hand. The innocent nature, attractive melodies, constrained technical demands, and a high level of stylistic integrity all contribute to the work's accessibility to younger pianists. This movement is a wonderful selection as an introduction to the concerto genre. (C major, level 4)

BERNSTEIN, Seymour (b. 1927) USA

Concerto ("for Our Time")

As explained by the composer in his introductory notes, this composition "is a strange mixture of the tragic and the absurd, and of a whole range of moods and feelings in the way we react to the world around us."

(Two pianos, Schroeder & Gunther)

1. *Gathering—Con brio (exuberantly)* (♩ = 88)

Fun and spirited, this movement maintains a vigorous tempo throughout. Tempo shifts are frequent, although the underlying energy of the work slows only in the laid-back "South Bristol Rag" portion of the movement. Melodic octaves transform into parallel 6ths, and quick figures alternate between the hands. The rag section involves thicker chords and a constantly moving bass line. The movement culminates in a *Presto* section that sends a musical wink to the listener. (D major, level 8)

2. *Lament for Vietnam—Adagio* (♩ = 50–54)

The rhapsodic writing of this *Lament* feels improvisational, as the soloist has the opportunity to repeat several figures as many times as desired. Tempo fluctuations add to the free feeling, as do the frequent changes of key center. This *grandioso* movement serves as a true arrival point, thicker in texture and more Romantic in nature than the rest of the concerto. The end drifts away in soft, slowly dying statements that are traded between Pianos I and II. (Polytonal, level 7)

3. *Jubilation—Allegro con brio* (♩ = ca. 132)

This entertaining movement is full of vim and vigor. Attentive listeners will notice snippets of familiar piano works: Clementi's *Sonatina in C Major, Op. 36, No. 1*; the *Musette in D Major* from the *Anna Magdalena Bach Notebook*; Stephen Foster's *Swanee River*; and Mozart's *Sonata in C Major, K. 545*. Rapid register shifts test the soloist. Frequent accidentals, quickly changing tonalities, and close choreography combine to raise the difficulty level of this movement above the previous two. Highlights include a well-written cadenza and an appearance of *Rhapsody in Blue*—leading to a spirited finish. (C major, level 9)

BLACHER, Boris (1903–1975) Germany

Blacher, who was born in China, was an important figure in the musical life of Berlin after World War II. His writing successfully combines traditional musical forms with more modern techniques. His later music employs modified serialism and electronics.

Piano Concerto No. 1, Op. 28 in A Minor

(Piano and orchestra, full score, Bote and Bock)

1. *Adagio—Presto* (♪ = 84; ♩. = 184)

The orchestra presents the opening *Adagio* section, while the piano ushers in the *Presto* section. The movement features through-composed writing, full of energy and vitality, but with little motivic cohesiveness. The piece fluctuates between repeated tones and moving lines, occasionally interrupted by angular figures comprised of the interval of a 4th. (Atonal, level 10+)

2. *Andante* (♩ = 60)

A nostalgic introduction in the piano finishes with a rhythmic jazz bass line in 10ths. After an orchestral interlude, the piano re-enters with greater Romantic fervor. In the *poco più mosso*, the piano adopts a single-note melody line with a relaxed jazz feel before returning to the introduction. This movement flows directly into the final movement. (Atonal, level 9)

3. *Allegro* (♩ = 184)

This exciting movement is characterized by grace-note decorations and scampering pianistic figures. Technical challenges include complex metric and rhythmic shifts, thick textures, and quickly changing registers. (Atonal, level 10+)

BOBER, Melody (b. 1955) USA

Concertino in Dance Styles

(Solo piano with piano accompaniment, two pianos, Alfred Music)

1. *Festive Dance—Joyously* (♩ = 92)

A bugle-like motive introduces this upbeat, attractive opening movement. Writing is mostly in two-line texture, with the right hand playing a singable melody over left-hand support. The second piano fills out the texture, making this work sound much more impressive than with the solo part alone. Repetitive figures in five-finger patterns repositioned in various octaves encourage mobility and accessibility for the early intermediate student. (C major, level 1)

2. *Shadow Waltz—Mysteriously* (♩ = 144)

Contrasting with the energy of the first movement, Bober's nostalgic waltz makes use of chromatic neighbor tones to liven up C minor five-finger-pattern melodies throughout this work. Traversing six octaves of the keyboard, the recurring opening melody varies in dynamic strength, embodying the "shadow" nature of the title. The solo line gains support from thick chordal structures and running eighth-note gestures in the second piano. These require careful listening in order to maintain alignment of the two parts. Syncopated pedaling is indicated and necessary to bring out the smooth legato required through many position changes. (C minor, level 2)

3. *Celtic Jig—With energy* (♩. = 92)

Dancing rhythms, combined with open 5ths and C major five-finger melodies, bring excitement to this final movement. Double-3rd motion in the solo right hand, combined with damper pedal use, will be the challenging part of this work for most players. Students will likely enjoy the choreography, which moves over seven octaves of the keyboard in this rousing finale. (C major, level 2)

BOUTRY, Roger (b. 1932) France

Berceuse and Rondo, pour Piano et Orchestre in A Minor

(Piano and orchestra, two piano reduction, Éditions Aug. Zurfluh)

1. *Berceuse—Andantino/più mosso* (♩ = 84–92, 116)

Based on simple thematic lines and sparse texture, this haunting movement in ABA form utilizes ostinato patterns to stunning effect. Attention to shaping long phrases is necessary, as is a careful balance between piano and orchestra. This is an effective movement for a less experienced but musical pianist. (A minor, level 3)

2. *Rondo—Allegro* (♩. = 66–72)

The opening theme is singable and easily identifiable in its numerous appearances in both the piano and the orchestra. This accessible composition presents a great opportunity to focus on memorization, as its clear chordal outlines are evident throughout the work. Idiomatic piano writing that makes excellent use of limited technical resources creates a delightful piece with a triumphant ending. (C major, level 4)

BOYKIN, Helen (1904–1997) USA

Concerto in F Major

A Classical study, this concerto is effective as a predecessor to studying the easiest Haydn concerto movements.

(Two pianos, Associated Music Publishers)

1. *Allegro* [♩ = ca. 112–120]

A charming and lighthearted movement, the *Allegro* offers predictable harmonic motion and characteristic Classical gestures. The composer has included frequent righthand arpeggios that are limited to a two-octave range, and can be redistributed easily between the hands for less adept players. A clearly defined sonata-allegro form makes this a great choice for a study in memorization. (F major, level 5)

2. *Andante* [♩ = ca. 76–84]

Written in ABA form, this reverent chorale is technically accessible. It does present a voicing challenge within the soloist's chords and between the Piano I and Piano II, which both occupy the same register. Lovely harmonic motion abounds, and the chordal texture in Piano II is contrasted with a singing melody over an arpeggiated accompaniment in Piano I. (C major, level 4)

3. *Allegro vivace* [♩ = ca. 120–132]

Rondo form (ABACA) organizes the final movement of this concerto. The animated A theme alternates with a cheerful melody in 3rds and a homophonic chordal statement. This memorable movement is a showcase for rapid finger technique and a great option for a student with small hands. (F major, level 5)

BOZZA, Eugène (1905–1991) France

Sicilienne et Rondo

(Piano and orchestra, two piano reduction, Éditions Aug. Zurfluh)

1. *Sicilienne—Tranquille* [♩. = ca. 50–56]

This lovely, pensive movement in §§ features a lilting piano melody often doubled at the octave. Two scalar passages, one purely chromatic and the other stepwise, present the biggest technical challenges. The orchestral reduction sets the harmonic tone for the movement, providing a foundation of lush 7th and 9th harmonies over the melody. (A modal, level 2)

2. *Rondo—Allegro moderato* [♩ = ca. 120–126]

Full of energy, this frolicking work has a childlike spirit. The movement opens with a simple melody doubled between the hands, barely reaching beyond a 5th. The following sections involve coordination similar to that of Hanon exercises and motives divided between the hands. Displaced accents shift the downbeat at times, while drastic dynamic changes capture the joking nature of the piece. A brilliant ending caps off an enchanting movement. (F major, level 4)

BURGESS JR., Henry (ca. 1720–1770) Great Britain

Burgess wrote six keyboard concertos that were published around 1740 and display the distinct influence of George Frideric Handel.

Concerto No. V in G Minor

(Harpsichord/organ and orchestra, full score, Concordia Publishing House)

1. *Andante—Allegro* [♩ = ca. 75, 116]

The opening *Andante* is most effective when played with double-dotted eighth notes. An energetic *Allegro* continues for the remainder of the movement. Keyboard and orchestra trade melodic statements, and the keyboard takes on a continuo role when the two parts play simultaneously. Constant 16th-note passages are the core of the keyboard writing, with the running notes often outlining chords, scalar passages, or sequences. Clarity and precision in finger technique are necessary. This is the most lengthy and challenging of Burgess's three movements. (G minor, level 8)

2. *Largo* [♩ = ca. 50]

This movement is an orchestral interlude with keyboard continuo and an oboe added to the string ensemble. No solo keyboard solo sections are present. (B-flat major, level 5)

3. *Allegro* [♩. = ca. 72]

The rapid tempo and large intervals (compared to the stepwise motion of the first movement) are the main technical challenges of this final movement. However, patterns fit easily in the hand. The keyboard and orchestra work together in the opening measures and at sectional cadences; at other times, the keyboard solo alternates with short orchestral statements. This precise, compact movement is appropriate for a student with strong fingers. (G minor, level 8)

BUSH, Geoffrey (1920–1998) Great Britain

A Little Concerto on Themes by Thomas Arne in D Minor

The themes used in this *Little Concerto* are taken from Thomas Arne's *Harpsichord Sonata No. 4 in D Minor* (first and second movements), *Harpsichord Sonata No. 7 in A Major* (first movement), and the *Concerto No. 3* (organ solo movement). Effective as a whole, the movements are too short to stand successfully on their own.

(Piano and string orchestra, full score, Elkin & Co.)

1. *Andante* [♩ = ca. 42]

A tragically beautiful main theme is ornamented with mordents, trills, and appoggiaturas. Hints of Baroque style permeate the composition, but the thick, dramatic chord work toward the end of the piece reveals the 20th-century origins of the composer. Bush does an exceptional job of weaving the melody back and forth between the piano and orchestra, altering small elements to propel the movement to a powerful finish. (D minor, level 7)

2. *Allegro* [♩ = ca. 108]

An energetic movement, this *Allegro* drives to the final chord. Agile fingers are required to negotiate the passagework, which includes trill decorations of the melodic line. This sparkling movement is attractive in its simplicity and a potential showpiece despite its short length. (A major, level 7)

3. *Siciliana* [♪. = ca. 38]

Suspensions amplify the tension and release of the phrases in this concise, lovely movement. The pianist reiterates two eight-measure phrases eloquently introduced by the orchestra. Attention to held notes is imperative to create the natural push and pull of the phrases. The movement concludes with an unresolved D minor harmony in the piano, leading directly into the final movement. (F major, level 5)

4. *Con spirito* [♩ = ca. 120]

A glittering finale to this concerto, the last movement sparkles with running 16th-note lines, trills, and predictable yet effective cadences. Careful planning and execution of fingerwork is crucial in the more rapid passages. It is an exuberant finish to the work, particularly when preceded by the *Siciliana* movement. (E major, level 8)

CAMBINI, Giuseppe Maria (1746–1825) Italy

Cambini was an Italian violinist who travelled to Paris with his string quartet, becoming well known in the 1770s and 1780s. He was a prolific composer of instrumental music for Parisian concert settings and concentrated his efforts on chamber works for strings or winds. He also wrote several symphonies, some vocal works, and solo concertos for violin or piano. Unfortunately, many of his works have been lost. Thoughtful phrasing and interpretive instructions have been added in this edition of his keyboard concertos. Parts for instrumentalists are included with the piano score.

Concerto in B-flat Major, Op. 15, No. 1

(Piano and orchestra, full score, Ricordi)

1. *Allegro* [♩ = ca. 120]

Alive with the vitality of the Classical era, the first movement opens with an extended orchestral introduction. The piano is showcased with minimal orchestral support and relies on clarity in extensive scalar passages, doubled 3rds, and bass accompaniment patterns typical of the period. An opportunity for a cadenza is indicated, but none is provided in this edition. This lovely concerto movement will beautifully showcase precise playing. (B-flat major, level 9)

2. *Rondo—Allegro ma non troppo* [♩. = ca. 92]

The piano introduces the primary theme, a breezy tune that alternates three complete statements of the melody with two contrasting sections. Filled with sparkling runs and rolling passagework, the music requires careful fingerings for clarity as none are provided. A cadenza preceding the final statement of the theme is mentioned but not included. This piece is appropriate for students who are ready for the early Haydn and Beethoven sonata movements. (B-flat major, level 10)

Concerto in G Major, Op. 15, No. 3

(Piano and orchestra, two piano reduction, Ricordi)

1. *Allegro* [♩ = ca. 144]

A captivating work, this opening movement can easily stand on its own. It features charming themes, alive with enthusiasm and energy, and is full of distinctive Classical-style characteristics. Statements of the theme in a minor key add contrast and depth to the mood. Technical challenges include control of scales, arpeggios, and broken octaves. A full cadenza is provided by the editor. (G major, level 9)

2. *Rondo—Allegretto* [♩ = ca. 92–96]

This vivacious gem includes lightness and humor sprinkled with drama. An editorial cadenza presents a show-case moment for the pianist, demanding a wide range of technical and musical control. Challenging for the pianist, this movement is a delight to learn and to perform. (G major, level 10)

CANNON, Philip (b. 1929) Great Britain, born in France

Concertino for Piano and Strings

Only 12 minutes long, this concerto is most effective when played in its entirety.

(Piano and string orchestra, full score, Novello Co., Ltd.)

1. *Allegro molto vivace* (♩ = 104)

Similar to Bartók's style, Cannon's writing brims with irregular lines, primitive rhythmic feeling, and open 5ths. The rapid tempo may be a challenge, but students will encounter numerous repetitions of patterns. A contrasting middle *espressivo e cantabile* section captures the mood of a Romantic melody. A short, brilliant cadenza restates each of the three main themes in four- to six-measure snippets. (A modal, level 8)

2. *Andante tranquillo* (♪ = 112)

The piano opens this movement with a wistful melody over a lightly pulsing bass, setting a contemplative mood that remains throughout the work. Following the opening, an orchestral statement of the initial melody is accompanied with cross-hand arpeggio outlines in the piano. This is a subtle but effective movement when approached with a high level of musicality. (A modal, level 7)

3. *Presto leggiero* (♩ = 168)

Nimble fingers and incessant energy are required for this sparkling work. As in the first movement, the composer combines a few easily executed patterns, including rapid broken triads, first-inversion chords, and cross-hand arpeggios. While no cadenza is incorporated, the *prestissimo* finish provides a fiery conclusion. (C major, level 8)

CARRÉ, John F. (1894–1966) USA

Concertino in C Major

Appealing and cleverly conceived technical patterns are plentiful, bringing a virtuosic impression to a technically accessible work. Piano II is equally matched in skill level and musical content.

(Two pianos, Schroeder & Gunther)

1. *Allegro maestoso* (♩ = 92)

The melodramatic opening statements clearly define the roles of soloist and orchestral accompaniment, but the movement's overall impact is decreased by somewhat uninspired musical ideas. (C major, level 5)

2. *Adagio* (♩ = 58)

The opening solo of the second movement is a beautiful and tender *Intermezzo*, a highlight of the concerto. (A minor, level 6)

3. *Allegro* (♩. = 120)

The last movement is a relaxed tarantella with distinct rhythms and motives, as well as a dazzling finale. Appropriate fingerings and pedal markings are provided throughout. (C major, level 6)

CHILCOT, Thomas (ca. 1707–1766) Great Britain

Chilcot wrote two sets of concertos for harpsichord. Each is in three movements and similar to the works of Antonio Vivaldi. His style features brilliant keyboard writing reminiscent of Domenico Scarlatti.

Keyboard Concerto in A Major, Op. 2, No. 2

This concerto is scored for keyboard, two violins, and cello.

(Harpsichord and string orchestra, full score, Oxford University Press)

1. *Allegro* [♩ = ca. 104]

Written in a crisp Baroque style, the *Allegro* forms the most substantial portion of the concerto. Perhaps more effective on the harpsichord, this work requires clean articulations, excellent control of close fingerwork patterns, and the ability to move easily between solo passages and *tutti* continuo playing. The movement has a jaunty feel and is delightful in performance. (A major, level 9)

2. *Largo* [♪ = ca. 69]

The performer is challenged to maintain a steady pulse during various subdivisions of the beat in this lyrical, flowing movement. Ornamentation adds to the beauty and complexity of the piece, while sequential phrases make the work more accessible to the intermediate pianist. (A minor, level 7)

3. *Tempo di gavotta* [♩ = ca. 92–96]

Short and sprightly in ABACA form, this concluding movement demands elegance and grace. The A theme is contrasted with phrases in F-sharp minor. This brief 42-measure work can be a fun collaboration between a piano student and a student string trio. (A major, level 7)

Keyboard Concerto in F Major, Op. 2, No. 5

Instrumentation for this concerto includes keyboard, two oboes, bassoon, and strings.

(Piano and string orchestra, full score, Oxford University Press)

1. *Allegro spiritoso* [♩ = ca. 112]

The first movement is in a delightfully regal style reminiscent of a dance piece. Sprinkled with sequences, Alberti bass motion, and ornamentation, the keyboard writing feels very natural in the hands. Opportunities for solo as well as *tutti* playing abound in this, the most sizeable of the three concerto movements. Chilcot's writing translates well to the piano, making it a suitable choice for a single concerto movement. (F major, level 10)

2. *Adagio* [♪ = ca. 54]

Intricate rhythmic subdivisions present the biggest challenge in this movement, but as the rhythmic passages are placed within the larger framework of the piece, effortlessly flowing lines emerge. This *Adagio* is a peaceful hiatus from the energy of the outer two movements and leads directly into the last movement through a final, unresolved harmony in the keyboard and strings. (D minor, level 10)

3. *Giga Allegro* [♩ = ca. 116]

Dancing in a celebratory manner, this final movement contains idiomatic writing that easily fits the hands. The keyboardist takes a lead role, introducing phrases that are repeated by the ensemble. Motivic melodic intervals in both hands extend the reach farther than in Chilcot's other concerto movements, and isolated trills on the top of melodic 3rds require control within the hand. This movement brims with humor and would be relatively easy to coordinate given the small size of the accompanying ensemble. (F major, level 9)

CLEMENTI, Muzio (1752–1832) Italy

Piano Concerto in C Major

(Piano and orchestra, full score, Ricordi)

1. Allegro con spirito [♩ = ca. 136–142]

An extended orchestral introduction presents the two main themes. Right-hand figures of octaves with inner 3rds and 6ths are used throughout the movement, making the piece more challenging for students with small hands. Pure scales and arpeggios with minimal alteration, along with a development section comprised of logical, sequential-key relationships, help the process of learning and memorizing this work. In the recapitulation, cross-hand playing and wide leaps in the melody lead to a cadenza written by the composer. (C major, level 10)

2. Adagio e cantabile, con grande espressione [♩ = ca. 48]

This lovely, lyrical movement suggests a seeming effortlessness. The steady eighth notes in the left hand guide the pulse, while the right hand artfully weaves melodic groups into the structure. Playing this fluid, Romantic melody over an unvarying left-hand bass pulse is the main challenge for the pianist. A cadenza is suggested but not provided in the score. (F major, level 9)

3. Presto [♩ = ca. 152]

A brisk tempo combined with demanding technical requirements, including rapid scales, arpeggiated segments, and decorative chromatic alterations, creates a thrilling movement. (C major, level 10+)

CORRETTE, Michel (1707–1795) France

Corrette was a French organist, composer, and teacher who bridged the late Baroque and newer Classical styles of writing. Most concertos of his time were designated for harpsichord or organ, but the pianoforte was added as a third possibility in the 1770s and replaced the harpsichord in practice by the late 1700s. Corrette scored his concertos for six instruments (three violins, viola, cello, and flute) with keyboard *obbligato*.

Concerto in A Major, Op. 26, No. 2

(Harpsichord/organ, flute, and string orchestra, full score, Schott Music)

1. Allegro [♩ = ca. 120]

Musically simple, the *Allegro* movement features clean and pianistic writing. Alberti bass patterns, cross-hand playing, sequences, and ornamentation at cadences add sparkle to a straightforward movement. It is appropriate for smaller hands, with isolated left-hand octaves as the largest intervallic requirement. This cheery, uplifting movement is equal in difficulty to easier intermediate sonatinas. (A major, level 7)

2. Adagio [♩ = ca. 46]

After a short *tutti* section, this movement opens with a solemn dialogue between the keyboard and violin. This musical idea serves as a precursor to the concluding statement of the short piece. Keyboard roles shift from continuo to interspersed solo statements. Unable to stand on its own, this movement provides the perfect contrast between the preceding *Allegro*, with its lightness and clarity, and the following *Giga*, which brings the work to a close. (A minor, level 6)

3. Giga—Allegro [♩. = ca. 126]

With a feeling of two beats per measure, the concluding *Allegro* vaults into a merry romp. The keyboard part fluctuates between chordal outlines and melodic, three-note groupings in stepwise motion. Once the pianist learns the initial patterns, it is simple to master. The quick tempo contributes to the impressive nature of the work in performance. (A major, level 7)

Concerto in D Minor, Op. 26, No. 6

(Harpsichord/organ, flute and string orchestra, full score, Bärenreiter)

1. *Allegro* [♩ = ca. 116–120]

Basic harmonic progressions abound in this unpretentious movement. The keyboardist takes on an accompani-mental role at the beginning and ending of the *Allegro*, and acts as soloist for the majority of the middle section. The middle section pairs the flute obbligato with the keyboard in a duet, with the keyboard playing cross-hand harmonies to support the flute melody. The energy of the perpetual 16th notes is an attractive element of the composition. Frequent Alberti bass patterns and moving figures in close position make this work a technically accessible choice as an intermediate Baroque concerto movement. (D minor, level 6)

2. *Andante* [♪ = ca. 80–86]

In two-part form, this stately movement resides in the same technical realm as the *Anna Magdalena Bach Notebook* pieces. The continued pairing of the flute and keyboard makes for an especially pleasing combination. A few rhythms look more complicated than they are to play. The piece has an ease and grace that elevate the work above its simplicity. (D minor, level 5)

3. *Presto* [♩ = ca. 120–126]

This energetic movement utilizes an appealing opening motive, driving phrases, and winding sequences to command attention. More involved passagework alternates with simple phrases, putting the technical level above the preceding movements. The middle section in F major brings a buoyancy that the surrounding gravity of D minor lacks. An opportunity for a short cadenza-like keyboard flourish presents itself before all instruments join together in a final unison statement of the main theme. (D minor, level 7)

DAVIS, Peter (b. 1962) USA

Davis wrote his *Spring Fantasy* as a young teacher to address the need for intermediate-level concertos that were accessible, exciting, appropriate for smaller hands, and easy to memorize. This six-minute work is scored for a youth orchestra.

Spring Fantasy: A Youth Concerto

(Piano and orchestra, two piano reduction, Pinner Publications)

1. *Lento assai—Allegro/Energico e non legato* (♩. = ca. 48–52, 126–144)

An animated fantasy, this one-movement work features triads in blocked and broken forms. The highly patterned piece employs some unexpected chromatic resolutions that provide additional spark. An opening woodwind duet leads to a whirling arabesque in the piano and then a dancing first theme in 6/8. The second theme is the inversion of the first theme at a slower tempo. A cadenza allows the student to display energetic passagework without straining technical control. (C major, level 6)

DIAMOND, David (1915–2005) USA

Concertino for Piano and Small Orchestra

(Piano and orchestra, full score, Southern Music Publishing Co., Inc.)

1. *Allegro con brio* (♩. = 72)

This movement features angular, rhythmically expressive writing in a multi-tonal framework. Right- and left-hand voices interact through imitation, contrary motion, and parallel statements. The writing is intervallic, rather than melodically based, with sections centered around prominent intervals of a 4th and 5th. The challenging work is full of angular writing and tricky passagework. (Atonal, level 10)

2. *Theme and Variations—Adagio* (♩ = 63)

A 24-measure theme slowly unwinds in an atonal construction, followed by 18 variations, some as brief as eight measures long. Typical to sets of variations, the individual settings contrast widely in mood, articulation, meter, and compositional devices. A brilliant finale brings the movement to a close. While the work as a whole is above a level 10, select variations do fall within the intermediate range. (Atonal, level 10+)

DUSSEK, Jan Ladislav (1760–1812) France

Concerto for Piano and Orchestra, Op. 49, in G Minor

Originally published as Op. 49, this work was revised and then released by Breitkopf & Härtel as Op. 50 in 1803. It represents a milestone in the transition between the late Classical style and early Romantic style.

(Piano and orchestra, full score, C. F. Peters)

1. *Allegro ma espressivo* [♩ = ca. 126–132]

The *Allegro* opens with an orchestral statement, and the dramatic entrance of the keyboard is set up with an exaggerated *pianissimo* ♭II–V cadence. The ensuing keyboard lines are largely comprised of three-octave scales and arpeggios, as well as thick chord statements in dotted rhythm. A lyrical second theme ventures into B-flat major. The extended development, continuing for 127 measures, builds to a climax before returning to the initial theme. (G minor, level 10+)

2. *Adagio* [♪ = ca. 66–72]

In three-part song form, the *Adagio* movement includes a wide scope of musical demands. The piano fulfills an accompanimental role through lyrical arpeggio outlines that support lush string harmonies. The middle section takes on a more dramatic feel, due to increased rhythmic values and a passionate outburst. No true cadenza is present, but Dussek creates the feel of one in a dramatic, left-hand octave melody combined with a right-hand octave chordal scheme. (E-flat major, level 10)

3. *Rondo—Allegro non troppo* [♩ = ca. 120]

This movement is reminiscent of Bohemian dances through its use of folk melodies and characteristic rhythms. Moments full of enthusiasm and energetic articulations are juxtaposed with singing melodies and more relaxed sections. Variety is provided to the G minor key center with visits to B-flat major and G major. (G minor, level 10+)

EBERL, Anton (1765–1807) Austria

Concerto for Piano and Orchestra in E-flat Major, Op. 40

(Piano and orchestra, full score, Ries & Erler)

1. *Allegro* [♩ = ca. 124]

Similar in style to Beethoven's concerto writing, this substantial movement is a distinctive Classical concerto choice. Employing the typical compositional devices of scales, arpeggios, and broken octaves, this piece is accessible to advanced students, despite its length. The themes are grandiose, and the music contains horn-call motives that are also popular in Mozart's writing. A keyboard cadenza is indicated but not provided, offering an opportunity for a more experienced student to create a unique statement. (E-flat major, level 10+)

2. *Andante* [♩. = ca. 42]

A beautiful and lilting movement, this *Andante* involves some thicker chords for the keyboard. Extended arpeggio passages put the pianist in an accompanying role as the orchestra adopts the main theme. The movement, satisfying yet uneventful, does not stand effectively on its own. (B-flat major, level 9)

3. *Rondo—Vivace* [♩ = ca. 90]

Crisp and Classical in spirit, a catchy rondo tune pervades the movement. The keyboard writing is built on a technical foundation of scales and arpeggios, with appearances of Alberti bass and limited ornamentation. The piano has numerous thematic statements supported by thin orchestration, as well as an *ad libitum* cadenza that leads into the final *Allegro* section. This work is a fitting substitution for an easier Mozart or Beethoven concerto movement, or for a student who enjoys exploring lesser-known repertoire. (E-flat major, level 9)

ECKSTEIN, Maxwell (1905–1974) USA

Concerto for Young Americans in C Major

(Piano and orchestra/band, two piano reduction, Carl Fischer)

1. *Moderate* (♩ = ca. 108, ♩ = 132)

This charmingly nostalgic movement brims with the usual concerto gestures—arpeggiated harmonic expansions, melodies within chords, cross-hand motions, and left-hand octave passagework. All elements combine to evoke the innocence of the past. (C major, level 9)

2. *Slow* (♩ = ca. 100)

A sentimental, dance-like second movement opens with a long orchestral introduction. The solo entrance in measure 19 requires careful voicing, as it weaves the main theme into arpeggiated figures. The chord textures of the first movement return, highlighted in moments where the support of Piano II is relegated to articulations only on strong beats. The challenge of more frequent cross-hand accompaniment adds to the difficulty of this slow movement. (F major, level 9)

3. *Quick—vivo* (♩ = ca. 120)

This movement's sprightly melody has the potential to charm both the performer and the listener with its subtle reference to quickstep music. The shortest of the three movements, this lively piece employs frequent syncopation and some quick register changes while limiting some of the technical demands of the preceding two movements. (C major, level 6)

EDWARDS, Matthew (b. 1968) USA

Edwards is an active teacher, pianist, composer, and editor. His concertos appear frequently on concerto festival and competition lists.

Concerto for Young Pianists

This score edition is accompanied by a CD containing a full performance of the concerto in addition to individual Piano II tracks for rehearsal or performance.

(Two pianos, Hal Leonard)

1. *Moderato* (♩ = 88)

This movement's tuneful melody is often presented in octaves between the hands. Edwards has included a number of meter changes, but the consistent quarter-note pulse eases the task for the pianist. A modal sound exists at times within the D minor framework. The movement creates a brilliant effect with limited technical demands. The solo line often interweaves with Piano II and takes the lead in a few places. (D minor, level 4)

2. *Adagio* (♩ = 66)

A lovely, nostalgic theme opens the second movement and requires careful attention to the voicing of the melody over a running 16th-note texture divided between the hands. A section of parallel 3rds brings increased drama, and an exalted climactic moment leads back to the introspective mood of the opening. (D minor, level 4)

3. *Animato* (♩ = 160–176)

The Piano II introduction sets a chaotic and playful scene in this closing movement that, although bolstered by syncopated accompaniment figures, does not extend to the solo part. A steady middle section dissipates the initial energy, moving through brief modulations before returning to the opening theme and a whimsical ending. (D major, level 5)

Piano Concerto No. 2 in G Major

(Two pianos, Hal Leonard)

1. *Maestoso* (♩ = ca. 126)

A majestic opening melody in octaves between the hands is combined with a soaring secondary theme. The rich Piano II texture and harmonic groundwork elevate this accessible work to a high musical level. Arpeggios in 6ths are the most advanced technique required in the solo part. (G major, level 5)

2. *Andante* (♩ = ca. 76)

A lyrical, Romantic movement, this *Andante* highlights beautifully crafted melodies over more active arpeggiated and chordal support in Piano II. Constant attention to musical phrasing and shaping provides the most effective performance. (D major, level 5)

3. *Allegro animato—Meno mosso* (♩ = ca. 152, 108)

The quirky, fun third movement involves great rhythmic complexity and technical range. The pleasing work offers an opportunity to explore musical expression. (G major, level 6)

ERDMANN, Dietrich (1917–2009) Germany

Concertino for Piano and Chamber Orchestra

Erdmann's chamber orchestra requires two violins, viola, cello, bass, flute, oboe, and clarinet.

(Piano and orchestra, full score, Edition Gravis)

1. *Allegro* (♩ = 120)

This energetic movement is more complicated to read than it is to execute technically. The harmonic structure may prove challenging to memorize, although motions and chords are frequently patterned. Hands are in limited ranges, making this appropriate for an adventurous student with small hands. The thin orchestral texture effectively showcases the pianist. After a four-measure quasi-cadenza, Erdmann writes a dramatic conclusion to the movement. (Polytonal, level 8)

2. *Andante cantabile* (♩ = 60)

Opening with a lyrical piano solo statement, this movement evades a traditional tonal center through-out. Frequent accidentals add to the complexity, although the music is not as demanding as the score appears. Demonstrating musical and emotional understanding is the biggest challenge for the pianist. (Atonal, level 8)

3. *Allegro vivace* (♩ = 100)

The most tuneful of the three movements, the *Allegro vivace* may be easier for students to understand due to fewer accidentals, more repeated motives, and many passages with hands-together melodies in unison at the octave. The movement is in ABA form. The opening motive returns to set up a final arpeggio run leading to an exciting, octave-filled finale shared by the piano and orchestra. (G modal, level 7)

FAITH, Richard (b. 1926) USA

Concerto for Two Pianos

This concerto was written specifically for two pianos, with no orchestration offered by the composer. The levels of the two parts are evenly matched.

(Two pianos, Shawnee Press)

1. *Allegro deciso* [♩ = ca. 120]

The opening and closing sections of the first movement are predominantly hands-together melodic doubling at the octave in Piano I, while a middle section offers opportunity to display lyrical voicing. Energetic drive throughout most of the movement culminates in a united Piano I/Piano II flourish at the close. Melodic construction of the main thematic material is in open 4ths and 5ths and chord outlines, although the key center often shifts. (Polytonal, level 5)

2. *Andante—flowingly* [♩ = ca. 76]

The second movement is Romantic in gesture, but not always in sound. The introduction and conclusion of the movement require an octave motion decorated by an upper grace note, which is difficult to play with small hands. Modal in sound, the *Andante* requires careful melodic projection in both parts, as they often occupy a similar range and register. (Polytonal, level 5)

3. *Vivace* [♩. = ca. 126]

Quickly changing musical ideas, tonal centers, and registers stand out in this final movement. The meter switches between various time signatures, with the eighth note remaining constant. Maintaining a steady pulse throughout the changes may be the most challenging element of the work. Numerous musical ideas occur several times each, forming a patchwork of themes. The last section is a dashing *prestissimo* in both parts, culminating in a dramatic *fortissimo* finale. (Polytonal, level 7)

FARJEON, Harry (1878–1948) USA

Phantasy Concerto for Piano and Chamber Orchestra, Op. 64

Much of Farjeon's oeuvre is written for the piano. His *Phantasy Concerto*, composed in one continuous movement, earned a Carnegie Award.

(Piano and orchestra, two piano reduction, Stainer & Bell)

Allegro con spirito/Adagio non troppo/Allegro/Presto [♩ = ca. 126, 60, 120, 192]

The concerto is filled with shifts in tempo, mood, and key center. Most individual ideas are not too difficult, but demands on the pianist include awkward hand position changes and fingerings, mixed meters, and a wide variety of beat subdivisions. The tonal center is C major, with limited use of accidentals. The piece is identified as a level 10 work based on the number of unique ideas presented and the technical demands of the writing, along with the extended length of the concerto (51 pages). (Polytonal, level 10)

FELICI, Alessandro (1742–1772) Italy

Felici, a Florentine composer of the mid-18th century, wrote four keyboard concertos. The F major concerto is the only one that has been published in a modern edition. Manuscripts of the other three concertos are housed in a collection at the University of Louisville. Felici died at the young age of 29.

Concerto per Cimbalo in F Major

(Harpsichord and orchestra, full score, Edizioni di Santis)

1. *Allegro moderato* [♩ = ca. 76–80]

Similar in nature to Mozart's writing, this *Allegro* movement is an appealing concerto to precede study of some of the more commonly played Classical concertos. Opening with a sprightly main theme in the orchestra followed by a piano restatement, the movement follows traditional form outlines and harmonic structures. The limited technical requirements include two-octave arpeggio patterns in the right hand, cross-hand playing, and a composed cadenza. (F major, level 7)

2. *Largo ed espressivo* [♩ = ca. 48]

The slow movement, complete with trills and Alberti patterns in the piano, works well as a continuation of the preceding movement but does not stand suitably on its own. Felici's cadenza is a one-measure connecting phrase and does not offer much opportunity for the pianist to stand out technically amid the placidity of the rest of the piece. (F major, level 6)

3. *Allegro assai* [♩ = ca. 126–132]

Flashes of brilliant passagework color this showy finale. Cross-hand technique, appearing in a more limited scope in the first movement, dominates the middle portion of this piece. With a grand finish to a relatively unknown but accessible work, this movement serves as a fitting vehicle for a student who plays with dramatic flair and a clear sound. (F major, level 6)

FRANÇAIX, Jean (1912–1997) France

Françaix began study with influential composition teacher Nadia Boulanger at the age of 10 and was considered by her to be one of her best pupils. A performance of his *Concertino* at the Baden-Baden music festival in 1932, with Françaix himself at the piano, brought about his first great success as a composer. A self-declared neoclassicist, his music displays the French traits of charm and wit, along with humor and irony.

Concertino for Piano and Orchestra in G Major

(Piano and orchestra, two piano reduction, Schott)

1. *Prelude—Presto leggiero* [♩ = ca. 120]

A lively romp introduced through an appealing opening motive is the basis for the entire movement. Energetic playing is required throughout. It fits well in small hands, with the largest reaches consisting of a few isolated right-hand octaves. Trickier to read than it is to technically execute, this movement employs frequently fluctuating key centers outlined in scales and chords. Quick bounces through staccato bass notes and chords require left-hand adeptness. A wide dynamic range adds to the drama of the prelude. (G major, level 8)

2. *Lent* [♩ = ca. 56]

This 31-measure meditation features an accompaniment of constant half notes in the second piano or orchestra. These half notes support Piano I's melody line that is doubled at the octave. The entire melody of the movement falls within the range of an octave. The movement presents a challenge in tone, line shaping, and the sustaining of long melodic structures. (G modal, level 1)

3. *Menuet—Allegretto—attacca* [♩ = ca. 138]

Pianos I and II are constructed of two alternating ideas: a staccato, arpeggiated melody that outlines tonic and dominant, and a contrasting chordal motive that moves back and forth between two harmonies (A minor and D7). A brief trio in A minor contrasts with the return statements of the two main themes. The movement ends with a long D7 chord, anticipating the opening of the fourth movement. (C major, level 3)

4. *Finale—Rondo—Allegretto vivo* [♪ = ca. 220]

After short second and third movements, the finale returns the vitality and enthusiasm of the opening prelude. A ⅝ meter with a consistent 3+2 subdivision creates an irregular, jaunty mood. Right-hand chromatic motion over a waltz-like leaping bass makes coordination with Piano II or orchestra tricky. The fun addition of glissandos in Piano I support the upbeat character of the concerto. (G major, level 8)

Concerto for Piano and Orchestra, Op. 19, in D Major

Movements 1, 3, and 4 fall outside the bounds of intermediate concertos and beyond the scope of this book.

(Piano and orchestra, two piano reduction, Schott Music)

2. *Andante* (♩ = 54)

In an easy, flowing ⅝ meter, this work is much more technically accessible than the surrounding movements. The composition begins and ends with a simply stated melody played at the octave between the hands. This same melody weaves its way between the piano and orchestra, sometimes occurring in both simultaneously. A short, eight-measure segment in the middle of the movement presents a thicker texture, with wider hand reaches and extended range. (D major, level 9)

FRANK, Marcel G. (1906–?) USA (born Austria)

Piano Concerto in E-flat Major, "Youth Concerto"

The three movements are to be played *attacca*.

(Piano and orchestra, two piano reduction, Henri Elkan Music)

1. *Brightly* (♩ = 112)

This rhythmically exciting, syncopated movement features consistent passagework with hands moving in similar motion. The quick tempo is interspersed with slower moments, including a particularly lovely theme played "slowly in a singing style." Musical demands include changing tempos, attention to detailed articulations, and contrasting styles. A 12-measure transition, improvisatory in nature, leads directly into the second movement. (E-flat major, level 7)

2. *Moderately* (♩ = 66)

In ABA form, this work contains a B section of outlined arpeggiated chords. The main theme forms an expansive, single-note line above an ostinato bass doubled by Piano II. The main motive, a combination of 8th notes, 32nd notes, triplets, and tied notes, is rhythmically challenging. (F major, level 5)

3. *Lively, and in steady rhythm* (♩ = 138)

The movement is dominated by a strong, brisk theme that incorporates dotted rhythmic figures and chromatic, jazzy alterations. Motives and gestures from the opening movement, including the first statement, return in combination with the jazzy theme to complete the concerto. It is effective as an individual piece. (E-flat major, level 6)

GALUPPI, Baldassare (1706–1785) Italy

Galuppi was a leading figure in the development of *opera buffa*. He also wrote a large quantity of harpsichord music and was one of the most popular performers of his time.

Concerto in F for Harpsichord and Strings

(Harpsichord and string orchestra, full score, Ricordi)

1. *Allegro, ma non troppo* [♩ = ca. 90]

A stately, highly ornamented movement, this *Allegro* is possibly better suited to the harpsichord than it is to the modern piano. With a simple orchestration of two violins and cello, the focus is on the keyboard throughout the movement. An arpeggiated middle segment sounds more involved than it is. (F major, level 9)

2. *Grave* [♪ = ca. 54]

The slow movement is regal, disguising a rather complicated rhythmic scheme. Technical demands are not great on their own, but when coupled with the implied elasticity of the pulse and the bel canto figuration of the melodic line, this movement becomes challenging. (B-flat major, level 10)

3. *Presto* [♩. = ca. 69]

A cheery movement containing few surprises, the *Presto* highlights the keyboardist over thinly textured string support. Ornaments and Alberti bass figuration are plentiful. Too brief to stand on its own, this movement works best in combination with the first two movements. (F major, level 9)

GOOLKASIAN RAHBEE, Dianne (b. 1938) USA

Rahbee is a pianist and composer who remains active internationally in workshop presentations, lectures, and master classes. A first-generation Armenian American whose father was a survivor of genocide, her music reflects a deeply rooted ethnic background. The strong influences of the Armenian language, her native tongue, and Armenian folk music figure prominently in her compositions.

Concertino No. 1, "Peasant Folk Dance," Op. 82

(Piano and chamber or string orchestra with optional percussion, two piano reduction, FJH Publishing Co.)

Allegretto (♩ = 92)

Opening with a bold statement of polychords, this concertino challenges musicians to engage in a modern melodic and harmonic language. Melodies exude an Armenian flavor and are initially a bit trickier to read than they are to play, due to the chromaticism in the lines and the juxtaposition of sharps and flats. The power of the introduction is balanced by a sprightly second theme, contrasted by a cantabile section. Each statement is reiterated until the movement culminates with a six-octave scalar passage and bombastic finish. (Polytonal, level 6)

Concertino No. 2, Op. 113, for Piano, Strings, and Percussion

(Piano and chamber orchestra, two piano reduction, self-published)

1. *Exhibition—Vivace* (♩ = ca. 120)

This highly energetic movement requires intricate rhythmic precision between the hands. The piece includes diminished-7th arpeggios and chromatic 3rds and 4ths in broken form. Punctuated by short statements of a passionate, interwoven melody, it is the most technically challenging movement of the *Concertino*. (Polytonal, level 9)

2. *Interlude—Adagio cantabile—gently rocking* (♩ = ca. 52)

Based on quartal (4th) harmony, this movement resembles a barcarolle. Issues of balance and line are the performer's foremost challenges. (Polytonal, level 4)

3. *Celebration—Allegretto—molto energico* (♩ = 170)

A steady pulse is a requirement in *Celebration*, as shifting meters and accents provide inconsistent rhythmic support. This movement uses quintal (5th) harmony, creating a primitive, forceful presence. It sounds more complicated than it is to play. (Polytonal, level 5)

Concertino No. 3, Op. 145

Concertino No. 3 is written for two pianos, but early-level string and percussion parts are also available. This edition also includes a CD with practice tempos as well as the performance tempo.

(Piano and string orchestra with percussion, two piano reduction, self-published)

Molto espressivo—Tempo giusto (♩ = ca. 152, 200)

Concertino No. 3 is a sparkling, enthusiastic work incorporating three-note chord clusters, repetitive accompaniment patterns, and cross-hand technique. Challenges include $\frac{5}{4}$ and $\frac{7}{4}$ time signatures and quickly shifting key centers. This composition serves as an excellent concerto for a student working on the skill of memorization, as patterns remain consistent and the piece can easily be divided into manageable sections. The overall effect of the piece is brilliant and uplifting. (Polytonal, level 5)

Urartu Rhapsodie, Op. 80, for Piano and Orchestra

This piece, in one continuous movement, is named after an ancient word for "Armenia."

(Piano and orchestra, two piano reduction, self-published)

Appassionato—Double the Tempo (♩ = 92, 184)

A powerful work, the *Rhapsodie* opens with a dazzling octave passage, a technique that returns several times throughout the piece. A fast-paced, triplet-arpeggio accompaniment in the solo line and a sincere, soaring Romantic melody over unusual left-hand arpeggio figures expand the eastern European motives. The composition culminates in a drive to the finish through the use of chord clusters in the solo piano. Technically demanding and emotionally stimulating, this work deserves to be widely known. (Polytonal, level 10)

GRAUN, Johann Gottlieb (ca. 1702–1771) Germany

An important instrumental composer of the pre-Classical period, Johann Gottlieb Graun primarily wrote symphonies, trio sonatas, overtures, and concertos, many of which were never printed. He is noted for teaching violin to Wilhelm Friedemann Bach.

Cembalo Concerto in C Minor

(Harpsichord and string orchestra, Kalmus)

1. *Allegro* [♩ = ca. 116]

A conventional first movement opens with a lively melody in the orchestra that is reiterated in the initial piano entrance. Scales, double 3rds, and Baroque non-legato articulation in the bass line are the core of the piece's technical elements. Small surprises may be found in a segment built of three-measure phrases, and the single-measure alternations between the tutti and solo in the recapitulation. This interesting piece highlights the common practices of the day. (C minor, level 7)

2. *Larghetto* [♪ = ca. 84]

Pleasantly lilting lines permeate this work, requiring careful attention to slurring and shaping for beautiful musical effect. The combination of the movement's short length and limited technical demands helps to highlight the intimate conversation that Graun has written between the keyboard and orchestra. Opportunities for added ornamentation are present throughout the movement. (E-flat major, level 6)

3. *Allegro* [♩. = ca. 80]

A rousing frolic in $\frac{6}{8}$, this *Allegro* uses lengthy sequences to maintain a sense of drama. The writing fits the hands well and would be suitable for a student with small hands. The final *tutti* phrase brings the keyboard and orchestra together in a grand C minor resolution. (C minor, level 7)

GREGOR, Čestmír (1926–2011) Czechoslovakia

From the introduction to this edition: "The piano part of the *Concerto Semplice* is written in an unconventional character, and due to this the work occupies a special place in contemporary music. Its interpretation requires an unusual technique of touch, sharpening of contrasts between staccato-legato, [and] economical pedal work … All this is a part of the entire conception of the concerto's unromantic simplicity."

Concerto Semplice

(Piano and orchestra, two piano reduction, Panton-Verlag Publisher)

1. *Con moto* (♩ = ca. 150)

This movement requires careful reading due to frequent accidentals in the body of the music. Written mostly in a thin, two-part texture with jagged motion, it is possibly more challenging than satisfying for the performer and listener. (Atonal, level 10)

2. *Moderato* (♩. = 60)

Written in ABA form, the *Moderato* features an expanded B section development. The return of the A section concludes with a 16-measure piano solo in a tuneful G major. Tricky hemiolas in $\frac{6}{8}$ and some thick textural moments are the biggest challenges. (Atonal, level 9)

3. *Con brio* (♩ = 140)

In rondo form, this movement begins with a peppy opening motive. The quick tempo, along with rapid register shifts and a variety of musical ideas, project this movement above a level 10. (Atonal, level 10+)

HALLORAN, Stephen (b. 1966) USA

Stephen Halloran studied composition with Joseph Schwanter, Samuel Adler, and Lukas Foss.

Piano Concertino

(Piano and orchestra, two piano reduction, self-published)

Allegretto (♩ = 96)

This one movement concerto is only 183 measures in length. Very pianistic in nature, the work fits the hands readily and contains repeated figures throughout. The bouncy, syncopated main theme is transferred between the hands in a number of key centers. A short *Andante* breaks up the consistently moving work. The ending continues with a return of the opening motive, moving with urgency into a rather amusing, somewhat unresolved final statement. (Atonal, level 7)

HATTORI, Koh-Ichi (b. 1933) Japan

Concertino for Small Hands

Piano II is equally matched in difficulty with Piano I.

(Piano and string orchestra, two piano reduction, Boosey & Hawkes)

1. *Allegro moderato* [♩ = ca. 126]

Based on a recurring melodic motive, the first movement of this work is woven together with thematic statements accompanied by a variety of styles and textures. While ranges are limited, atypical harmonies create challenges in the areas of coordination and memorization. (Polytonal, level 7)

2. *Adagio ma non troppo* [♩ = ca. 60–70]

A tuneful melody and relatively simple accompaniment patterns combine to produce the most accessible of Hattori's concerto movements. With the melody weaving between the solo Piano I and Piano II lines, the piece is a particularly fine motivic study. It culminates with a beautifully crafted concluding statement within a flowing arpeggiated figure. (F major, level 6)

3. *Vivace* [♩ = ca. 136]

Few moments of rest in a constantly moving 16th-note rhythm define the introduction of this energetic movement. A lively ⅝ meter provides orchestral focus over a solo ostinato pattern. The final lines, displaying an orchestral tremolo supporting an ascending chromatic solo line, conclude with driving chords in the solo and orchestra. Hattori's *Vivace* is an intense and stimulating work. (B-flat major, level 7)

HAYDN, Franz Joseph (1732–1809) Austria

Of the many concertos attributed to Franz Joseph Haydn, only Hob. XVIII, Nos. 3 (F Major), 4 (G Major), and 11 (D Major) have been deemed irrefutably authentic. The two *Divertimenti* (XIV:3 and XIV:4) and the *Concerto in F Major* (XVIII:F1) are the most accessible of Haydn's keyboard concertos. Many of the keyboard concertos bearing Haydn's name were not written for one particular instrument but marked "clavicembalo ò fortepiano," opening them to performance on a wider variety of keyboard instruments.

Concertino in C Major (Divertimento), Hob. XIV:3

This *Concertino* was written for keyboard and three string players—two violins and cello or bass. String parts are of an appropriate level for student players. A score edited by George Anson and published by C. F. Peters is particularly well designed for young students, with fully realized ornaments, fingerings, and a short, composed cadenza. It is an excellent choice for a first student concerto by a master Classical composer.

(Piano and orchestra, two piano reduction, C. F. Peters, Boston Music Co.)

1. *Allegro moderato* [♩ = ca. 132]

Composed in a two-part texture, the first movement has a left-hand accompaniment of triads, mostly in root position or first inversion. Coordination challenges for an early intermediate student are diminished through a limited demand on the player's hand span. Themes are crisp and clean, with minimal development. (C major, level 3)

2. *Menuetto* [♩ = ca. 58]

In ABA form, this work contains no accidentals and very clear chord patterns. Each section of the piece is only eight measures long. The accompanying trio brings lyrical contrast to the lightness of the minuet, with the left hand mostly in a single-note line. It is a charming movement with restrained technical demands. (C major, level 2)

3. *Allegro di molto* [♩ = ca. 116]

This short, pleasant movement, approximately one minute of performance time, presents two main ideas and a *codetta*. Much of the movement is in five-finger position, with only a few scalar motions and hand-position extensions in the right hand. The clarity of Haydn's writing leaves great possibilities for study in balance and shaping. (C major, level 3)

Concerto in C Major, Hob. XIV:4

(Piano and orchestra, two piano reduction, Boosey & Hawkes)

1. *Allegro* [♩ = ca. 120]

Haydn's first movement is a beautiful representation of simplicity and charm. A very sparse orchestral accompaniment makes it one of the easier concerto movements to coordinate as an ensemble, opening the possibility of a student string group as collaborators. Compositional elements include scalar patterns in C major and G major, limited right-hand 3rds, and Alberti bass outlines in expected progressions. Hand span does not reach beyond an octave. A cadenza is a possibility but not a necessity, depending on the experience of the pianist. (C major, level 5)

2. *Menuet and Trio* [♩ = ca. 104]

The *Menuet and Trio* is similar in level of difficulty to J. S. Bach's easier works from the *Anna Magdalena Notebook*. Writing is in a sparse texture with left-hand blocked intervals under a repeated motive in the right-hand line. Melodic rhythms fluctuate between duple and triple subdivisions of the beat. The movement presents the grace of a minuet and trio on a moderate technical scale, with opportunity to capture the elegance of the dance's style. (C major, level 4)

3. *Finale* [♩ = ca. 132]

A lively, spirited movement, this work places demands on the player that are mostly centered around 16th-note arpeggios divided between the hands. The main challenge for the pianist is keeping the pulse even and steady in these passages. Two musical motives prevail: the opening theme combines a scale with following melodic 3rds, and the second theme presents chord structures distributed between the hands in 16th-note motion. (C major, level 4)

Concerto in F Major, Kleines Konzert, Hob. XVIII:3

(Piano and string orchestra, two piano reduction, Schott Music)

1. *Allegro* [♩ = ca. 88–92]

An elegant opening movement, the *Allegro* features moments of exciting and unexpected harmonies. The most difficult passages involve diminished-7th arpeggios. Scalar sections are predictable in direction and fit well in the hand. A cadenza is included. (F major, level 8)

2. *Largo cantabile* [♩ = ca. 40]

Technically accessible while musically mature, this movement is an excellent vehicle for studying the ornamentation typically employed on repeats or reiterated thematic statements. It requires an exceptionally refined sense of style with a great deal of musical nuance. A cadenza is provided. (C major, level 8)

3. *Presto* [♩ = ca. 138–152]

This driving, energetic movement offers little opportunity for rest in the solo piano. Technical demands focus on incessant right-hand 16th-note figurations with left-hand bass support. The development brings dramatic harmonic motion with continued right-hand figurations, and the fast tempo causes these challenges to be even more exacting. (F major, level 9)

Concerto in G Major, Hob. XVIII:4

(Piano and orchestra, two piano reduction, many standard editions)

1. *Allegro moderato* [♩ = ca. 96–100]

This bright, sunny movement is full of Haydn's spirit. It features accessible harmonic progressions and an easily identifiable structure that includes a cadenza opportunity. Technical requirements are limited to arpeggios, scalar motion, and isolated octave passages. (G major, level 8)

2. *Adagio cantabile* [♩ = ca. 44–48]

This slow movement is beautifully lyrical and sublime. Technical refinement and stylistic nuance are the main challenges, requiring a musically mature ear and sense of timing. The composer offers the opportunity for an improvised cadenza. (C major, level 7)

3. *Rondo—Presto* [♩ = ca. 156]

An attractive and sparkling work, this movement is slightly more accessible than the popular D major concerto (Hob. XVIII:11) but a fine substitute for it. Challenges include the energetic tempo, tricky passagework, the need for ultimate clarity of sound, and the overall endurance of the pianist. A fully notated cadenza is present. (G major, level 10)

Concerto in F Major, Hob. XVIII:7

(Piano and string orchestra, two piano reduction, Kalmus)

1. *Moderato* [♩ = ca. 69]

Galant in style, this *Moderato* demands absolute clarity in articulation, as the writing is without complexity and yet showcases the pianist quite prominently throughout the movement. A perfect choice for the student with smaller hands, this work has minimal technical requirements aside from short scalar runs and decorative trills and turns. The pianist's left hand is relegated predominantly to pulsing eighth notes, often in two-note texture but occasionally on a single note. It is a charmingly simple movement. (F major, level 5)

2. *Adagio* [♪ = ca. 69]

The strings and an animated left hand in the keyboard provide consistent pulse, while the melodic line rolls through the keyboardist's right hand with deep emotional longing. A mature sense of timing and pacing is important to keep the melody from becoming too strict. This movement is musically demanding, rather than technically challenging. (D minor, level 5)

3. *Allegro* [♩ = ca. 132]

Vivacious in spirit, the *Allegro* is a direct opposite to the preceding *Adagio*. Students will delight in the Classical elements here, including sparkling runs, repeated left-hand patterns, and characteristic cadences. Despite a few tricky ornaments amid the running passages, most of the movement is propelled forward in a very natural way. (F major, level 5)

Concerto in G Major, Hob. XVIII:9

(Piano and string orchestra, full score, Schott)

1. *Allegro* [♩ = ca. 120]

The *Allegro* opens with the orchestra playing a straightforward statement of a motive later heard in the keyboard, presented with little elaboration. The intensity of the music increases as the movement progresses, resulting in heightened rhythmic activity and greater coordination demands in the development. Brilliant dialogue between the piano and orchestra artfully weaves the soloist with the strings throughout. (G major, level 9)

2. *Adagio* [♪ = ca. 56–60]

Powerfully expressive, this movement challenges even mature pianists to reach to the depths of its emotive energy. Although not overly difficult technically, the movement's slow tempo may be difficult for a young player to execute successfully, given the demands on the performer's attention for the creation of extremely long lines filled with intricacies of shaping and articulation. It is a gorgeous, but rather lengthy, middle movement that would not stand on its own without the the first and last movements. (G minor, level 9)

3. *Tempo di menuetto* [♪ = ca. 148]

The final movement exudes refinement and polish within keyboard writing of a sparse texture, often with only two single lines. The pianist must avoid rushing the constantly moving triplets that weave their way throughout the piece. Some beautifully intimate moments offer opportunities for the soloist to play with a more refined approach as opposed to the need to project over the orchestra, as is often the case in concerto playing. (G major, level 8)

Concerto in D Major, Hob. XVIII:11

This is Haydn's most popular piano concerto and a frequent choice for concerto contests and festivals.

(Piano and orchestra, two piano reduction, many standard editions)

1. *Vivace* [♩ = ca. 144]

The first movement is a true display of Haydn's vibrant compositional style. Demands include scalar passages, 16th-note figures of broken chords, and precisely directed articulation. It contains undeniably attractive writing and includes a cadenza. (D major, level 10)

2. *Un poco adagio* [♪ = ca. 66–69]

The slow tempo of this piece requires constant attention to phrasing, with its inherent tension and release. Figurative elaborations and decorative gestures require a solid sense of pulse. A cadenza is included. The movement is an excellent choice as an artistic vehicle for a musical student. (A major, level 9)

3. *Rondo All'Ungherese—Allegro assai* [♩ = ca. 160–172]

Also published under the title *Kinder Concerto*, this movement is a highly energetic romp, driven yet capricious in character. Multiple modulations present the rondo theme in transient key centers. It is a true *tour de force*. (D major, level 10+)

Concerto in F Major, Hob. XVIII:F1

This concerto is another captivating Haydn work and possible alternative to the popular D major concerto (Hob. XVIII:11).

(Piano and orchestra, two piano reduction, International Music Co.)

1. *Allegro moderato* [♩ = ca. 120]

A *tutti* section presents an unusual opening, pairing the piano and orchestra in a simultaneous statement of the main theme. This introduction is followed by a restatement of the theme in the piano, supported by thin orchestral chord structures. Charming themes, with some tricky chromatic neighbor-note figuration, serve as hallmarks of this movement. A cadenza is followed by a final collaborative statement of the first theme. (F major, level 8)

2. *Andante* [♩ = ca. 86]

This short movement captures a lovely minuet style. The primary theme is heartfelt, but the contrasting middle section lacks thematic significance. With the majority of the piano solo doubled in the orchestra, this piece is less successful in highlighting the soloist. (B-flat major, level 5)

3. *Presto* [♩ = ca. 166]

A highly energetic work, this movement contains technical demands including arpeggios and staccato clarity within the fast tempo. The second section presents the same thematic ideas in G minor and B-flat major, punctuated by a contrapuntal piano statement. (F major, level 8)

HERTEL, Johann Wilhelm (1727–1789) Germany

Highly regarded by his contemporaries as both a composer and a keyboard performer, Hertel was portrayed by the noted 18th-century lexicographer Ernst Ludwig Gerber as one of the "most tasteful composers" in the second half of the century.[5] Hertel, a prolific composer of over 45 symphonies and 48 concertos, is best known for his sacred works and concertos for keyboard and violin.

Keyboard Concerto in E-flat Major

Hertel writes for a small group of strings, with the addition of two horns in E-flat.

(Harpsichord or fortepiano and orchestra, full score, A-R Editions)

1. *Allegro con spirito* [♩ = ca. 108–112]

Written in concerto-sonata form, this jaunty movement introduces the keyboard through a jagged opening motive in the second exposition. It is replete with ornamentation, rapid choreographic shifts at the keyboard, and 16th-note passages that do not always lie easily in the hand. Rapid passagework, including alternating 16th notes between the hands, also challenges the soloist's ability to achieve a clear, even sound throughout the work. It is an effective vehicle for a student with quick fingers and a sense of flair. (E-flat major, level 9)

2. *Largo, con sordini* [♪ = ca. 58]

Piquant chromaticism punctuates this slowly winding work, creating a sense of both longing and unrest. The piece presents musical challenges in phrasing and direction. Thin orchestration supports the keyboard writing, helping to emote yearning in the moving keyboard lines. This movement would be difficult to program on its own, but it is very effective in contrast to the concerto's outer two movements. (C minor, level 7)

3. *Allegro* [♩ = ca. 138–144]

An unassuming eighth-note scale ushers the keyboard into to this final movement, hardly hinting at the swift passagework, carefully designed keyboard choreography, and twisting harmonic resolutions to come. Drama abounds, with nods to the minor mode and 16th-note flurries that generate rhythmic intensity. Expected cadential formulas and short trills relay the affectations of the early Classical period effectively. This movement is enjoyable to play, with its combination of technical and musical demands. (E-flat major, level 9)

Keyboard Concerto in F Minor

The scoring for the *Keyboard Concerto in F Minor* is for chamber strings only.

(Harpsichord or fortepiano and string orchestra, full score, A-R Editions)

1. *Allegro con spirito* [♩ = ca. 126–132]

Angular chromatic writing is a hallmark of this intense movement. Drama permeates through use of the minor mode, dotted rhythms, rapid ornamentation, and distinct sequential chromatic passages, all resolving into unexpectedly innocuous cadential gestures. Frequent orchestral breaks divide the keyboard statements into rather manageable sections, both for memorization and for pacing. Some tricky fingerwork and precise rhythmic coordination will test the technique of the keyboardist, but the overall effect of the work is striking. (F minor, level 9)

2. *Largo* [♩ = ca. 54]

Only 78 measures long, this movement serves as a short breath of fresh air, easing the dramatic tension of the surrounding movements. A portrait of Classical restraint, the *Largo* features a pulsing eighth-note bass line in the strings and keyboard under a delightfully tuneful, winding melody. Thirty-second note gestures take on an easy feel, and trills add a most appropriate decoration. A cadenza opportunity presents itself, but none is provided in this edition. (F minor, level 7)

---

[5] Ernst Ludwig Gerber, *Historisch-Biographisches Lexicon der Tonkünstler*, vol. 1 (Leipzig: Johann Gottlob Immanuel Breitkopf, 1790), 629.

3. Allegro [♩ = ca. 120]

In this third movement, Hertel ventures back to the writing style of the *Allegro con spirito* with an opening keyboard gesture built of rising 3rds and 4ths, followed by a syncopated falling line. The 16th-note passages traded between the hands demand careful attention for consistency. Sequential motivic episodes pervade the movement, and rapid register changes ramp up the energy, driving straight to the final cadence without respite. (F minor, level 8)

HILLER, Ferdinand von (1811–1885) Germany

Hiller was a German virtuoso pianist who studied with Johann Nepomuk Hummel. In 1828 he moved to Paris, where his circle of friends included Chopin, Liszt, and Berlioz. As a firm musical conservative, he regarded the New German School critically.

Concerto in F-sharp Minor, Op. 69

(Piano and orchestra, two piano reduction, G. Schirmer)

1. Moderato, ma con energico e con fuoco [♩ = ca. 92]

Beautifully Romantic in sentiment and technical skill, this movement is beyond the confines of the intermediate level of concerto movements. (F-sharp minor, level 10+)

2. Andante espressivo [♩ = ca. 56–60]

In the spirit of the great Romantic concertos, this slow movement is complete with sweeping melodies voiced in octaves, left-hand arpeggio accompaniment support, and running right-hand lines that incorporate chromatic decoration over orchestral melodies. It opens with a piano solo statement in a regal, stately mood, later picked up by the orchestra. Some lovely dramatic moments are framed by memorable melodies. This movement could stand alone as an effective introduction to the technical demands of Romantic-era piano concertos. (D major, level 10)

3. Finale: Allegro con fuoco [♩ = ca. 136]

A wonderfully effective finale, this movement presents a combination of tempo, texture, and quickly shifting ranges that puts it beyond the skill set of the intermediate pianist. (F-sharp minor, level 10+)

HOFFMEISTER, Franz Anton (1754–1812) Germany

Hoffmeister's reputation rests on his work as a music publisher. He established one of Vienna's first music publishing businesses, printing his own music as well as that of Haydn, Mozart, Beethoven, and Clementi. He composed numerous concertos, including a popular concerto for the viola.

Concerto in D Major, Op. 24

(Piano and orchestra, two piano reduction, C. F. Peters)

1. Allegro brioso [♩ = ca. 126]

Although written in an unmistakably Classical style, this movement has less inspiration than comparable Haydn and Mozart concerto movements. An extended orchestral introduction leads into the piano solo entrance. Demands include expected scalar and arpeggiated figures, clarity of articulation, and an original cadenza. The movement is rather long, with a number of large orchestral statements during which the soloist plays along in continuo style, written out in the modern edition. (D major, level 9)

2. Adagio [♩ = ca. 50]

In a cantabile style, the *Adagio* contains lovely yet predictable harmonic progressions. Some rhythmic pacing through notated values and ornamental figures is showcased in the piano solo. The slow tempo demands long phrasing, shaping, and a solid grasp of the movement's form. (D minor, level 8)

3. *Allegretto* [♩ = ca. 100]

A charming, straightforward opening theme decorated by trills is elaborated upon in a theme and variations treatment, although the variations are not specifically identified as such in the score. Variations include the addition of scales and arpeggios in both hands, passing-note and neighbor-note ornamental decoration, and key shifts to D minor and F major. The return of the original theme moves to more closely juxtaposed D major and D minor statements. A brief cadenza leads to the sparkling finale, combining the piano and orchestra in a unified declaration. (D major, level 9)

HOOK, James (1746–1827) Great Britain

Hook was an early proponent of the pianoforte and performed concertos on it frequently.

Keyboard Concerto, Op. 20, No. 2 in C Major

(Piano and orchestra, full score, Oxford University Press)

1. *Allegro moderato* [♩ = ca. 116]

This fetching galant-style movement is full of scalar passages, sequences, and imitative treatment of a secondary theme. The writing fits the hands naturally and fingerings, although not provided in this edition, come readily. The bass writing generally follows a few typical accompaniment patterns, and the right hand bears responsibility for much of the piece's ornate activity. This work is a nice alternative to some of the easier Haydn concerto movements. (C major, level 8)

2. *Andante* [♪ = ca. 78–84]

Concise and tender, this movement requires careful attention to specific articulation and dynamic markings. Constructed using only a few distinct motives, the technical content should not be difficult for a student to master. The main keyboard theme comes back in its entirety three times and is immediately echoed by the orchestra in each iteration. (C minor, level 6)

3. *Rondo: Allegretto* [♩ = ca. 104]

In a condensed ABACA form, this *Rondo* includes frequent scales in their purest forms, creating a work that is easily readable and innate in feel. Its delightfully regal and sparkling texture, featuring dotted rhythms and scalar passages, creates a striking close to the work when the concerto is performed in its entirety. (C major, level 7)

HUMMEL, Johann Nepomuk (1778–1837) Austria

A pupil of Mozart, Hummel succeeded Haydn as music director for the Esterházy family in Eisenstadt, Austria. As a virtuoso pianist, he wrote a large number of works for piano.

Concertino for Piano and Orchestra, Op. 73, in G Major

In the Viennese Classical style, this concerto is a piano version of an earlier mandolin concerto.

(Piano and orchestra, two piano reduction, Neil A. Kjos Music Company)

1. *Allegro moderato* [♩ = ca. 120]

The opening theme of Hummel's first movement is very direct, but the ♫ rhythm and ornamentation add decorative interest and a heightened level of difficulty. Active right-hand figuration includes scalar passages combined with arpeggios, broken 3rds, and a section of right-hand triplets in which the melody reinforces the strong pulses. An attractive composition, it would be a great introduction to the more involved Mozart or Haydn piano concertos. (G major, level 9)

2. *Andante grazioso* [♩ = ca. 58–60]

This movement is an elegant and appealing theme and variations. The piano solo introduces the theme, followed by an orchestral statement and then variations in triplets, C minor with sharp right-hand rhythms, and 32nd-note figurations. The movement effectively concludes with a brief *codetta*. (C major, level 7)

3. *Rondo* [♩. = ca. 90]

The *Rondo's* upbeat, happy opening theme is inviting to play. A contrasting A minor section displays quick modulations and rapid passagework. It requires clean fingerwork and would be effective for teaching a clear, sparkling Classical sound. (G major, level 8)

JACOB, Gordon (1895–1984) Great Britain

Gordon Jacob was a lecturer at The Royal College of Music in London for 40 years. He wrote over 700 musical works and maintained a more conservative compositional style amid the popularity of atonality and serialism.

Concertino for Pianoforte and String Orchestra in D

(Piano and string orchestra, full score, Oxford University Press)

1. *Allegro con spirito* (♩ = 126)

The opening piano statement in this movement sets the tone for the piece—one of celebration and exuberance, with a fresh harmonic foundation and underlying energy. The pianist is required to move quickly through the keyboard choreography, including rapid succession of motives and thick but easily identifiable major and minor chord structures. The piece is initially difficult to read, but musical patterns make it easier to master. (D modal, level 9)

2. *Andante* (♩. = 44)

Replete with accidentals and unexpected harmonic shifts, the *Andante* is particularly challenging to read. Jacob's writing, beginning with a simple melodic statement doubled at the octave, morphs into Romantic phrases and then into a somewhat ethereal sound. The piece builds to several climaxes led by the piano, the second in the context of an unmarked cadenza. The conclusion of the movement returns to the feel of the opening—quiet and unsettled. (A modal, level 9)

3. *Allegro scherzando* (♩ = 120)

The energy and enthusiasm of the opening movement returns in the form of broken 7th chords and quartal (4th) harmonies. This charming, quirky work presents a memorization challenge, due to its rather abstract *espressivo* and imitative D minor sections. (D modal, level 9)

Concerto for Piano and Orchestra

(Piano and string orchestra, two piano reduction, Oxford University Press)

1. *Allegro assai* [♩ = ca. 128]

Full of vitality and energy, this engaging movement contains technical skills that are appropriate for level 10. However, given the large number of distinct ideas presented in this movement, the combined level ventures beyond the scope of this book. (Polytonal, level 10+)

2. *Adagio* [♩ = ca. 42]

A winding, enigmatic orchestral introduction is startlingly interrupted by the piano entrance in a sweeping, grand style with thick chords and octaves. The keyboard settles into a more traditional role after this initial burst of sound. The right hand voices the melody in chords over an undulating bass accompaniment. The conclusion of the movement returns to the tranquillity of the opening, finishing with a D-flat major chord ringing with ghostly effect in the piano. (Polytonal, level 10)

3. Allegro risoluto [♩ = ca. 76]

A striking display of energy and technical dexterity, this movement is beyond the scope of this study. (Polytonal, level 10+)

JIRKO, Ivan (1926–1978) Czech Republic

Piano Concerto No. 3 in G Major

(Piano and orchestra, two piano reduction, Schott Music-Panton)

1. *Allegro* (♩ = 80)

This energetic and playful movement evokes the punctuated orchestral writing and lean pianistic textures of Shostakovich. The work is written in sonata form with three principle themes: the first announces the start of the journey with a fanfare; the second conjures a mysteriously lyrical mood; and the third projects a proud attitude with a strutting rhythmic figure. The economical piano writing creates excitement through passages doubled at the octave, perpetual triplet motion, changing meters, extensive use of the higher registers with both hands, and angular note patterns. The energy of the movement dissipates into a delicate ending. (G major, level 10)

2. *Andante tranquillo* (♪ = 80)

An expressive and expansive movement in contrast to the jubilant *Allegro*, the second movement opens with a meditative theme in the strings, followed by two subsequent themes played by the piano. The second theme is more playful and direct, and the third casts a somber mood over the movement. Melodies doubled at the octave and triadic shapes in both blocked and two-note slur patterns comprise the stark piano sonority. Moments of biting dissonance in the orchestra create intensity in this otherwise tender, meditatively lyrical piece with a nationalistic character. (B minor, level 9)

3. *Allegro vivo* (♩ = 126)

A constant stream of musical ideas provides a feeling of spontaneity to this joyful and rousing work that is strongly reminiscent of Ravel's concerto in the same key. Toccata passages in single and double notes utilize a wide range of the piano, while rising and falling arpeggio figures provide yet another virtuosic element. The orchestra and piano alternate passages of rest throughout the movement, allowing the other to step fully into the spotlight. (G major, level 10)

JUNG, Helge (1943–2013) Germany

Konzert für Klavier und Kammerorchester, Op. 11, in F

(Piano and chamber orchestra, two piano reduction, VEB Deutscher Verlag)

1. *Ballade—Allegro moderato* (♩ = 84–92)

This movement is technically accessible yet harmonically elusive. The work often demands a full sound from the pianist, as it projects thin melodic lines over the richer orchestration. The *Ballade* presents a dramatic effect overall, despite the aural and musical challenges. (F modal, level 7)

2. *Variationen—Andante con moto* (♩ = 60–66)

Based on a Ukrainian folksong, this set of four variations includes a march and several lyrical settings of the tune. Some very harmonious moments arise in the midst of more angular writing. (E minor, level 7)

3. *Toccata—Allegro con brio* (♩. = 104–116)

Perhaps the most charismatic of the three movements, the *Toccata* energizes with its glissandos, primitive sounds, and a final *subito più mosso* that builds to a dramatic end. This movement fits the hands well and requires bold playing. (Polytonal, level 8)

KABALEVSKY, Dmitry (1904–1987) Russia

Most of Kabalevsky's compositional output in his later years was for children and youth. Only one advanced piano work was written after the Op. 50 *"Youth" Concerto.*

Piano Concerto No. 3 ("Youth"), Op. 50, in D Major

Kabalevsky's Op. 50 concerto contains the inscription *Dedicated to Soviet Youth.* Additional concertos for violin (Op. 48) and cello (Op. 49) were also written expressly for the education and enjoyment of young musicians.

(Piano and orchestra, two piano reduction, MCA Music)

1. *Allegro molto* (♩ = 132–138)

The first movement of Op. 50 is very playful, with a sense of youthful exuberance. The tuneful second theme brings to mind the soaring compositions of Rachmaninoff. A dramatic cadenza involving an *accelerando* leads into an *Allegro molto* section, where a melody constructed on 3rds and 6ths sings out over interspersed left-hand octaves. A driving tempo with sharp accents carries energy throughout the movement. (D major, level 9)

2. *Andante* (♩ = 72)

This movement is bookended by sections that present a simple thematic statement at the octave in the piano and repeated by the orchestra. The pianist takes on an accompanimental role in the middle of the work, spreading arpeggios between the hands. Continued drama leads to the most challenging section of the movement, both in accelerated tempo and in technical facility and clarity. (G minor, level 8)

3. *Presto* (♩ = 132–144)

An exuberant, rousing spirit pervades the opening piano theme. The middle *marciale* section is very militaristic, with a thicker chord texture setting it apart from the high-velocity outer sections. A short cadenza leads dramatically to a Romantic restatement of a theme from the first movement, pushing through to a *prestissimo* finale. (D major, level 9)

Rhapsody on a Theme of the Song "School Years," Op. 75, in G Minor

(Piano and orchestra, two piano reduction, MCA Music)

Allegro moderato (♩ = 126–132)

Kabalevsky dedicated this one-movement work in theme and variations form to young musicians of the Volga area. The 10 variations follow three stanzas of the song, illustrating the beginning, continuation, and completion of the years spent in school. The last two variations and the coda present a tableau of a culminating graduation ball. The variations cover a wide range—angular to lilting phrases, sparse to thicker textures, and various tonalities. The final variation is a waltz, with the right hand creating sweeping gestures with increasing intensity over a jumping left-hand bass. The *con fuoco* coda, complete with accents and *marcatissimo* indications, drives forward to a fermata and a concluding retrospective statement of the "School Years" theme. (G minor, level 10)

Piano Concerto No. 4 ("Prague"), Op. 99, in C Minor

Written specifically for students, this attractive work presents a wide emotional range.

(Piano and orchestra, full score, MCA Music)

1. *Allegro molto e energico* [♩ = ca. 136–148]

A brisk opening leads to the main theme, an off-kilter waltz stated as a piano solo and then accompanied by the orchestra. An extended middle portion challenges the pianist with double 3rds. A wonderful moment is created in the piano, with syncopated chords planing upward by half steps, leading to a more expansive, improvisatory chordal section. The ghostly statement of thematic fragments creates a stunning mood, dissipating into a recapitulation to round out the movement. (C minor, level 10)

2. *Molto sostenuto. Improvisato* [♩ = ca. 48]

This introspective movement is punctuated by moments of intensity. The introduction moves freely in triplets which take on a driving, forceful nature in the middle section. Intervals of a 9th in both hands reserve this work for students with bigger hands. It is a beautifully emotional and dramatic work. (A minor, level 8)

3. *Vivo* [♩ = ca. 98–102]

Parallel 7th chords, supporting the main theme in the piano, begin this movement. A sprightly melody, constructed of 3rds in both hands, propels the initial section forward. Rapid changes of key and mode occur frequently throughout the piece. Brisk 16th-note runs present one of the bigger challenges when coupled with the quick tempo, while easily readable stepwise patterns relieve some of the difficulty of the learning process. A final return of the opening melody, in root-position 7th chords in both hands, successfully completes the work. (C major, level 10+)

KASSCHAU, Howard (1913–1994) USA

Candlelight Concerto in F Major

(Piano and band, two piano reduction, Sam Fox Publishing Co.)

Maestoso/Allegro appassionato e con abbandono (♩ = 92, ♩ = 84)

This multi-sectional piece—at times reminiscent of Tchaikovsky, Debussy, and Gershwin—has a tendency to edge into melodrama. Four-note chords in unfamiliar voicings and harmonies require attention, but the writing is idiomatic. A wide range of dynamics, tempo changes, and the full keyboard are explored. Sweeping arpeggiated figures, divided between the hands, should be played with smooth choreography. It is especially appropriate for the performer who has large hands and wants to perform a full-sounding, yet less technically demanding, work. This concerto is an appropriate precursor to the study of a movement from a standard Romantic-era concerto. Piano II (levels 6–7) is considerably easier than the solo piano part. (F major, level 10)

Concerto Americana, for Piano Solo and Band and Singing/Humming Audience in C Major

Concerto Americana is dedicated to Australian pianist Percy Grainger. Although somewhat dated in its thematic content, the piece recalls a bygone era and would be a clever choice for a patriotic celebration.

(Piano and band, two piano reduction, Schroeder & Gunther)

1. *Fast* (♩ = 116)

Popular and familiar tunes, including "Camptown Races," "Home on the Range," and "Arkansas Traveler," create the thematic basis for this work. The pianist is often playing the tune divided between or doubled by the hands. Kasschau treats the ballad "Home on the Range" in a Romantic manner, inserting rolled chords and thick harmonies into the piano's statement of the song. Text is included in this edition, encouraging audiences to join in singing or humming the familiar tunes. (C major, level 6)

2. *Slowly* (♩ = 56)

The slow movement is based on the spiritual "Swing Low, Sweet Chariot." This heartfelt rendition utilizes thickly voiced jazz harmonies, extending into three piano staves in the first verse, in order to add the desired richness to the overall sound. The writing creates an improvisatory impression and will be most effective when played with an appropriate amount of rubato. (F major, level 8)

3. *Fast* (♩ = 126)

American classics, including "Dixie (I Wish I Was in Dixie)," "Oh! Susanna," and "The Battle Hymn of the Republic," combine to create the framework for the last movement. The "Dixie" and "Oh! Susanna" segments bring charm and humor to the work, but the true star of this movement is the arrangement of "The Battle Hymn of the Republic." The band and audience take over its melody while the piano plays a treatment reminiscent of the opening of Tchaikovsky's *Piano Concerto No. 1*. The effect produces a rousing finish to the concerto and will undoubtedly bring an audience to its feet. (C major, level 8)

Concerto in C Major

This work adheres closely to the typical form of a Classical concerto. The Piano II/Orchestra part (levels 4–5) is slightly less difficult than Piano I.

(Piano and orchestra, two piano reduction, Schroeder & Gunther)

1. *Allegro* (♩ = 108–112)

A spirited piece with very appealing and upbeat themes, this movement displays Classical clarity through limited harmonic language. Written in sonata-allegro form, it presents some challenging technical elements including quick register and clef changes, although written in limited hand ranges suitable for smaller hands. A short scalar cadenza line, offering a spotlight moment for the pianist, leads to the recapitulation. (C major, level 6)

2. *Canzonetta—Andantino* (♪ = 126)

The movement opens with a lyrical solo for Piano I with limited chordal support from Piano II. The lightly rocking, left-hand *piano* chords in the solo form a repetitive foundation for the cantabile melody. This melody is traded between the bass left hand of Piano I and the treble right hand of Piano II in the B section, making careful voicing of the melody an important consideration. (G major, level 6)

3. *Allegro moderato* (♩ = 116)

In a lively finish to the concerto, the *Allegro moderato* presents some unusual fingering patterns, unique in their use of chromatic and neighbor tones in the melody. However, once the figures are mastered, repetitions occur with limited variation. Arpeggios in the middle section are fingered for smaller hands, incorporating a left-hand crossing motion for the top notes, but may be refingered to fit the two hands without crossing. In this *Allegro moderato*, Kasschau creates a pleasant, largely repetitive movement. (C major, level 6)

Country Concerto for Young Pianists in C Major

(Piano and orchestra, two piano reduction, G. Schirmer)

1. *Allegro* [♩ = ca. 120]

Despite the quick tempo, the difficulty of this piece is mitigated by stationary left-hand positions, decorated with neighbor tones that are also present in the opening melodic motive. A contrasting theme utilizes common broken-chord patterns in the left hand. This snappy, energetic movement is easy to read despite a few short forays into E-flat and A-flat major. (C major, level 5)

2. *Andante, molto moderato* [♩ = ca. 100]

An opening cadenza-like elaboration in Piano I precedes the nostalgic, pensive waltz feel that occupies this movement. A contrasting, angular middle section, driven by dotted rhythms in the melody, is echoed in the repeated chords of Piano II. A satisfying conclusion is provided in a return to the original theme, this time in E major. (E minor, level 5)

3. *Vivace* [♩. = ca. 132]

This animated movement, sounding more difficult than it is to read or play, requires crisp staccato articulation throughout. The melody is found in the left hand of Piano I at times, and the voicing is facilitated by the simultaneous presence of the melody line in Piano II. Rapid register changes present the greatest technical challenge of the movement. A grand finale, with constantly moving eighth notes distributed between Pianos I and II, crafts an impressive ending to a reasonably uncomplicated composition. (C major, level 5)

The Legend of Sleepy Hollow (A Program Concerto)

Based on the story by Washington Irving, Kasschau's programmatic work creates themes for each of the three main characters: Ichabod, the local schoolmaster; Katrina Van Tassel, the student who

Ichabod hopes to marry; and Brom Bones, the rival suitor. The piece is a fitting choice for a Halloween recital, with the possibility of different students playing each of the three movements to present the work as a whole.

(Piano and orchestra, two piano reduction, G. Schirmer)

1. *Idyll: Andante teneramente* [♩ = ca. 68]

A Romantic setting of the story's opening is painted with arpeggios, thick harmonies, and heartfelt melodic lines. The shortest of the three movements, this piece is a great introduction to the sentiment and technical demands of Romantic music in the more limited scope of intermediate-level writing. (Polytonal, level 8)

2. *Of Ichabod, Katrina, and Brom Bones: Moderato—Allegretto scherzando* [♩ = ca. 86–90, 108]

The character motives are introduced in this movement—Ichabod as a jaunty, slightly quirky dotted figure; Katrina as a dreamy melody over pulsing chords; and Brom Bones in menacing, chromatically descending chords in a low register. Quick register shifts, thick textures, and chromaticism decorate the solo lines. The pianist has many opportunities to engage in character portrayal by capturing the diverse moods. (Polytonal, level 10)

3. *The Chase: Presto—Andante piacevole* [♩. = ca. 86–92, ♩ = ca. 60–64]

This chaotic chase is depicted in a tarantella feel, with wild gestures outlined in chromatic lines. Kasschau's writing includes long descending figures in the solo punctuated by staccato chords, edgy grace notes, and chromatic tones doubled between the hands a whole step apart. The driving 6/8 meter sweeps to a *fortissimo* climax, followed by a short *Adagio* and then a return to the first movement's heartfelt melodic theme. The rapid tempo along with complex writing move this finale beyond level 10. (C minor, level 10+)

KASSERN, Tadeusz Zygfryd (1904–1957) Poland

Teenage Concerto

The concerto form and many technical aspects of piano writing are widely explored in this work, although the thematic material might not sustain student interest. The accompaniment, for which orchestral parts are available, is sparse in texture, often doubling or restating but never competing with the solo part. The two parts frequently interplay, and many moments feature the soloist alone.

(Piano and orchestra, two piano reduction, G. Schirmer)

1. *Allegro risoluto* (♩ = ca. 120)

Dramatic, bitonal opening chords against a strong orchestral figure lead to a quasi cadenza. The entire movement is characterized by repetitive rhythmic figures with unpredictable note patterns and running passages doubled at the octave. The constant and varied articulations are challenging. An extended cadenza derived from the opening material sounds impressive. (F major, level 5)

2. *Andante tranquillo* (♩ = ca. 72)

The solo piano presents a gentle, eight-measure melody with attractive harmonies. As the orchestra enters, the soloist accompanies with a rippling texture of bell-like triplet patterns for the remainder of the movement. An augmented variation on the opening theme enters halfway through the movement. (F major, level 4)

3. *Presto* (♩ = 168)

This quick, lighthearted movement features multiple sections in various keys and changes of tempo. Note patterns are conveniently designed to fit the hands with frequent passages doubled at the octave or with octaves in the right hand alone. Two cadenzas allow the soloist to demonstrate both cantabile and presto characters. The prestissimo coda is delightful. The length and tempo of this movement are considerations in its difficulty level. (F major, level 7)

KIMES, Kenneth Francis (1920–1981) USA

Rainbow Concerto

A concerto in the Romantic style with a true sense of drama and grandeur, this composition is bold and heroic throughout, with colorful harmonies. Although highly patterned, the piece requires a refined technique, particularly in chordal textures and octave playing. Another challenge for the student centers on achieving a full sound without force. The writing in both piano parts is equal, with active rhythms and thick harmonies. The score is marked with pedaling, phrasing, and articulation.

(Two pianos, Clayton F. Summy Co.)

1. *Heroic Reds and Greens* (♩ = ca. 76)

A large range of the piano is explored using dramatic themes and gestures in triad and octave textures. The climax features ascending dominant-7th chords in the style of Tchaikovsky. (C major, level 6)

2. *Capricious Pastels* (♩. = ca. 56)

This waltz movement is fresh with contemporary harmonies. The interplay between Piano I and Piano II provides many rewarding ensemble moments. (C minor, level 6)

3. *Majestic Blues and Purples* (♩ = ca. 90)

An Impressionistic opening is followed by a broad theme in quarter notes. Blocked four-note chords, frequent chromatic alterations, and the use of *8va* for the majority of the movement make reading difficult. The work concludes with a flashy cadenza and a grand coda. (D major, level 7)

KIRNBERGER, Johann Philipp (1721–1783) Germany

Kirnberger was one of the leading theorists and commentators on music of the 18th century, while his reputation as a composer is of less significance. He was introduced to the fugues of J. S. Bach around 1738 and moved to Leipzig to study with the master for two years. His widely published theoretical works had a profound effect on the legacy of Bach.

Concerto in C Minor

Long-attributed to Wilhelm Friedemann Bach, this work is strongly reminiscent of J. S. Bach.

(Harpsichord and string orchestra, two piano reduction, Schott (Eickemeyer))

1. *Allegro* [♩ = ca. 104]

An energetic and well-written work, the *Allegro* brims with characteristics of the Baroque era. The influence of J. S. Bach can be heard in the thick scoring, rolling counterpoint, and insistent continuo, while the solo is generally in a two-part texture. Performers should be encouraged to add embellishments in addition to those provided by the editor. (C minor, level 9)

2. *Adagio* [♩ = ca. 50]

Biting dissonances in the orchestral harmonies create a deeply expressive mood. The solo part is not prominently featured but serves in the continuo role for most of the movement, except when the orchestra rests. The cadenza offers the best opportunity for the soloist to shine. The realized figured bass results in rolled chords with a few linear moments, and the chords allow for dramatic and poignant phrases within the texture. (F minor, level 7)

3. *Presto* [♩. = ca. 69]

The final movement reflects a strong and emphatic character with rapid 16th notes, often divided between the hands for a virtuosic effect. The contrapuntal treatment of the 32nd-note motive is heard frequently in all the parts, creating an irresistible cascade of flourishes. Although mostly in a two-voice texture, the movement is placed at a higher difficulty level due to its speed. Writing is brilliant for the keyboard and the ensemble. (C minor, level 10)

KOŽELUCH, Leopold (1747–1818) Bohemia

Concerto in D Major, Op. 25

Koželuch was a highly prolific composer with over 400 works to his credit. He wrote 23 piano concertos, all but two of them dating from the 1780s, before his tenure in the court of Emperor Francis II, where he served as the immediate successor to Mozart in 1792. Koželuch's concertos reflect the same Viennese Classical style that Mozart perfected.

(Piano and orchestra, two piano reduction, Breitkopf & Härtel)

1. *Allegro* [♩ = ca. 66]

Bright and cheerful, the lightly scored orchestra allows the piano to shine in this *Allegro*. The work is written in sonata form, and the solo presentation of the secondary theme is an interesting feature for the period. A fully developed cadenza displays elements associated with *Sturm und Drang*. The left hand is active and independent, and some toccata-like passages in conjunction with the right hand require careful choreography. This edition provides no fingerings or articulation markings, although ornamentation suggestions are offered. It is a delightful substitute for more familiar Classical-era concertos. (D major, level 9)

2. *Moderato* [♩ = ca. 60]

This work is written in cut time, with the piano line creating a sustained, lyrical melody while the orchestra provides minimal support. An abundance of embellishments added to the rhythmically ornate line requires a strong sense of pulse. The prominence of the piano provides an opportunity for the performer to display control of tone and rhythmic expressivity. (B-flat major, level 10)

3. *Andante con variazioni* [♩ = ca. 80]

This attractive, Classical-style movement features a theme and seven variations, concluding with an *Allegretto* finale. The orchestra presents the theme alone, with the piano entering at Variation 1 with the left hand. The remainder of the set (with the exception of an orchestral Variation 3) focuses attention on the pianist's right hand with gradually increasing note values and ornamentation in each new variation. The delicate filigree of the passagework lies easily in the hands. The *Allegretto* provides liveliness to the solo and is a fitting culmination to this jubilant work. (D major, level 10)

KRAEHENBUEHL, David (1923–1997) USA

Marches Concertantes: A Short Piano Concerto for Young People

The three distinct and rather lengthy movements each have a different march character, featuring engaging 12-tone compositional style with a tonal center. This work is technically patterned and pianistic.

(Piano and band/orchestra, two piano reduction, Carl Fischer)

1. *Marche rondeau—Briskly* (♩ = 132–144)

This energetic and rewarding march fully explores the range of the piano. Included are varied articulations, incorporation of the extreme ends of the keyboard with gestures that rapidly traverse a wide range, and use of the damper and sostenuto pedals. (12 tone, level 7)

2. *Marche solennelle—Mournfully* (♩ = 50)

A funereal mood is created, with Kraehenbuehl utilizing Impressionistic colors to great effect. Dynamics grow to a sustained *fortissimo* before quickly receding. A high level of musical sophistication is required to capture the solemnity. (12 tone, level 7)

3. *Marche vite—Briskly* (♩. = 160)

Themes and patterns from the first movement return, some slightly varied and others exactly as first presented. Overall performance effect is impressive in texture and sound. However, a lack of contrasting material and rhythmic variety might become problematic in maintaining student interest. (12 tone, level 7)

Rhapsody in Rock: A Concerto in One Movement for Piano

The four sections of this piece are meant to be played *attacca*, but they could be played separately. Kraehenbuehl's contemporary chords and patterns do not fit the hand easily at first. The Piano I and II parts, although often in different textures, are evenly matched in difficulty and are effective for two students to play. Band and orchestral parts are available for rental.

(Piano and band/orchestra, two piano reduction, Carl Fischer)

1. *Lazily* (♩. = 100)

This section features a "call and response" texture between the Piano I solo and Piano II accompaniment. The composer cleverly uses § meter to achieve a written swing rhythm. The cadenza in this section lacks unique, interesting material, but students may enjoy the popular style. (Blues in A, level 3)

2. *Going* (♩ = 120)

A quick alla breve work with a syncopated solo part, this movement features a boogie-woogie accompaniment. A variety of treatments of the Piano I material help to build intensity. Satisfying rhythmic interplay between the parts signals the climax of this section. Doubling the melody between the hands occurs at different intervals, and more involved textures add interest toward the end. (Modal, level 7)

3. *Broadly* (♩ = 92)

The opening measures of this ballad-style section present a solo statement marked *molto rubato*. The texture is comprised largely of triadic patterns and accented harmonic intervals, creating a punctuated *marcato* articulation within a pedaled sonority that contrasts nicely with the flowing *dolce cantabile* theme occurring later. Effective ensemble writing between Pianos I and II is featured here, in the shortest section of the piece. (F major, level 5)

4. *With energy* (♩ = 120)

The final section is the most "rock style," featuring blues scale patterns and syncopations in both hands. There are repetitive patterns throughout and the ending is flashy. This final movement would work particularly well as a stand-alone piece. (Blues in G, level 7)

KUHLAU, Friedrich (1786–1832) Denmark, born in Germany

Piano Concerto in C Major, Op. 7

This early work is grandiose, exuberant, and surprisingly mature in the breadth of its themes and its sensitive awareness of style. Modeled after Beethoven's *Piano Concerto in C, Op. 15*, this composition would make an excellent alternative for a performer with flair and strong fingers.

(Piano and orchestra, two piano reduction, Bisel Classics)

1. *Allegro* [♩ = ca. 132]

Flourishes of rapid scalar, arpeggiated, and broken-chord patterns incorporate a wide range of the keyboard in this pianistic movement. A fermata is indicated for the inclusion of a cadenza. A commanding presence in both the solo and orchestra is required for effective performance. (C major, level 10)

2. *Adagio* [♩ = ca. 50]

The beautifully embellished piano texture requires musical and interpretive maturity and a secure rhythmic sense. The cantabile melody, combined with the key of A-flat major, creates a luxurious sound. Allusions to Beethoven are frequent, including treatment of harmony and texture in the piano and orchestra. The work provides a challenging but worthwhile musical endeavor for a sensitive and thoughtful performer. (A-flat major, level 10)

3. *Allegro* [♩ = ca. 132]

This thoroughly compelling rondo demonstrates Kuhlau's dexterity as composer and pianist. The interaction between the piano and orchestra crackles with excitement, and the overall effect is one of ceremonial splendor. Extended use of the damper pedal as indicated by the composer throughout the movement, particularly in the arioso-like cadenza, is another homage to Beethoven. Agility within and between the hands should be equal, and articulations should be pronounced. A rousing coda concludes the work. (C major, level 10)

LANCEN, Serge (1922–2005) France

Concertino

The *Concertino* is a well-crafted work in a dashing and vibrant style that displays the mid-20th century French penchant for chromaticism and extended harmonies within a diatonic framework.

(Piano and orchestra, two piano reduction, Hinrichsen Edition/Peters Edition)

1. *Allegro* (♩ = 106)

A simple and carefree attitude permeates this movement, with light textures and a continuous eighth-note pattern in scalar passages and broken-chord figurations throughout. The piece fits the hands well with only a few exceptions. The use of pedal should be carefully considered to support the articulation and to maintain harmonic and linear clarity. (C major, level 9)

2. *Andante* (♪ = 84)

The soloist presents the expressive theme four times throughout the movement, each time following a statement by the orchestra. With each statement, the original theme is transposed either up or down a half step to create an eerie sense of uncertainty. Colorful harmonies in the left-hand broken-chord accompaniment feature some very wide stretches. (G major, level 9)

3. *Allegro* (♩ = 92)

According to the score, the thematic material is based on a popular Lebanese melody. Toccata-like textures propel the music forward in four-note chords, octaves, and single-line melodies distributed between the hands. The chromatic harmonic language will likely be challenging to learn and memorize, although the writing is highly patterned. (C major, level 10)

LANTIER, Pierre (1910–1998) France

Concertinetto

(Piano and orchestra, two piano reduction, Éditions Auguste Zurfluh)

Andantino [♩ = ca. 90]

A charming one-movement work with a hint of Impressionism and exoticism, this composition features mildly contemporary harmonies in the orchestration. The fingerings are clear and instructive for achieving articulation and efficiency of motion. It is an appropriate piece for a student whose musical intellect exceeds technical ability. (C major, level 4)

LARSSON, Lars-Erik (1908–1986) Sweden

Concertino, Op. 45, No. 12

The *Concertino's* outer movements use unconventional tonality, a feature of Larsson's eclectic compositional approach. Many passages are doubled at the octave. This challenging work is worth the effort. (Piano and string orchestra, full score, Carl Gehrmans Musikforlag)

1. *Allegro molto* (♩ = ca. 152)

Instead of thematic material, this movement creates appealing textures and sound palettes in a pseudo-minimalist style, resulting in clever shapes and patterns that fit the hand well. A chorale-like *dolce* theme provides contrast intermittently. (Atonal, level 10)

2. *Andante con moto* (♩ = 92)

Wistful and meditative, the second movement contains planing harmonies and repetitive gestures. Rhythmic activity increases throughout the movement. There are independent and angular lines in each hand, as well as multiple key changes. (A major, level 10)

3. *Allegro scherzando* (♩. = ca. 112)

This movement is a captivating, folk-style gigue with rhythmic flamboyance. A meditative pastorale section features a leaner texture with piano and solo strings, before revisiting elements from the first movement to conclude the work. It is an excellent choice for a performer with agile fingers. (Modal, level 10)

LINEK, Jiří Ignác (1725–1791) Czech Republic

Linek is a late-Baroque, provincial Czech composer who skillfully combined the rustic, tuneful, and energetic elements of Czech folk music with the influence of modern musical trends from Prague.

Concerto in F Major

The concerto grosso form is employed in all movements of this Classically-styled work, with a Baroque aesthetic that features prominent ornamentation throughout.

(Harpsichord and orchestra, full score, Heinrichshofen [Edizioni Pegasus])

1. *Allegro moderato* [♩ = ca. 108]

Figurations and ornaments will require hand-position adjustments and careful fingerings in this joyful, energetic movement. A stable sense of pulse is necessary to negotiate the rhythmic patterns. (F major, level 9)

2. *Andante* [♩ = ca. 62]

An expressive movement with simple musical textures, the cantabile line is decorated with trills and grace notes, requiring secure rhythmic control for musical execution. (B-flat major, level 8)

3. *Allegro* [♩ = ca. 116]

Classical-style passagework abounds in this jaunty movement, including broken-octave and Alberti bass accompaniment patterns in the left hand, and scalar and triadic shapes in the right hand. The movement takes an idiomatic approach to the keyboard. (F major, level 8)

MANEN, Christian (b. 1934) France

Concertino

The composer wrote this piece either for a very specific ability level or a specific individual, as he indicates at the top of the score, "for (18 months of) piano and orchestra." The technical demands indicate an understanding of the young pianist's development in the first years of study.

(Piano and orchestra, two piano arrangement, Éditions Auguste Zurfluh)

1. *Gai et très rythmé* (♩ = 88)

This high-spirited movement is engaging from the very start, and features a French style reminiscent of Francis Poulenc. The punctuated, simple, and somewhat sparse solo statements doubled at the octave are given forward momentum by the incessant eighth notes and playful dissonances in the orchestra. The young student may find the simplified versions of textures in the development section useful. Syncopation, frequent rests, and a harmonic language that deviates from the basic C major framework are the potential difficulties. (C major, level 1)

2. *Aimable et avec souplesse/Final—Presto* (♩ = 104, 184)

Tender melodies derived from French folk songs are divided between the hands or doubled at the octave. The dynamic range of *pianissimo* to *fortissimo* is impressive for a compact piece with an overall gentle demeanor. The *presto* arrives *attacca,* and the solo focuses on rapid wrist rotation in contrary motion. The orchestra and solo piano alternate musical statements and lead to a final *fortissimo* cluster on the lowest piano keys, to be played "with the fist." (C major, level 2)

MARGOLA, Franco (1908–1992) Italy

Kinderkonzert

Margola was an important Italian composer of the 20th century, writing in an energetic Neoclassical style influenced by Igor Stravinsky. Bright and sunny themes and passagework in the solo part are featured along with detailed orchestration.

(Piano and orchestra, two piano reduction, Ricordi)

1. *Allegro* (♩ = 132)

This pianistic and musically advanced work features refined and engaging writing for the agile player. Many shifts of harmony and borrowed chords add to both the difficulty and attractiveness of this piece. (A minor, level 10)

2. *Aria (Larghetto)* (♩ = 63)

This spirited *da capo aria* is in neo-Baroque style, with a clear sense of structure and line. (F major, level 10)

3. *Allegro spigliato* (♩ = 168)

Expert use of meter and rhythm is apparent in this composition's phrasing and at the cadences. An extensive cadenza reiterates many themes encountered in the movement with interesting and sudden stylistic shifts. It is not as technically difficult as the first movement, but features engaging and charismatic writing with a dazzling effect. (A minor, level 10)

Terzo Concerto

This ambitious work features expanded tonality and some jazz influence. It is an appropriate choice for a student with a keen musical intellect and a fondness for modernism.

(Piano and orchestra, two piano reduction, Edizioni Curci)

1. *Allegro assai* (♩ = 138)

Despite the somewhat angular writing, the hand positions feel natural and patterns easily fit the hand. Careful attention to fingerings during the learning process will be necessary. The right hand demands facility, while the left hand is an accompaniment, apart from some textures doubled at the octave. A faster middle section is to be played alla breve. This effective piece is derived from contemporary harmonic idioms. (Expanded tonality, level 10)

2. *Andante disteso* (♩ = 88)

An Impressionistic quality permeates this melancholy movement in sonata-rondo form. The lack of a key center and a clever use of irregular and overlapping phrases with two distinct, independent lines make it musically appealing and challenging for the performer. Left-hand counterpoint creates another layer of melodic interest. The orchestral accompaniment is minimal until the B section. (Expanded tonality, level 10)

3. *Vivo con spirito* (♩ = 84)

A quirky, fun movement in the style of Dmitri Shostakovich, this work features patterns that are well conceived for efficient and speedy performance. It is the only movement that has a tonal center. A substantial cadenza before a restatement of the opening theme and a swift coda build to an exciting ending. (A minor, level 10)

MARTINI, Giovanni Battista (1706–1784) Italy

"Padre Martini" was an accomplished composer, music theorist, music historian, and internationally renowned teacher. Among his students were J. C. Bach, W. A. Mozart, and Christoph Gluck.

Concerto in C Major

Martini's works demonstrate the stylistic trends in piano concertos of the pre-Mozart period outside Germany. All movements are in binary form, and the ritornello form is favored, though with modifications indicative of the period.

(Harpsichord and string orchestra, full score, S. A. Edizioni Suvini Zerboni)

1. *Allegro sostenuto* [♩ = ca. 98]

The primary challenge of this movement lies in creating seamless transitions between the various rhythm patterns. Fingerings are provided. A virtuosic cadenza is included before the final orchestral entrance. (C major, level 8)

2. *Larghetto* [♪ = ca. 54]

The soloist is featured by presenting thematic elements in longer phrases, while the orchestra takes on a supportive accompanimental role, with less clear distinctions made between soloist and *tutti* sections. Some exotic ideas in the melody color the harmonic minor mode. (C minor, level 6)

3. *Allegro molto* [♩ = ca. 120]

An exuberant display with prominent orchestral *tuttis*, this movement utilizes distinctly different thematic material in the solo, establishing its independence from the larger ensemble. The tempo requires agile fingerings. (C major, level 8)

4. *Allegretto* [♩ = ca. 110]

A simple minuet with short phrases in dotted rhythms, this movement is led by the soloist. According to instructions in the score, the *Allegro molto* is customarily repeated after the *Allegretto* has been played. (C major, level 6)

Concerto in D Major

(Harpsichord and orchestra, two piano reduction, Classici Musicali Italiani)

1. *Allegro* (♩ = 120)

A spirited and virtuosic work in ritornello style, this movement features brilliant, running 16th notes. The solo material is completely different from that of the orchestral *tuttis* and features Baroque-style keyboard figurations in sequences and repeated phrases with a consistent orchestral accompaniment. (D major, level 7)

2. *Andante* (♪ = 80–84)

This mournful movement demonstrates an adventurous, masterfully executed harmonic sense with contrapuntal textures in the orchestra and a cantilena-style solo. The left hand doubles the cello continuo throughout. Effective and concise, the work is filled with unexpected twists and deep emotion. (D minor, level 5)

3. *Allegro* (♩ = 126)

The solo presents new thematic material after the opening *tutti*. It features frequent use of repeated patterns in compact hand shapes and clever use of the parallel minor key. This final movement is a motivating work in terms of fingerwork and rhythms. (D major, level 6)

Concerto in F Major

This edition from 1943 is considered useful for its "revision and reduction" for two pianos, despite the excessive liberties taken during editing. Each of these movements makes a natural transition from the orchestra to the piano.

(Harpsichord and orchestra, two piano reduction, Classici Musicali Italiani)

1. *Allegretto* (♩ = 92–96)

Buoyant and bubbly, early-Classical homophonic writing pervades with a rolling triadic accompaniment in triplets against a right-hand melody. It showcases rising arpeggiated patterns followed by fast, falling scales. The solo and *tutti* material are clearly differentiated. Quick finger execution is needed for passagework in a limited range. (F major, level 8)

2. *Lento* (♪ = 66)

A wistful quality permeates the aching harmonies and cantabile lines, crafted in clear phrases. This movement would be suitable to aid a younger student in learning how to integrate simple ornaments into a very linear melody. (F minor, level 6)

3. *Allegro* (♩. = 60)

This dance in ⅜ has an improvised quality in its rhythmic patterns and cadenzas, for which Martini composed two different versions. The technical requirements emphasize scale playing in the right hand. (F major, level 7)

4. *Balletto Spiritoso* (♩ = ca. 112)

The *Balletto* is a light, dance-like form associated with the Italian madrigal. A distinguishing feature is the "fa-la-la" refrain at the end of the sections, which Martini imitates in punctuated interruptions from the orchestra. An insistent and active left-hand part imitates the continuo, while the right hand plays sequences and repetitive patterns. (F major, level 7)

Concerto in G Major

The inclusion of a fourth movement, as in this concerto, was rare in its time. It is a very attractive piece for the motivated and facile performer, particularly one who displays a fondness for Baroque repertoire.

(Harpsichord and string orchestra, full score, G. Zanibon—Padova)

1. *Spiritoso* [♩ = ca. 104]

This commanding work is full of vitality and combines Baroque sensibilities with a masterful, progressive blend of binary and ritornello forms. (G major, level 9)

2. *Andante* [♪ = ca. 66]

The stunningly beautiful and highly embellished melody of this *Andante* creates rhythmic complexities. It combines deeply expressive harmonies with some unexpected and delightful twists to create a powerful musical statement. (G minor, level 9)

3. *Allegro* [♩ = ca. 68]

Sequence and repetition of rapid triplet figures in the right hand are features of this quick, jaunty dance in cut time. (G major, level 9)

4. *Vivace* [♩. = ca. 72]

This poised minuet in ⅜ cleverly plays with expectations of each regular, eight-measure phrase. (G major, level 9)

MAYR, Johann Simon (1763–1845) Italy, born in Germany

Mayr was one of the leading opera composers in Italy and was the teacher of Gaetano Donizetti. His music has a foundation in the Classical tradition and conforms to early 19th-century Italian tastes. His numerous concertos are important works that fill a gap left in the concerto genre by Italian composers who abandoned their grand instrumental tradition in favor of opera.

Concerto No. 1 in C Major

This first concerto is a well-crafted work with a style borrowed from Viennese Classicism. The piano is prominently featured throughout, with supporting accompaniment from the orchestra, scored for two oboes, two horns, and strings. The facility needed to achieve smooth tone and articulation adds to the level of difficulty.

(Piano and orchestra, two piano reduction, Boccaccini & Spada Editori)

1. *Allegro moderato* [♩ = ca. 72]

Full of sparkling personality, this attractive piece would serve as a fitting substitute for a Mozart concerto. A consistently transparent texture is maintained without any overly demanding passagework. A stylish, fully developed cadenza is provided by the composer. (C major, level 9)

2. *Andantino grazioso* [♩ = ca. 96]

The *Andantino grazioso* makes a simple musical statement with a rolling triplet accompaniment in a flowing tempo. There are no significant technical or musical challenges, making this a good piece for focusing on balance and consistency of tone. (F major, level 7)

3. *Rondo Allegro* [♩. = ca. 98]

A jovial and energetic movement, this *Rondo Allegro* includes quick 16th-note runs in the right hand. The brilliant technical patterns are designed for efficient execution. The solo piano is featured in short cadenzas between sections and would be appropriate for developing rapid finger movement. (C major, level 9)

Concerto No. 2 in C Major

This lengthy, fully formed work in the spirit of Mozart aims to delight. The orchestration is scored for strings, two oboes, and two horns.

(Piano and orchestra, two piano reduction, Boccaccini & Spada Editori)

1. *Allegro moderato* [$\textstyle\downarrow$ = ca. 68]

Many of the popular effects of the Classical piano concerto are found in this piece. Extended 16th-note passages require careful attention to tone, shape, and momentum, but they fit easily in the hand (with the exception of some odd register shifts). Two cadenzas are provided by the editor. (C major, level 9)

2. *Andantino con variazioni* [$\downarrow$ = ca. 96]

A charming theme with six variations, this movement explores various filigree and decorative patterns. Some awkward left-hand accompaniment patterns involving octaves and position changes on the keyboard are not always intuitive. It is technically and musically the most difficult movement of the concerto. (F major, level 10)

3. *Allegro moderato* [$\downarrow$ = ca. 90]

This rollicking rondo resembles a hunting song. Features include attractive, logical shapes in the melodic phrasing and triadic patterns of the left hand, with the right hand featuring repetitive figurations. (C major, level 9)

MEUNIER, Gérard (b. 1928) France

Concertino "Charlotte"

This well-written, three-movement work contains moderate contemporary harmonies and clear formal structures. The letters in the word *Charlotte* serve as material for subtle motives and themes in each movement. Accessible for a young student, there are many breaks for the soloist. The composer gives no tempo markings other than the provided metronome indications.

(Piano orchestra, two piano reduction, Editions Henry Lemoine)

1. ($\downarrow$ = 126)

An energetic piece, this opening movement has patterns that are doubled at the octave. Varied dynamics and detached articulations in the solo part will help develop tone projection. An active accompaniment in the orchestra provides most of the textural interest. (D mixolydian, level 3)

2. ($\downarrow$ = 60)

A melody accompanied by chordal textures and independently moving lines is followed by a simple descant above the orchestra. (A minor, level 3)

3. ($\downarrow$ = 108)

An effective jazz-style piece, the movement is dedicated, "Hommage à Lionel Hampton." The walking bass line in the orchestra sets the stage for the soloist to perform a syncopated version of the "Charlotte" theme, doubled at the octave. A chromatic ostinato pattern in the left hand doubles the orchestra while the trumpets play rhythmic, *fortissimo* chords. Although not indicated, the rhythm may be swung. (A major, level 3)

MIER, Martha (b. 1936) USA

Concerto in Classical Style

This piece was commisioned by the Southwest District of the Ohio Music Teachers Association for their annual Concerto Auditions in Cincinnati. Although written for solo piano with piano accompaniment, the interaction between the parts clearly establishes the roles of soloist and orchestra. Piano I and Piano II are equally difficult. The score provides excellent fingering suggestions, pedal indications, and articulations.

(Two pianos, Alfred Music)

1. *Allegro* (♩ = 112)

The delightful theme comprised of scales and triads, the shape of the line, and the symmetrical phrases effectively capture the spirit of the Classical style. There are some surprises in form, particularly with the placement of the effective cadenza. (C major, level 6)

2. *Larghetto cantabile* (♩ = 63)

Similar to many slow sonatina movements, this work showcases a cantabile melody over a rolling triadic accompaniment. Effective rhythmic and melodic textures alternate between Piano I and Piano II. (F major, level 5)

3. *Allegro marcia* (♩. = 126)

This energetic rondo in 6/8 meter evokes a tarantella character, with only a few tricky technical passages. A sunny, contrasting A major section spins a long melody over a sustained accompaniment. An extended cadenza utilizes rhythmic groupings and quick harmonic rhythm to create excitement, and the skillful use of a measured trill leads to *tempo primo* with stylistic flair. (C major, level 5)

Concertino in Jazz Styles

(Two pianos, Alfred Music)

This accessible piece will introduce students at the late elementary level to the sounds of jazz through Mier's signature compositional style.

1. *Blue Light Special—Moderately* (♩ = 96)

The appealing harmonies and "swing" rhythm in Piano II provides a full, supportive texture to Piano I's melody doubled at the octave in straightforward rhythms. Although the note groupings are mostly written within five-finger patterns, the student is required to execute some sophisticated fingerings. Finger substitutions, frequent thumb crossings, and independence of the fingers account for the difficulty of this movement. (C major, level 2)

2. *Starlight Jazz—Smoothly* (♩ = 112)

The 3/4 meter, long melodic phrases, "blue" notes, and minor key establish the mood of this movement in ABA form. Increased activity in the key of C major defines the B section before a winning cadenza returns to the opening A section. Broken triads and use of pedal throughout for both performers create a rich sonority. (A minor, level 3)

3. *Strolling Along the Boardwalk—Jauntily* (♩ = 92)

This movement is based on the 12-bar blues chord progression, with the eighth notes played in a swing style as indicated by the ♪♪ = ♪³♪ marking. The blocked harmonic textures in the left hand accompany blues-inspired riffs in the right hand that students will enjoy playing. It is a motivating piece with an impressive ending. (F major, level 2)

MILFORD, Robin (1903–1959) Great Britain

A distinctive English composer of the early 20th century, Milford suffered artistically in the face of the avant-garde establishment that was in vogue during the 1950s and 1960s.

Fishing by Moonlight, Op. 96

(Piano and string orchestra, full score, Hinrichsen Edition)

Andante espressivo [♪ = ca. 76]

Fishing by Moonlight is a one-movement work inspired by a painting of the same title by Dutch artist Aert van der Neer (1603–1677). Milford showcases the ability to condense a mood or atmosphere into surprisingly simple textures through sophisticated and original writing with Romantic tendencies, contemporary harmonic coloring, and lush string writing. A *doppio movimento* middle section is characterized by Neoclassicism and sweeping lines. Diverse rhythms augment this work's complexity, and some figures may initially pose challenges. It is a fine work for a mature student with a solid sense of pulse. (C minor, level 10)

MILLER, Beatrice A. (1923–2015) USA

Concerto No. 1 in A Minor

This piece contains appealing and memorable themes, as well as flowing patterns and rich voicings in Piano II that make for an overall robust sonority. The chordal textures and some octave passages will require an appropriate hand size.

(Two pianos, Summy-Birchard Inc.)

1. *Con energia* (♩ = 76–80)

A clever relationship between motives appears in the themes of this sonata-allegro movement. Piano I requires solid hand independence and familiarity with various chord shapes. (A minor, level 6)

2. *Adagio* (♩ = 50–54)

This movement captures the essence of Chopin. Use of harmonic pedaling is indicated, and triads with inversions in the left hand are featured. Right-hand voicing will need careful consideration. (G major, level 6)

3. *Con allegria* (♩ = 104–112)

Repetition of material makes this lengthy movement less daunting, but the phrasing can be monotonous if not carefully planned. The captivating B section and an impressive cadenza, reminiscent of Beethoven, are delightful. (C major, level 7)

MOZART, Wolfgang Amadeus (1756–1791) Austria

The 23 piano concertos of Wolfgang Amadeus Mozart were composed throughout his active compositional life. They can be organized into four periods, with the first group composed in Salzburg between 1773 and 1780. The remaining concertos were composed in Vienna. Mozart's rise and fall in popularity with the Viennese public is correlated with each year's output of new concertos. The second group includes the three concertos written during the summer of 1782. The third group includes 12 masterpieces written between 1784 and 1786. The fourth group includes the final two concertos of 1788 and 1791.

The piano concertos are the most personal works of Mozart, having been written to showcase the composer's keyboard prowess in public performances. His catalogue of piano concertos represents not only the "coming of age" of a virtuoso composer and performer, but also of a genre and an instrument, as they were the first to be written specifically for the pianoforte. Because the modern pianoforte was able to effectively balance with the orchestra, it could serve not only as a tonal equal but also as a dramatic and musical protagonist. The fusion of symphonic and concerto elements came to fruition in these works, and Mozart truly liberated the orchestra from its previous position of mere accompanist to more of a symphonic role, elevating the piano concerto to a position of high stature and prominence.

Concerto in F Major, K. 37

The outer movements are arrangements of sonata movements by Hermann Raupach and Leontzi Honauer respectively, while the second movement is likely by Mozart. It is scored for strings, oboes, and horns.

(Piano and orchestra, two piano reduction, Oxford University Press)

1. *Allegro* [♩ = 132]

Energized and radiant with dramatic turns, this movement contains a variety of broken-chord figures and scalar passages. (F major, level 8)

2. *Andante* [♪ = 96]

This poised and stately movement in ⅜ contains some rhythmic complexities within an expressive context. A cadenza is provided by the editor. (C major, level 8)

3. [♩ = 132]

Mozart gave no tempo marking for this movement. A spirited rondo, the movement has more intricacies between the hands than in the other movements. It features frequent Alberti bass accompaniment patterns. The score indicates a repeat of the opening A and B sections, while ornamentation becomes prominent from the C section to the end. A cadenza is provided by the editor. (F major, level 9)

Concerto in B-flat Major, K. 39

These arrangements of sonata movements by Hermann Raupach and Johann Schobert are scored for strings, oboes, and horns.

(Piano and orchestra, two piano reduction, Oxford University Press)

1. *Allegro spiritoso* [♩ = 126]

The *Allegro spiritoso* movement features a graceful quality with elegant right-hand figuration and rhythmic interest. The orchestral *tuttis* introduced here by Mozart demonstrate his desire to add creative touches to Raupach's source material. A cadenza is provided by the editor. (B-flat major, level 9)

2. *Andante* [♩ = 72]

At times dreamy and other times bold in its suspensions and half-step clashes, this movement shows the potential of a composer who would rise to heights of true genius. Mozart added a short introductory prelude and a more elaborate melodic line to Schobert's finely drawn melodic structure. The triplet figure provides a consistent pulse throughout. (F major, level 7)

3. *Molto allegro* [♩ = 80]

In a buoyant and playful style with primarily non-legato articulation, this finale movement showcases clever technical patterns, particularly in the middle section. It is a rewarding and technically accessible work for a performer with agile fingers. A cadenza is provided by the editor. (B-flat major, level 9)

Concerto in D Major, K. 40

These arrangements of sonata movements by Leontzi Honauer, Johann Gottfried Eckard, and C. P. E. Bach are scored for strings, oboes, horns, and trumpets.

(Piano and orchestra, two piano reduction, Oxford University Press)

1. *Allegro maestoso* [♩ = 132]

This movement is full of drama and lyricism, with substantial right-hand passagework and ornamentation over a consistent left-hand Alberti bass. It includes the only original cadenza provided by Mozart in the four early concertos. (D major, level 9)

2. *Andante* [♪ = 76]

Effective treatment of a decorated legato line flows over a broken-triad accompaniment. There are minimal position changes, with patterns lying readily in the hand, and a prominent use of trills. (A major, level 9)

3. *Presto* [♩. = 88]

A quick ⅜ meter suggests a "returning from the hunt" spirit. Figurations and harmonic structure align closely with the original material. The movement features highly energetic and engaging scale passages. The use of rotation in both hands will be key in executing patterns at the correct tempo. (D major, level 9)

Concerto in G Major, K. 41

These arrangements of sonata movements by Leontzi Honauer and Hermann Raupach are scored for strings, flutes, and horns.

(Piano and orchestra, two piano reduction, Oxford University Press)

1. *Allegro* [♩ = 126–132]

This rhythmically straightforward movement includes an Alberti bass accompaniment. The performer will need a comfortable technique to capture the charisma. A cadenza is provided by the editor. (G major, level 10)

2. *Andante* [♪ = 88]

This hauntingly poignant movement from Raupach is a gem among the four early concertos. A diversity of rhythms augments the work's complexity and expressive power. A successful performance requires musical maturity. (G minor, level 9)

3. *Molto allegro* [♩ = 116]

Irresistible, signature Mozartian flair is captured in the exciting themes and animated interaction with orchestra. A highly embellished melodic line with an abundance of ornamentation requires careful attention to balance between and within both hands. The cadenza is by the editor. (G major, level 10)

Concerto in D Major, K. 107, No. 1

The three concertos of K. 107, written in 1771–1772, are near-literal arrangements of piano sonatas by J. C. Bach from his *Six sonates pour le clavecin ou le piano forte, Op. 5*, with slight orchestrations added as accompaniments. Mozart held J. C. Bach in very high esteem and used one of his themes in the slow movement of the *Concerto in A Major, K. 414* as a memorial tribute upon Bach's death. The works offer an inventive use of the original source material and can be effectively performed as piano quartets.

(Harpsichord and string orchestra, full score, Schott Music)

1. *Allegro* [♩ = ca. 138]

This joyous, entertaining chamber music has attractive and simple string parts. Engaging characters and themes are used throughout, and patterns translate well to the piano. A lengthy and effective cadenza is provided. (D major, level 8)

2. *Andante* [♪ = ca. 90]

An active left hand provides momentum for the ensemble as well as the foundation for the right hand. The movement is elegant and graceful with prominent ornamentation and varied articulations in both hands. It also features an expressive cadenza. (G major, level 8)

3. *Tempo di menuetto* [♩. = ca. 126]

This simple and immediately appealing movement includes consecutive non-legato harmonic 3rds in the right hand. A trio section in D minor is strikingly different in character and attitude, with pizzicato strings providing extra variety. (D major, level 7)

Concerto in G Major, K. 107, No. 2

(Harpsichord and string orchestra, full score, Schott Music)

1. *Allegro* [♩ = ca. 130]

Mozart's solo part is derived from the ritornello of the orchestra, but with new thematic material introduced by the soloist during the first entry. It is pleasant, predictable, and always charming. Technical demands are similar to more difficult sonatina movements, with scale patterns in the right hand accompanied by Alberti bass patterns. (G major, level 8)

2. *Allegretto* [♩ = ca. 70]

Binary form is used for this theme and each of its four variations. String parts are characterized by various approaches to syncopation. Rhythmic activity becomes busy at times with increasingly active interaction between the soloist and the strings. The melody and accompaniment require careful balance between the hands. (G major, level 8)

Concerto in E-flat Major, K. 107, No. 3

(Harpsichord and string orchestra, full score, Schott Music)

1. *Allegro* [♩ = ca. 142]

This spirited movement features appealing material in the strings and rapid ornamental figurations in the keyboard. A clearly delineated development section portrays a strongly contrasting character. Perky keyboard gestures add a touch of humor. The tempo and the variety of intricate technical patterns contribute to the difficulty of this movement. No cadenza is provided. (E-flat major, level 9)

2. *Allegretto* [♩ = ca. 68]

A cantabile melody unfolds above a gently rocking accompaniment. The middle section of this rondo features a restless 16th-note pattern divided between the hands. The performer may choose to explore opportunities for ornamentation in addition to what is already indicated in the score. (E-flat major, level 8)

Concerto in D Major, K. 175

The *Concerto in D Major, K. 175* represents Mozart's first fully original concerto written as a showpiece for the young virtuoso himself to perform. Mozart continued to perform this work until the year of his death. It was strikingly unique, brilliant, and unmatched at the time. The sense of grandeur is heightened in the orchestration by the addition of trumpets and timpani. In 1782, Mozart revised the concerto to adapt it to the changing tastes of his audiences by replacing the original final movement with a Viennese rondo. (See *Concerto Rondo in D Major, K. 382*.)

(Piano and orchestra, two piano reduction, many standard editions)

1. *Allegro* [♩ = ca. 126]

The solo part demonstrates a new level of brilliance and technical challenge. Figurations are remarkably fresh and resourceful, particularly when compared with other works of the period. The more independent and robust orchestral accompaniment provides an admirable complement. The cadenza was composed by Mozart. (D major, level 10)

2. *Andante ma un poco adagio* [♩ = ca. 48]

Elegant and refined, this minuet displays Mozart's understanding of dramatic intent and vocally inspired melodies. The student should possess a sure sense of balance and control of touch. The cadenza was composed by Mozart. (G major, level 8)

3. *Allegro* [♩ = ca. 132]

With youthful exuberance, Mozart blends fugal imitation in sonata-allegro form with an *opera buffa* character, as if to demonstrate his masterful grasp of composition by the age of 18. This technical masterpiece displays exhilarating scales, broken octaves, and dashing broken chords. (D major, level 10)

Concerto in B-flat Major, K. 238

Mozart completed three concertos in 1776: K. 238, 242 (for three pianos), and 246. All three are similar in orchestration and structure. They were written to allow the soloist to display skill while entertaining a small gathering of listeners. The *Concerto in B-flat Major, K. 238* is the most demanding of the three, rivaling concertos of Mozart's admired colleague J. C. Bach, yet it also is the least flamboyant. (All three movements end with a *piano* dynamic level.) According to Dutch musicologist Marius Flothuis, "This is the earliest example of 'orchestral chamber music,' a hallmark of many of Mozart's mature concertos."[6] Mozart provides cadenzas for all three movements.

(Piano and orchestra, two piano reduction, many standard editions)

1. *Allegro aperto* [♩ = ca. 132]

The *Allegro aperto* refers to a definite and obvious allegro tempo. *Allegro aperto* is defined as "an *allegro* with broad, clear phrasing." The movement follows the basic principles of the sonata, with short ritornellos and a concise, fantasia-like development section. Included are frequent octave demands and extended 16th-note runs. (B-flat major, level 10)

2. *Andante un poco adagio* [♩ = ca. 56]

One of Mozart's finest slow movements of the early concertos, this *Andante* features an expressively singing line that gently weaves in an uninterrupted ⅜ flow. A brief four-measure development section is transitional. The orchestration provides a special color to this movement, with muted pizzicato strings and flutes instead of oboes. There are no particular technical difficulties, but the movement is musically sophisticated. (G major, level 9)

3. *Allegro* [♩ = ca. 92]

This simple, stately rondo finale does not include the bravura displays that Mozart would normally employ in such a work. Alternations between duple and triple rhythms can be challenging. (B-flat major, level 9)

Concerto in C Major, K. 246

Written for the Countess Lützow of the fortress Hohensalzburg, this concerto lacks the outward brilliance of others from this period. However, enough facility is required in the outer movements to suggest that Lützow was an accomplished pianist. Mozart performed the work often and used it in his teaching; the latter likely explains why there are three sets of cadenzas of varying degrees of difficulty in the work. The relative technical simplicity of this concerto makes it ideal for young students.

(Piano and orchestra, two piano reduction, many standard editions)

1. *Allegro aperto* [♩ = ca. 138]

This movement represents Mozart's keyboard style within the concerto genre, making it an excellent introductory work. The textures and passagework, with predominant scales and Alberti bass, are similar to his sonatas at this level. (C major, level 9)

2. *Andante* [♩ = ca. 104–108]

This beautiful movement hints at the great slow movements in Mozart's later concertos. Rapid rhythmic

---

[6] Marius Flothuis, *Mozart's Piano Concertos* (Amsterdam: Editions Rodopi, 2001), 13.

figures, incorporating 32nd and 64th notes, can be intimidating at first glance. The detailed articulations provide stylistic and expressive gravitas. (F major, level 9)

3. *Tempo di menuetto* [♩ = ca. 126]

The rondo finale is a good-natured minuet that whisks along freely without pronounced technical difficulties. Embellishments require rapid execution. (C major, level 9)

Concert Rondo in D Major, K. 382

(Piano and orchestra, two piano reduction, many standard editions)

Allegretto grazioso [♩ = 76]

This *Concert Rondo* stands as a superb representation of Mozart's style and impeccable concerto writing. He was delighted with this piece and referred to it as a "gem" in a letter to his father, Leopold. Written as a substitute for the last movement of the *Piano Concerto in D Major, K. 175*, the *Rondo in D Major* is not actually a rondo but rather a set of variations. A slow, expressive *Adagio* and an *Allegro* hunting song in ⅜ provide contrast, and a cadenza written by Mozart segues into a rousing coda. It is an excellent piece to study facets of Mozart's keyboard writing, requiring agile fingers to execute extended trills, voicing within each hand, and rapid passagework. (D major, level 10)

Concert Rondo in A Major, K. 386

(Piano and orchestra, two piano reduction, many standard editions)

Allegretto [♩ = ca. 64]

One of Mozart's most graceful works, this composition is comparable to the *Rondo, K. 382* and was written in the same year. The piece was believed to be unfinished by Mozart due to the absence of the final pages upon the manuscript's sale by Constanze Mozart in 1799. The autograph went through a tumultuous period of being sold, separated, and scattered by its various owners. Well-intentioned arrangements were made of the original, including a solo piano version published by Cipriani Potter in 1839. Alfred Einstein used Potter's arrangement and only two pages of the score to reconstruct the work in a 1936 publication. Exhaustive efforts to gather and reassemble 90 percent of the autograph resulted in a 1962 edition by Paul Badura-Skoda and Charles Mackerras, and the final pages, which were discovered in the British Library in 1980 by Alan Tyson, are now incorporated into some scores. The *Rondo in A Major, K. 386* is similar in style and spirit to the *Concerto in A Major, K. 414*, written around the same time yet with different instrumentation. The themes are bright and cheerful, and the piece maintains a consistent tempo and a joyful character throughout. While there is no surviving cadenza by Mozart, notable musicians and scholars, including Paul Badura-Skoda and George Szell, have written convincing possibilities. The performer needs a refined technique for passagework and ornamentation. (A major, level 10)

Concerto F Major, K. 413

A mannered and orderly concerto, this work is reminiscent of the galant style of J. C. Bach.

(Piano and orchestra, two piano reduction, many standard editions)

1. *Allegro* [♩ = ca. 144]

One of only three concerto first movements by Mozart in ⅜ time, the *Allegro* is also notable for the number of themes—upwards of 10—that Mozart presents throughout the exposition. A new theme in C minor starts the development section. The playful and amiable character is created with rapid scale and alternating-note passages and cross-hand patterns. A cadenza is provided by Mozart. (F major, level 9)

2. *Larghetto* [♩ = ca. 69]

This sweet, yet somewhat ordinary, movement in binary form adds color through melodic figuration and embellishment. An ever-present Alberti bass in the left hand provides stability. The wide variety of rhythmic groups and detailed articulations will require attention. A cadenza is provided by Mozart. (B-flat major, level 9)

3. *Tempo di Minuetto* [♩ = ca. 136]

The third movement shares many of the same qualities of the first movement, but with a more convincing use of form and melodic development. Passagework fits the hands well and may be particularly effective for the student with smaller hands. A poised finale, it features nuanced interactions between orchestra and soloist. (F major, level 9)

Concerto in A Major, K. 414

A close relative of the *Concerto in F Major, K. 413*, this concerto strives to be agreeable to the listener with a general character of refinement and sophistication. Mozart frequently used this work in his own performing and teaching, and he wrote two complete sets of cadenzas for it.

(Piano and orchestra, two piano reduction, many standard editions)

1. *Allegro* [♩ = ca. 144]

A graceful sweetness permeates the movement, and the piano writing is fresh and spirited. Mozart's compositional inventiveness is on full display with six major subjects in the first movement alone, two of which appear in the development section. As pianist and author Charles Rosen writes, "Mozart uses melodies at once so complex and so complete that they do not bear the weight of development."[7] (A major, level 10)

2. *Andante* [♩ = ca. 66]

The solemn theme for this movement in sonata form is based on the first bars of an orchestral overture by J. C. Bach, as homage to the recently deceased composer who had a significant impact on Mozart. The key of D major takes a strikingly reverent stance with a development section in A minor. The recapitulation presents an ornamented and florid restatement. Chordal textures are prominent. (D major, level 9)

3. *Allegretto* [♩ = ca. 72]

A light and gentle rondo, this movement includes an orchestral refrain in $\frac{2}{4}$ time. The solo part contains many contrapuntal moments, primarily in the left hand, that will demand clear voicing. (A major, Level 9)

Concerto in C Major, K. 415

The *Concerto in C Major, K. 415* is conceived on a more brilliant and grand scale than the other two concertos from this period. Mozart employs his largest orchestra yet with strings, oboes, bassoons, horns, trumpets, and timpani.

(Piano and orchestra, two piano reduction, many standard editions)

1. *Allegro* [♩ = ca. 132]

A military march rhythm opens the movement. The orchestral introduction presents four themes and builds to a proud and mighty climax before the piano enters, somewhat timidly by contrast, with new material. Mozart's penchant for counterpoint is reserved for the orchestra, while the solo piano displays conventional virtuosity in scalar and sequential patterns. An effective showpiece, this *Allegro* features expressive underpinnings as demonstrated in the contrasts of major and minor mode in the second theme. Mozart has provided a vigorous cadenza to conclude the movement. (C major, level 10)

2. *Andante* [♩ = ca. 58]

Cast in ABA form in F major, this slow middle movement originally contained ideas in C minor that now survive as the *Adagio* interludes in the finale. Its unpretentious character is underscored by florid cantilena melodies that spin effortlessly. The musical execution of these melodies presents the soloist with the greatest challenge of the movement. (F major, level 9)

3. *Allegro* [♩. = ca. 88]

Although executed with logic and craftsmanship, the form of this whimsical movement is unconventional

---

[7] Charles Rosen, *The Classical Style* (New York: W. W. Norton & Company, 1998), 218.

for a divertissement finale: a double-exposition within a sonata-rondo form. Features include elaborate and somewhat humorous *Adagio* interruptions in the tonic minor in $\frac{2}{4}$ and the alteration of the rondo section each time by either developing one of three themes or inserting a new one altogether. The result, ABACABA, is a symmetrical and balanced ternary rondo form. Unexpected dramatic changes and the brilliant vivacity of the solo part, which is in control the entire time as if teasing and taunting the orchestra along the way, make this the most appealing movement of the concerto. (C major, level 10+)

Concerto in E-flat Major, K. 449

The *Concerto in E-flat Major, K. 449* was the first piano concerto Mozart composed after K. 413, 414, and 415, written 15 months later. Within the subsequent three years, Mozart would compose a dozen masterpieces that constitute one of the most significant contributions to the canon of the keyboard concerto, establishing himself as the preeminent composer of the genre. The concertos from 1784–1786 are notable for their complex and daring structure, the integral relationship between the solo and orchestra, rich and resourceful orchestration, and a deeper commitment from Mozart in regards to his own emotional investment in the music.[8]

Generally regarded as his first mature work in the genre, Mozart's *Concerto in E-flat Major* was composed for his student Barbara Ployer, for whom K. 453 would also be written. Although it is scored for strings and paired oboes and horns, it may be played with only string accompaniment. Considered to be a pivotal work in his stylistic reinvention, Mozart described this concerto in a letter to his father as "a concerto of peculiar kind."[9]

(Piano and orchestra, two piano reduction, many standard editions)

1. *Allegro vivace* [♩ = ca. 152]

A restless and unstable mood is created by the triple meter. This is one of three Mozart piano concertos with a first movement in $\frac{3}{4}$ time. The use of minor mode also adds to the operatic drama. The vigorous keyboard part dialogues prominently with the orchestra, acting more as a member of the ensemble rather than as featured soloist. The cadenza, the only one that Mozart provided for the concerto, was written for Ployer. (E-flat major, level 9)

2. *Andantino* [♪ = ca. 100]

The agitation of the first movement is replaced with elegance and grace in the dominant key of B-flat major. This tender cantilena presents two contrasting themes, stated first by the orchestra and then decorated by the piano in delicate figurations. The pianist will need to focus attention on four-note chord textures, ornamentation, accompaniment patterns, and pedaling for clarity and style. (B-flat major, level 9)

3. *Allegro ma non troppo* [♩ = ca. 100]

Full of *opera buffa* spirit with contrapuntal ingenuity, the finale is crafted around a single theme that is varied, decorated, and developed by the soloist and the orchestra. The mixture of rondo and variations creates an invigorating romp that is deservedly one of Mozart's most adored finales. The *moto perpetuo* solo part, brisk without being breathless, coupled with the articulations and the contrapuntal textures, presents the greatest technical demands of the concerto. (E-flat major, level 10)

Concerto in D Major, K. 451

The *Concerto in D Major, K. 451*, along with K. 449 and K. 450, was written within a six-week period in the winter of 1784. Mozart's confidence as a composer is on full display in this concerto, complete with the largest orchestra of his concertos to date. The ensemble includes the celebratory presence of trumpets and timpani, as well as an increased level of virtuosity in the solo part designed to "make the performer sweat," according to Mozart.[10]

---

[8] C. M. Girdlestone, *Mozart's Piano Concertos* (London: Cassel & Company Limited, 1978), 175.
[9] Alfred Einstein, *Mozart: His Character, His Work* (New York: Oxford University Press, 1945), 301.
[10] Ibid.

(Piano and orchestra, two piano reduction, many standard editions)

1. *Allegro assai* [♩ = ca. 138]

The *Allegro* is the first work in which Mozart achieves the masterful realization of the "symphonic concerto" with intricate and intimate engagement between the piano and orchestra, particularly the winds. Two bravura passages prominently feature the piano, which otherwise is rarely independent. Chromatic and diatonic scales, arpeggios, broken chords, and octave passages provide technical dazzle. Mozart's cadenza includes a level of virtuosity that is otherwise absent from the movement, complete with cross-hand figurations. (D major, level 10+)

2. *Andante* [♩ = ca. 84]

The second movement is surprisingly cast in rondo form and, much like the finale of K. 449, is based on a theme that is varied each time it appears, most notably in the orchestration. The sensuous and sinuous *Andante* melody is full of chromaticism, and the prominent use of sustain pedal connects it further to an expressive style. Of interest is the section in C major where Mozart includes only an outline of the melody, providing a fine opportunity for the performer to display talent as an extemporizer. (G major, level 9)

3. *Allegro di molto* [♩ = ca. 144]

The powerful and dramatic final movement is one of the most monumental examples of sonata-rondo, Mozart's main contribution to the growth of musical form.[11] The solo is comprised of a steady flow of decorated 16th-note passages derived from the three or four themes within the movement. After the cadenza, the change from 2/4 to 6/8 ushers in a rousing rhythmic coda and a fitting close to this innovative concerto. (D major, level 10)

Concerto in B-flat Major, K. 456

This work was written in 1784 for Maria Theresia von Paradis, a friend of the Mozart family and blind pianist, who was planning a tour of Paris. Smaller in scope and much less ambitious than the other five concertos from this period, it is nonetheless the work of an inspired master. Mozart provided cadenzas for the first and second movements.

(Piano and orchestra, two piano reduction, many standard editions)

1. *Allegro vivace* [♩ = ca. 152]

After a lengthy orchestral *tutti* stating multiple themes, the piano enters with its own previously unheard original thematic statement. Mozart's favorite march-like rhythms are present but not prominent. Many different pianistic patterns are explored throughout in the service of elegance rather than virtuosity. (B-flat major, level 9)

2. *Andante un poco sostenuto* [♩ = ca. 50]

This movement features a simple song-like theme with an exquisite set of five variations plus a sizeable coda. A deep melancholy pervades throughout the variations, which are centered mainly in the accompaniment and piano ornamentation. The shape and direction of these lines require a developed musical sense. Broken octaves may pose the greatest technical challenge for students with small hands. (G minor, level 9)

3. *Allegro vivace* [♩. = ca. 108]

This rondo movement in 6/8 includes a brief piano statement that is taken up by a substantial orchestral *tutti* in several motifs throughout. The development section in B minor is an unexpected cloud that is soon dispelled back to B-flat major. Dialogue between piano and orchestra maintains the buoyant, jubilant feel. (B-flat major, level 10)

---

[11] Girdlestone, *Mozart's Piano Concertos*, 233.

Concerto in F Major, K. 459

Mozart wrote this work for his own use. It is the last of the six concertos composed in 1784. It reflects the confidence and joy of the master working at his creative peak, "content with radiating a mood of youthful happiness, irresistibly cordial."[12] It is scored for flute, two oboes, two bassoons, two horns, and strings.

(Piano and orchestra, two piano reduction, many standard editions)

1. *Allegro* [♩ = ca. 154]

The influence of the opening melody and its dotted rhythm provides unity to the movement. The orchestral presence is as important as the solo, with many instances where the solo serves in an accompanying or decorating role. Broken triads and arpeggiated figures in triplets dominate the texture. (F major, level 9)

2. *Allegretto* [♩. = ca. 40]

The idea of a slow movement in such an ebullient work would seem to counter Mozart's message, so he opted instead for an elegant *Allegretto* in §. While the first movement relied on a repetitive rhythmic gesture, diversity of rhythm is favored here. The solo piano spins long lines, interacting with the orchestra in the style of chamber music. (C major, level 9)

3. *Allegro assai* [♩ = ca. 162]

The use of fugato textures in a finale, characteristic of symphonic works, is brought to the concerto genre in this movement. Juxtaposing homophonic and contrapuntal textures are not thematic, but rather restricted to a three eighth-note motif. The piano entrance after the lengthy orchestral *tutti* is marked with virtuosic flourishes—scales, arpeggios, and broken octaves. The movement can easily stand on its own, and it provides an exciting climax to the entire concerto. (F major, level 10)

Concerto in C Major, K. 467

Mozart composed this work just four weeks after the monumental *Concerto in D Minor, K. 466*, and the contrast between the two could not be more striking: passion and conflict on one hand, calm and majesty on the other. This concerto is sometimes referred to as the "Elvira Madigan Concerto" due to extensive use of the *Andante* movement in a film of that name. Like the *Concerto in D Minor*, it is scored for a large orchestra (flute; pairs of oboes, bassoons, horns, and trumpets; timpani; and strings). The inclusion of clarinets in the concertos occurs in the next work, K. 482 in E-flat major. No original cadenzas survive.

(Piano and orchestra, two piano reduction, many standard editions)

1. *Allegro maestoso* [♩ = ca. 132]

Although the character marking is *maestoso*, the first subject is a march on tiptoes with an *opera buffa* attitude, while the second subject is incomparably sunny. The soloist is on prominent display in this expansive movement with brilliant keyboard figurations. Simultaneous use of the two hands in passagework is more persistent than in previous works. The writing demands virtuosity in arpeggios and broken octaves. (C major, level 10+)

2. *Andante* [♩ = ca. 56]

The piano cantilena is continuous throughout this most cantabile of *Andantes*.[13] The gently undulating triplets murmur in muted strings and the left hand of the piano, except for three heart-stopping measures. Irregular phrases give the impression of improvised song, and the long expressive leaps from one register to another imitate the operatic cavatina.[14] Simple yet deeply poignant, the main contribution of the piano here is to sing, which provides the greatest challenge to the performer. (F major, level 9)

---

[12] Ibid., 285.
[13] Ibid., 344.
[14] Rosen, *The Classical Style*, 238.

2. *Allegro vivace assai* [♩ = ca. 160]

The level of inspiration in the first two movements provides an excellent opportunity for comedic relief, which comes in the form of this lighthearted sonata-rondo in strict form that emulates the *opera buffa* so typical of Mozart's finales. In comparison to the Olympian aspirations of the first movement, this is content to be less ambitious and quite compact. Although the piano part is diminished in vitality and virtuosity, the patterns lie easily in the hands and the interaction with the orchestra is lively and inspired. (C major, level 9)

MYSLIVEČEK, Josef (1737–1781) Czechoslovakia

In the 1770s, Mysliveček was one of the most celebrated opera composers in Italy. His friendship with the Mozart family and his devotion to Wolfgang are documented in the letters of Leopold Mozart. In Mysliveček's work, Mozart found a model of the Italian style, with its graceful melodies and elegant rhythms.

Concerto No. 2 in F Major

An appealing piece, it serves as an inviting substitute for works by Haydn or Mozart.

(Harpsichord and orchestra, two piano reduction, Boosey & Hawkes)

1. *Allegro con spirito* (♩ = 132–138)

This movement is sprightly and melodically pleasing with a variety of articulations and accompaniment patterns in the early Viennese Classical style. The editor has provided fingerings and a suitable cadenza. (F major, level 7)

2. *Larghetto* (♩. = 50)

The simple texture in 12/8 features a cantabile line with expressive half steps and clear phrasing against rolling triads. The orchestra is sparse aside from the *tutti* prelude, interlude, and postlude. (D minor, level 7)

3. *Tempo di menuetto* (♩. = 126)

The Minuet, Trio I, and Trio II each have a different character and key. Sections are concise, but repeats can add to their overall length in this relaxed movement with a delightful lilt. (F major, level 5)

NELHYBEL, Vaclav (1919–1996) USA, born in Czechoslovakia

Cantus et Ludus

This piece is scored for solo piano, 17 wind instruments, string bass, and percussion.

(Piano and wind ensemble, full score, Ars Nova Music Press)

Sostenuto (ad libitum)—Con brio [♩ = ca. 110]

Cantus and *Ludus* are to be played without interruption. *Cantus* (song or chant) is a search for an idea and its formulation—an expressive, organized improvisation. *Ludus* (game) is a tightly organized game played according to established rules. Rhythmic and metric polyphony, duality of vertical organization, tonal space, texture, and instrumental timbres create a steadily mounting sense of tension and excitement. The piece explores register and percussive treatment of the piano with some use of contemporary notation. It features highly patterned writing with textures doubled at the octave and divided figures between the hands. An effective performance requires a rhythmically sound performer skilled in chordal textures and nontraditional piano writing. (D modal, level 10)

Passacaglia

(Piano and orchestra, full score, Franco Columbo Inc.)

Allegro marcato [♩ = ca. 126]

The orchestra forcefully introduces an eight-measure ground bass followed by a more serene version of the thematic material. The piano enters with the ground bass in the left hand and ostinato motives in the right hand while the orchestra provides rhythmic and textural elements. As the piece progresses, the prominence of the piano increases; more rhythmically active variations are presented in the right-hand pattern with each repetition of the ground bass. The composition ends on a triumphant D major chord with full orchestra. It is an original work with limited technical demands besides frequent octaves and four-note chords. Rhythmically challenging due to variations of beat emphasis within the ¾ meter, it features clever orchestration and combinations of themes and motives. (D dorian, level 7)

NICHELMANN, Christoph (1717–ca. 1762) Germany

Nichelmann studied composition with Wilhelm Friedemann Bach, Georg Philipp Telemann, and Johann Joachim Quantz. He served with Carl Philipp Emanuel Bach as harpsichordist for the Royal Ensemble of King Frederick the Great. Nichelmann was best known during the 18th century for his solo keyboard works, including unaccompanied keyboard concertos. The earliest examples of accompanied keyboard concertos were written by J. S. Bach in Leipzig between 1730 and 1733, a period that coincides with Nichelmann's student days at the Thomasschule in Leipzig. Bach's works had a significant influence, and Nichelmann was among the first to compose in this new medium, eventually writing 16 keyboard concertos, with his earliest manuscript appearing in 1740.

Concerto in A Major

This accessible work blends the older Baroque styles with the newer pre-Classical musical aesthetics that were increasingly popular with Nichelmann and his contemporaries. Fermatas in the first and second movements indicate where the performer may insert an original cadenza.

(Harpsichord and string orchestra, full score, A-R Editions Inc.)

1. *Spirituoso* [♩ = ca. 132]

Midway through the movement, the texture shifts from melodic statements to an array of virtuosic broken chords and arpeggiated figures divided between the hands in the style of Scarlatti. Idiomatic writing requires consideration of articulations for ease of mobility on the keyboard. (A major, level 9)

2. *Adagio* [♩ = ca. 40]

Presenting a wide range of emotion, from yearning to melancholy, this movement is an excellent example of German "sensitive style" writing. It is harmonically adventurous, with expressive use of chromaticism. (F-sharp minor, level 9)

3. *Allegro* [♩ = ca. 112]

Although Nichelmann had access to pianos, this movement is clearly intended for the harpsichord. The rapid unisons and frequent changes of direction within the lines are virtuosic, but less efficient and some-what awkward on the piano. Redistribution is a possible solution. (A major, level 10)

Concerto in E Major

Structurally solid and rhythmically exciting, this work features prominent, idiomatic writing for the solo instrument. The ritornello provides the fundamental drive, and the musical texture is derived from conventions of earlier Baroque style. According to the comments in the score, the keyboard player is expected to fulfill the continuo role when inactive as a soloist.

(Harpsichord and string orchestra, full score, A-R Editions Inc.)

1. *Allegrissimo* [♩ = ca. 72]

A new theme in the solo part contrasts with the opening ensemble material, and distinctions between the solo and accompanying parts are evident. Solo sections contain extensive passagework, often in toccata style, clearly conceived for and by a keyboard performer. Such excellent keyboard writing demands technical dexterity. (E major, level 10)

2. *Andante* [♪ = ca. 90]

An *attacca* transition leads to stately dotted-rhythm figures in $\frac{3}{8}$, introduced by the solo keyboard. The solo passages are brief and elaborate, with much ornamentation and rhythmic activity that will require careful planning for execution. (G major, level 9)

3. *Vivace* [♩ = ca. 120]

A restless spirit permeates the lively writing. Fingerings and clear articulations will facilitate the rapid passage-work in this brilliant work for a performer seeking to display virtuosity. (E major, level 10)

NIEMANN, Walter (1876–1953) Germany

Niemann wrote more than 150 works for solo piano, many of which are character pieces. He was one of the few German composers to explore Impressionism.

Piano Concerto No. 1 in C Major, Op. 153

This engaging contemporary work emulates various styles with an admirable use of the orchestra throughout. A brilliant selection, it is an impressive and original showpiece.

(Piano and string orchestra, two piano reduction, C. F. Peters)

1. *Allegro marcato ed energico* (♩ = 116–120)

Rapid and appealing toccata-like figurations are introduced by the orchestra and picked up by the solo piano, doubled at the octave. A lush secondary theme is reminiscent of Rachmaninoff. (C major, level 9)

2. *Molto tranquillo e soave* (♩. = 40)

A theme and six variations based on an old Dutch lullaby feature strikingly different characters for each variation. An abundance of specific details and directions are provided in the score pertaining to articulation, tone color, and tempo. A dazzling cadenza leads to a quiet ending. Pianistic writing abounds with attractive harmonies and textures. (G major, level 10)

3. *Vivace giocoso* (♩. = 116–120)

The indication *Alla gagliarda* refers to the galliard, an athletic dance from the Renaissance, characterized in the fugal opening by leaps and other similar figures. The solo part is full of winning spirit and features animated interaction with the orchestra. A cadenza restates the quiet theme from the second movement before the animated fugue subject begins a rousing coda. (C major, level 9)

NOONA, Walter (b. 1932) and Carol (b. 1935) USA

The Noonas' concertos provide an excellent introduction to the student concerto genre, as well as ensemble playing at differing levels. Each one displays a clear pedagogical approach to the technical and musical development of the young pianist. The tempo markings provided will ensure a steady and fluent performance at the early stages of training. The pieces are arranged for two pianos, and accompaniment tracks are available with both piano and orchestral versions at practice and performance tempos.

Concertino in D Minor

Each movement begins with an introduction in Piano II to set the tempo and character. There is unity across the movements, and themes are comprised of technical and rhythmic patterns appropriate for the level. A cadenza is featured in each movement.

(Two pianos, Heritage Music Press)

1. *Allegro* (♩ = 100–112)

A grand *fortissimo* opening in Piano II leads into the solo statement with a sneaky D minor five-finger melody in the left hand accompanied by syncopated right-hand chords. The material is repeated frequently and with some variation. The piece emphasizes five-finger patterns and triads, both blocked and broken. An exciting cadenza features pedaled arpeggiated triads. (D minor, level 2)

2. *Semplice* (♩ = 100)

This attractive waltz features a five-finger pattern melody and a variety of patterns over a simple recurring harmonic progression in the left hand. Pedal is used throughout to blend harmonies, and phrase indications are provided sporadically. (F major, level 2)

3. *Allegro con brio* (♩ = 138–164)

This syncopated dance evokes a Hungarian spirit. The technical patterns in this piece, combined with Piano II interaction and a showy cadenza, drive forward to a *fortissimo* finale. (D minor, level 2)

A First Concerto in D Minor

(Two pianos, Heritage Music Press)

1. *Allegro con brio* (♩ = 144–152)

The serious, energetic character of the orchestral introduction is the only part of the movement in the key of D minor. The solo enters in G minor, with F major and E-flat major appearing prominently. Textures include parallel motion, tetrascale passages, Alberti bass figurations, and triadic structures. The piece is engaging as a two-piano work with exciting interaction between the parts. The orchestration is sparse but effective. (D minor, level 4)

2. *Andante* (♩ = 88)

A cantabile melody emphasizing the B-flat major scale unfolds over a pleasing harmonic progression presented in a variety of broken-chord patterns and textures. Pedaling is indicated and should be encouraged for expression. (E-flat major, level 4)

3. *Presto* (♩. = 152)

The finale is substantial and satisfying in content. The rollicking theme is comprised of two-note slurs separated by an octave within the D minor five-finger pattern. Some harmonic intervals in the left hand may pose a challenge for smaller hands. A transition through various keys leads to a cadenza with flashy note patterns, followed by a driving *accelerando* to a dynamic finish. This effective writing sounds more difficult than it is. (D minor, level 4)

Little Concertino in C Major

(Two pianos, Heritage Music Press)

1. *Allegro con brio* (♩ = 116)

The simple melodic and rhythmic material is presented in clear four-measure phrases. It features occasional expansion out of the five-finger pattern in the right hand. A doubled-3rd texture is prevalent. The accompaniment provides frequent breaks for the soloist. (C major, level 1)

2. *Flowing* (♩. = 60)

This attractive waltz is written in the F major five-finger pattern. The brief cadenza is marked by some clever and expressive note patterns. (F major, level 1)

3. *Fast!* (♩ = 126)

Repetitive figurations create distinct and memorable themes for an energetic rondo. Hand position changes are easy to find by sight and feel. The accompaniment includes a variety of articulations. A cadenza marked *ad libitum* is comprised of chords and scalar material. (C major, level 1)

OLSON, Lynn Freeman (1938–1987) USA

Celebration! A Youth Concerto

Originally written for piano and rhythm ensemble, this work was also arranged for two pianos by the composer. It provides an attractive vehicle to feature a young pianist's talents in a performance with peers.

(Piano and rhythm ensemble, two piano reduction, Alfred Music)

1. *Brisk and Brilliant* (♩ = 126)

A clear tone is needed to convey the folksy character. Highly patterned in a variety of five-finger positions, the work combines engaging accents and rhythms into an exciting musical effect. (C dorian, level 3)

2. *Revolving, turning* (♩ = 176)

Sustain pedal use, glissandos, and planing triadic harmonies create an Impressionistic quality suggested by the movement's evocative title, "Night Lights." Five-finger patterns and rolling arpeggios are divided between the hands. The movement offers an excellent opportunity to reinforce wrist rotation. (C major, level 2)

3. *With Snap!* (♩ = 126)

Rhythm instruments effectively capture the "parade" spirit. This movement contains many pedagogical concepts and skills, including articulation, hand crossings, toccata-like textures, and contrasting themes. Musical ideas are crafted in logical, clear phrases, and the patterns lie easily in the hand. The fingerings provided in the legato phrases are well planned. (C major, level 3)

OLSON, Kevin R. (b. 1971) USA

Concerto Bravo

This dynamic two-piano work is evenly matched in difficulty between the parts and skillfully uses sonority. It features frequent repetition of rhythm and note patterns throughout each movement. Use of parallel harmony supports the intervallic structure, chord shapes, and fingering.

(Two pianos, FJH Music Company Inc.)

1. *With rhythmic drive* (♩ = 160)

Syncopations, ostinato patterns, and meter changes combine with distinctly contemporary harmonies and melodies to create an impressive musical effect. (A major, level 8)

2. *Freely; with expression* (♩ = 132)

The movement features evocative harmonies and provides a good opportunity to develop rhythmic expression. Many exposed solo moments in Piano I, with increasingly involved contributions from Piano II, lead to an emotional climax. (D major, level 8)

3. *With drama and intensity* (♩ = 120)

The attractive, toccata-like texture displays a Spanish flavor. It includes a clear melodic presentation in the top of the right hand and dramatic crossover flourishes in Piano I. The ensemble demands precision in the execution of unison rhythmic patterns. (B-flat major, level 8)

PAISIELLO, Giovanni (1740–1816) Italy

Paisiello spent his early career in the service of Catherine the Great in Russia. One of the most prolific opera composers of the late 18th century, he composed a total of 80 works. This operatic influence is evident in his eight keyboard concertos. Although they bear some superficial similarities to Mozart's concertos, they lack the sophisticated counterpoint and motivic playfulness of those masterworks.

Concerto No. 1 in C Major

(Harpsichord and orchestra, two piano reduction, Carisch)

1. *Allegro* [♩ = ca. 120]

A substantial work, this movement captures the spirit of Mozart from the very beginning, particularly in the treatment of the orchestra. Highly idiomatic, it makes a successful transition to the piano. Broken octaves, chords, and toccata passages create an appealing technical display. The Alberti bass accompaniment in the left hand is a constant presence. A cadenza is provided by the editor. This *Allegro* is an excellent substitute for Haydn or Mozart concerto movements. (C major, level 10)

2. *Larghetto* [♪ = ca. 76]

Paisiello's expressive gestures are sincere, but the overall effect is slightly unusual. The movement tends to meander through intricate, florid phrases without a stable identity. Rhythms are challenging for a student who lacks a secure sense of pulse. (F major, level 10)

3. *Allegro* [♩ = ca. 132]

A lighthearted and playful rondo, this movement has a main theme that sounds like a simple children's song. Although lengthy, it is technically accessible and not musically demanding. (C major, level 9)

Concerto No. 2 in F Major

The simplicity of this concerto's solo part is due to the modest keyboard capabilities of the Grand Duchess in Russia, for whom the piece was written. It is an excellent first concerto or a substitute for the easier Haydn and Mozart concertos.

(Harpsichord and chamber orchestra, full score, G. Ricordi)

1. *Allegro* [♩ = ca. 120]

This movement has an amiable, light character with the texture and difficulty of an intermediate-level sonatina. It can produce pleasing musical results with an economy of elements. The majority of the movement features five-finger pattern melodies over an Alberti bass accompaniment and sequential motion. A brief cadenza is included. (F major, level 7)

2. *Largo* [♩ = ca. 56]

The *Largo* is a suitable selection for a student who is uncomfortable with hand-position changes, since the position shifts are limited and the notes fit easily in the hand. Rhythmic variety provides interest within the simple texture. (C major, level 7)

3. *Allegretto* [♩ = ca. 116]

A jubilant rondo, this movement abounds with Baroque characteristics in orchestration and clear harmonic direction. The assertive solo part playfully weaves varied patterns with the orchestra. (F major, level 8)

Concerto No. 5 in D Major

(Harpsichord and orchestra, two piano reduction, Boccaccini & Spada Editori)

1. *Allegro moderato* [♩ = ca. 88]

A bright, cheerful spirit displays a vocally oriented melodic style. The movement has a unique quality due to compositional experimentation through the inclusion of small cadenzas to define the sonata form sections. It includes creative rhythmic figures and harmonies. A more lengthy cadenza, written by the editor, appears in the customary location. (D major, level 8)

2. *Largo* [♩ = ca. 48]

A desolate quality permeates the introduction, with redemption arriving in the B section. Beautifully transparent textures support a cantabile melody. The gently syncopated string accompaniment adds a desperate, pleading expression. In a final inquisitive gesture, the movement hangs unresolved on the V chord. (D minor, level 6)

3. *Allegro* [♩. = ca. 72]

Sparkling patterns with high-energy rhythmic flair are found in both the piano and orchestra. Paisiello continues to defy expectations by beginning the return of the A section in the remote key of B-flat major. (D major, level 7)

PASQUET, Jean Emerson (1896–1977) USA

Concertino in G Minor

(Two pianos, J. Fischer & Bro.)

Allegro maestoso / Adagio / Allegro molto (♩ = 96, 48, 168)

This attractive piece features virtuosic patterns and many extended solo episodes with passages divided between the hands or with lines doubled at the octave. Although written as a one-movement piece, it could easily be played as individual movements. The understated character of the second piano serves as an orchestral accompaniment. (G minor, level 8)

PEHKONEN, Elis (b. 1942) Great Britain

Concerti with Orchestra

(Piano and orchestra, full score, Universal Edition)

Adagio (♩ = ca. 56)

As indicated in the score, "The word *concerti* refers to the practice of such composers as Vivaldi and Corelli of writing for alternating groups of soloists." This work requires four groups of performers: piano, instrumental quintet (flute, clarinet, trumpet, violin, and cello), percussion, and orchestra. The piano provides short but complex cadenzas that contrast with the other groups. Frequent changes of tempo indicate mood shifts as well as variation of speed. Contemporary notational techniques include clusters, and improvisatory and *senza tempo* passages are found throughout. The combination of instruments and the approach to timbre and texture demonstrate a Webern influence. The piece requires 50 performers, and according to the score, "It would make for a better performance if three conductors were used." (Atonal, level 10)

PESKANOV, Alexander (b. 1953) USA, born in Ukraine

Peskanov is an accomplished pianist and prolific composer who has contributed an abundance of consistently engaging and musical repertoire for the genre. He includes patterns that fit the hand well and is able to derive a wealth of thematic material from five-finger patterns in the elementary works. In advanced works, he creates challenging patterns and textures that evoke masterworks of the genre. There is a clear focus on pedagogical principles at each level. All concertos are titled "for piano and orchestra," and the roles of Piano I and Piano II are clearly as soloist and orchestra. Each concerto is arranged for two pianos, and full orchestral parts are available from the composer. Teachers will find these works satisfying for technical development and interpretive growth, and students will love the choreography of the hands and the dazzling effect created with the Piano II orchestral accompaniment.

Concert Fantasy

The term "fantasy" implies compositional freedom and inventiveness, an apt description of this substantial work, which is sometimes referred to as *Concerto No. 11*.

(Piano and orchestra, two piano arrangement, Classical Video Concepts, Inc.)

1. *Amoureux—Andantino cantabile ma non troppo* (♩ = 92)

Primarily written in the treble clef, the pianistic textures sound impressive and rich for the level, and the harmonic colors are strikingly different from other Peskanov works. Clearly indicated note distribution between the hands and fingerings are provided in the score. The solo part interacts and engages with the orchestra, making this an especially effective two-piano work. (C major, level 6)

2. *Nostalgia—Andante con moto* (♩ = 92)

This is a contemplative movement with a popular sound and themes that are evocative of cinematic scores. Simple yet moving, this piece should easily attract and engage young students. (F-sharp minor, level 5)

3. *Cakewalk—Playfully* (♩ = 104)

A rhythmic and motivic homage to a popular cakewalk by Debussy, this movement captures the spirit and the character of the dance. The soloist and orchestra take turns alternating between thematic material and accompaniment patterns, and the texture stays simple enough throughout for the intermediate student to successfully manage. The pianistic writing includes a few changes of tempo, meter, and key. (E-flat major, level 6)

Concerto No. 1 for Piano and Strings

This bright, sunny piece features memorable, Classically inspired themes throughout. Inventive textures in the solo part create passagework that sounds more difficult than it is. Piano II is slightly more difficult than the solo part. It provides support through solid harmonic voicings and textures, sensitive dynamic markings, and contrasting articulations. The score provides clear articulations and suitable fingerings, and it includes a CD with a full performance track and an accompaniment track for practice.

(Piano and string orchestra, two piano reduction, Willis Music)

1. *Allegro con brio* (♩ = ca. 96)

Energetic and playful, this movement features the melody in octaves, rising and falling broken chords, and phrases that are traded between the hands. A brief cadenza appears as a retransition back to the opening material. (C major, level 5)

2. *Andante cantabile* (♩ = ca.72)

The simple, expressive cantabile line is accompanied by swelling chords. As the movement progresses, the tempo and rhythmic activity increase, finally arriving at an *Agitato con passione* before returning to the opening character. Pedaling is clearly marked. (F major, level 5)

3. *Allegro ma non troppo* (♩ = ca. 72)

A repeated-note motive fills the movement in both parts. Variation in articulations of similar phrases requires careful study and integration. The movement consists of three sections that contrast in key and thematic material. A rousing *Vivace* closes the work. (C major, level 5)

Concerto No. 2 "Ukrainian Concerto"

This piece was written in memory of the composer's grandmother, Esther.

(Piano and orchestra, two piano reduction, Classical Video Concepts, Inc.)

1. *Allegretto ma non troppo* (♩ = 92)

Thematic material is based on Ukrainian folk music, predominantly doubled at the octave or as arpeggiated figurations with minimal blocked chords. The cadenza cleverly returns the piece to the opening material. (F minor, level 6)

2. *Andante cantabile* (♩ = 60)

A sorrowful, pleading melody features two-note slurs, reflecting grieving sobs. Excellent interaction between the Piano I and Piano II parts creates a rich sound, with use of the higher register intensifying the emotion. (C-sharp minor, level 6)

3. *Allegretto scherzando* (♩ = 132)

Written in the style of the traditional Ukrainian dance called a *Hopak*, this spirited movement features virtuosic patterns such as repeated notes, rapid arpeggios, hand crossings, broken-chord passages, and alternating notes between the hands. The piece ends loudly and proudly. (F minor, level 7)

Concerto No. 3 "Maryland Concerto"

(Piano and orchestra, two piano reduction, Classical Video Concepts, Inc.)

1. *Joy—Allegro con brio* (♩ = 132)

According to the composer, this movement "reflects on the birth of a child and the beginning of life." Short motives that utilize firm fingers are cleverly repeated, inverted, and varied to produce an effective musical result. A surprise ending is a special delight. (C major, level 3)

2. *Lullaby—Andante cantabile* (♩. = 52)

Piano I introduces the theme, which is reminiscent of Scandinavian folk music. Written entirely in the treble clef, Piano I alternates between the theme and an accompaniment. A secure sense of rhythm is necessary to navigate frequent shifts between $\frac{3}{4}$ and $\frac{6}{8}$. (F major, level 3)

3. *Journey—Allegretto scherzando* (♩ = 112)

The carefree theme of the introduction yields to a rollicking carousel theme in the B section that combines with the exciting Piano II accompaniment. (C major, level 3)

Concerto No. 4

(Piano and orchestra, two piano reduction, Classical Video Concepts, Inc.)

1. *Allegro scherzando* (♩ = 88–92)

The character of this *Allegro scherzando* is stately but lighthearted, evoking the spirit of Haydn's symphonies. It focuses on broken major, minor, and diminished triads and two- and three-note slurs. (G major, level 3)

2. *Andante cantabile* (♩ = 76)

A beautiful cantabile line modeled after the early operatic works of Christoph Gluck permeates this movement.

The use of treble clef throughout allows the student to focus on consistent, balanced tone between the hands. Two-note slurs imitate expressive sighs. (E minor, level 3)

3. *Allegretto con moto* (♩ = 120)

This spirited rondo features technical and rhythmic patterns used in various combinations. Sixteenth-note scales are divided between the hands, and the slurred phrases coincide with the musical gestures throughout. (G major, level 4)

Concerto No. 5

Each movement offers variety in terms of style and technical approach.

(Piano and orchestra, two piano reduction, Classical Video Concepts, Inc.)

1. *Moderato con moto* (♩ = 88)

The rhythmic and thematic elements provide a Slavic flavor to this movement. This is the slowest of the three movements, with a cadenza in the middle and a dramatic tempo change for the coda. The texture of Piano I alternates between motives doubled at the octave and more florid passagework. (E minor, level 8)

2. *Allegro e scherzando—Andante cantabile* (♩ = 96, ♩ = 69)

This is an excellent piece for students to play sweeping melodies and grand harmonic colors in the vein of Rachmaninoff. A gorgeous C major section, a majestic *tutti* statement of the theme, and a shimmering cadenza propel the music back to the opening *Allegro*, which pays tribute to Ravel. (E major, level 7)

3. *Allegro con fuoco* (♩ = 80)

The Classical style and the humor of Haydn and Mozart, along with some elements of Shostakovich, are on display in this movement. The solo part features playful motives, often in five-finger patterns similar to some of Peskanov's elementary concertos. A prevalence of hands-together passages and varied articulation will require a developed technique. (E minor, level 7)

Concerto No. 6 "Royal Concerto"

An excellent introduction to the Classical style and a clear fondness for Mozart is evident. This concerto is designed for the young pianist, with simple melodic gestures that fit the hand and a variety of articulations, characters, and rhythms throughout.

(Piano and orchestra, two piano reduction, Classical Video Concepts, Inc.)

1. *At the Royal Court—Allegretto con moto* (♩ = 144)

A jubilant, theatrical opening theme with trumpet calls punctuates the solo part. A single-note texture is prevalent throughout, with occasional segments in which both hands play together in parallel rhythms. The cadenza is effective. (G major, level 3)

2. *Lacrimosa—Lento e cantabile* (♩ = 60)

The slow movement is a nod to Mozart and the "Lacrimosa" movement from his famous *Requiem*. It is a lamenting work with slurs that portray weeping. In the two-piano arrangement, the combination of parts sounds like a Classical slow movement for solo piano. Diligence with rhythmic values and melodic line is essential. It is a beautiful showpiece for an expressive player. (G minor, level 3)

3. *Pirate's Cove—Allegro con brio* (♩ = 144)

A playful and good-humored rondo, this work has a title inspired by the jaunty "yo ho ho" rhythmic pattern of its main theme. The opening statement in the solo piano is restated with accompaniment, and the soloist and orchestra alternate roles throughout. A brief cadenza leads to a rousing finale. (G major, level 3)

Concerto No. 7 "Anniversary Concerto"

(Piano and orchestra, two piano reduction, Classical Video Concepts, Inc.)

1. *Allegretto con moto* (♩ = 120)

Whimsical and flashy with influences of Prokofiev and Shostakovich, this movement includes multiple key changes and extensive use of chromaticism within patterns. The secondary theme features an ambling cowboy song that returns later in the cadenza. It is a fine selection for the student comfortable with various keys and technical patterns. (E-flat major, level 9)

2. *Sognante* (♩ = 84)

An attractive and elegant showpiece for an expressive player, this piece begins with a simple statement of the theme and grows into a rich texture of flourishes and melody. The soloist is featured prominently, with the orchestral accompaniment primarily providing harmonic support. This beautiful love song emulates the style of a bygone era. (E-flat major, level 9)

3. *Andantino tranquillo* (♩ = 144)

This movement is based on a motive from an old Jewish song that the composer's grandfather would sing during family gatherings. Klezmer and Hassidic influences are evident. It features engaging rhythmic vitality and a flamboyant coda. (E-flat major, level 9)

Concerto No. 8 "Spring Concerto"

This attractive work includes memorable themes, distinctive characters, consistent challenges, and satisfying textures in all movements. It is an excellent work to develop the intermediate student's skills in the concerto genre and to further understanding of the Classical style.

(Piano and orchestra, two piano reduction, Alfred Music)

1. *Allegro—Tempo di marcia* (♩ = 120)

The cheerful style of Haydn and early Beethoven is captured in this sonata-form movement with Alberti bass figurations and graceful patterns that lie naturally in the hand. (G major, level 5)

2. *April Scherzo* (♩. = 92)

A charming piece, it calls to mind a rider on horseback. Cast in ABA form, the B section gracefully navigates through three keys before returning to C major. The return of the A section requires an awareness of the distinctions from the first A statement. Triadic patterns in blocked and broken form are featured throughout. (C major, level 5)

3. *Sunset Reverie* (♩ = 72)

The slow movement is heartfelt and nostalgic with expressive, two-voice counterpoint in the solo piano. (E minor, level 5)

4. *May Rondo* (♩. = 92)

A playful rondo captures the energy and exuberance of the Classical style with attractive themes and appealing interactions between piano and orchestra. It is a motivating piece that focuses on solo passagework with variety and bravura. (G major, level 5)

Concerto No. 9 "Boston Concerto"

Concerto No. 9 was written in memory of the brave at the 2013 Boston Marathon.

(Piano and orchestra, two piano reduction, Classical Video Concepts, Inc.)

1. *Andante—Allegro ma non troppo* (♩ = 120)

Charming, sunny themes are distributed between the hands in a single-note texture. Written in sonata form, the movement includes a brief cadenza that includes a return of the opening material. There are no challenging rhythms in the solo part, but the ensemble requires attention to syncopation in the accompaniment. It is a lengthy movement with much repetition. (C major, level 3)

2. *Improvvisa e spaventosa—Andante maestoso* (♩ = 60)

Two forceful and dissonant chords symbolize the explosions that shook the city of Boston that day. A sorrowful, questioning melody with a rich orchestral accompaniment creates a poignant musical statement. The left hand's role is expanded by various accompaniment patterns and through doubling of the melody at the octave. (F minor, level 4)

3. *Molto allegro e con spirito* (♩ = 132)

Written to represent the "unbroken spirit of Bostonians," this music is filled with optimism and resolve. Energetic melodic material fits the hands well. Interaction between the hands requires a strong rhythmic sense. (C major, level 4)

Concerto No. 10 "Italian Concerto"

(Piano and orchestra, two piano reduction, Classical Video Concepts, Inc.)

1. *Divertimento—Allegro con spirito* (♩ = 92)

This lighthearted, amusing romp captures the 18th-century style with playful interactions between soloist and orchestra. Written in the treble clef throughout, the music is constructed of patterns that lie naturally in the hands, with prominent use of stepwise motion and broken triads and occasional harmonic intervals. Two-note slurs are used frequently. (G major, level 3)

2. *Romance—Andante cantabile* (♩ = 60)

An expressive melody and attractive harmonies combine to create a winning piece. The melody is often divided between the hands or doubled at the octave, and the orchestra part is harmonically supportive. (E minor, level 3)

3. *Tarantella—Allegretto e scherzando* (♩. = 92–104)

The engaging choreography is produced by five-finger patterns with identical technical requirements for both hands. The contrasting B section in the parallel minor key introduces a new accompaniment pattern and shifts the focus to the solo part. Bass clef is used sparingly. (G major, level 3)

Concerto No. 12 "Gypsy Concerto"

(Piano and orchestra, two piano reduction, Classical Video Concepts, Inc.)

1. *Voyage—Allegro con brio* (♩ = 96)

This substantial movement contains a variety of articulations and textural combinations in an effective and patterned style. Thematic material is comprised of both motivic and soaring gestures that create a sense of anticipation and excitement. The essence of traveling and motion is captured in the rhythmic drive, the interplay between soloist and orchestra, and the frequent modulations and key changes. An appealing cadenza leads to a *Quasi-Andante* middle section that is a vast departure from the opening energy. The piece returns to its opening character, and the *Vivace* coda makes clever use of texture, reminiscent of a train arriving at its final destination. (C major, level 7)

2. *Ghost Waltz—Allegretto grazioso* (♩. = 72)

This evocative movement features Chopinesque melodies in F minor, with a lighthearted, Viennese-style B section in the parallel major. The solo part uses various textures: a left-hand waltz accompaniment with right-hand melody, a single-line melody between the hands, and some doubling in 6ths and octaves. The repetitive nature will bolster student confidence, and the programmatic element will engage the imagination. (F minor, level 4)

3. *Gypsy Violin—Presto vivace* (♩ = 84)

This closing movement is a tribute to virtuoso gypsy violinists, with a nod to the great *Hungarian Rhapsodies* of Franz Liszt. The multi-sectional form alternates between C minor and C major. The right hand features continuous 16th-note passagework, while the left hand provides harmonic accompaniment. The increasingly showy solo part and the rhythmic dance attitude are sure to please both performer and audience. (C minor, level 8)

Concerto No. 13 "Azery Rhapsody"

This is the most technically advanced and musically demanding of Peskanov's concertos. The three movements are based on the modes or "maqams" that are used in the folk music of Azerbaijan.

(Piano and orchestra, two piano reduction, Classical Video Concepts, Inc.)

1. *Muğam—Rubato maestoso—Spirito* (♩ = 66, ♩ = 90)

A type of folk song or prayer, this *Muğam* uses augmented intervals, minor seconds, and the Mustar and Shahnaz modes to create its exotic sound. The character is attained through frequent changes of tempo and texture. Highly complex and rapid rhythmic patterns will require precision in the solo and accompaniment parts for an integrated ensemble. This is a challenging work to achieve musicality beyond the notes. (Modal, level 10)

2. *Leyli and Majnun—Allegretto con moto* (♩. = 92)

Leyli and Majnun are the characters' names from an Azerbaijani love story akin to *Romeo and Juliet*. Modal scales will require some familiarity with the patterns, shapes, and sounds. The through-composed movement is substantial in length, requiring the performer to have a clear sense of the architecture for direction and clarity of interpretation. A wide variety of textures and pianistic patterns demands a developed technique. (Modal, level 10)

3. *Dilbaz Horses—Molto Allegro* (♩ = 89)

This unrelenting, driving toccata captures the galloping nature of this famous breed of horse from Azerbaijan. It is based on the same mode utilized in the second movement. Rapid passages, often doubled at the octave, are interchanged between both piano parts, making this a particularly thrilling and effective work for two pianos. Careful attention must be given to tempo, ensemble precision, and balance. A facile repeated-note technique is necessary. (Modal, level 10)

PFEIFFER, Johann Michael (ca. 1750–ca. 1800) Germany

Concerto in G Major

Written for a "budding virtuoso" in the time of transition between the harpsichord and the fortepiano, this concerto reflects the broader array of sounds possible on the hammered instruments. It is an excellent example of the pre-Classical piano concerto immediately prior to its fully established form.

(Harpsichord and string orchestra, full score, Nagels Verlag Kassel)

1. *Allegro moderato* [♩ = ca. 84]

An elegant and charming piece, this movement is similar in style to Mozart. Chordal and scalar textures prevail. Elaborate and refined ornamentation, emphasis on melody and harmony, and subtle dynamic differences are indicative of the Rococo style. Suggestions for cadenzas are provided. (G major, level 5)

2. *Adagio* [♩ = ca. 60]

An intimate interlude, the *Adagio* is crafted with light textures, flowing rhythms, and simple harmonies. This brief and expressive movement could appeal to a young student. (C major, level 3)

3. *Allegretto* [♩. = ca. 108]

A bright rondo, the *Allegretto* includes concise musical ideas and an active string accompaniment. Musical material and technical requirements are similar to those found in sonatina movements. (G major, level 4)

PITFIELD, Thomas Baron (1903–1999) England

Concerto No. 2 "The Student"

The influence of notable contemporary English composers such as Ralph Vaughan Williams and Percy Grainger is evident in this work.

(Piano and full orchestra, two piano reduction, Hinrichsen Edition)

1. *Allegro giocoso* (♩ = 152)

Titled "Dance-Prologue," this spirited movement showcases thin textures and economy of material that give way to octave runs, blocked four-note chords, and differing articulations in each hand played simultaneously. The result is not always pianistic. The B section alternates between tonal and octatonic patterns. This piece is best suited for the agile performer with a passion for the avant-garde. (C major, level 8)

2. *Allegro fluido* (♩ = 144)

The "Interlude on White Keys" is playfully written with subtle references to beginning piano exercises. The use of modality provides variety to the material and presents technical challenges, particularly in regards to the indicated tempo. With proper fingerings, the quick passages can be efficiently executed. The middle section, marked *Andante teneramente e flessibile*, provides a brief reprieve. (C modal, level 8)

3. *Theme—Andante espressivo* (♩ = approx. 76)

The orchestra presents a beautifully harmonized version of the English folk song "The Oak and the Ash," followed by three contrasting variations that are radical departures from the source material. The first variation, *Allegro scherzando*, is creative with the rhythmic vitality and articulation suggested by the $\frac{5}{8}$ meter. The second variation, marked *Poco sognoso ma grazioso*, is for solo piano and requires skilled voicing and lyrical playing. The finale, *Allegro articolato*, is technically demanding with some awkward piano writing. (C minor, level 9)

PLATTI, Giovanni Benedetto (ca. 1692–1763) Italy

Platti spent his career at the Episcopal court of Würzburg, composing sacred and secular works for a small musical establishment comprised of princes and bishops. He wrote 11 keyboard concertos, but only nine exist today. Platti's concertos provide valuable confirmation of the early appearance of certain stylistic features, particularly in relation to form. His innovative devices for form exhibit the same thematic relationships, key relationships, and internal proportions typical of works from the end of the 18th century.

Concerto in A Major

(Harpsichord and orchestra, full score, A-R Editions, Inc.)

1. *Allegro ma non tanto* [♩ = ca. 76]

Free approach to dissonance, a characteristic of the galant era, is employed in this work. Rapid passagework falls into familiar finger patterns. A strong sense of pulse is established in the left-hand accompaniment figures. The orchestral accompaniment is sparse during the solo sections. (A major, level 9)

2. *Largo* [♩ = ca. 76]

The influence of German music is demonstrated here through a rich tonal palette. Supplemental ornaments may be added to embellish the cantabile lines. An improvised cadenza is required at the fermata. (E major, level 7)

3. *Allegro* [♩ = ca. 120]

Employing a clever manipulation of the traditional ritornello form, this work has vocally-oriented melodic patterns that evoke the style of Handel. Equal technical difficulties are presented in both hands. Proper execution of the rhythmic challenge ♪♩ against triplets has long been a point of dispute. The movement is witty and charming. (A major, level 9)

Concerto in C Minor

The *basso continuo* is realized in this score and can serve as a second piano accompaniment.

(Harpsichord and string orchestra, full score, Carisch)

1. *Andantino molto mosso* [♪ = ca. 84]

An expressive first movement opens in a stately ⅜ meter with contrapuntal melody lines. Substantial solo sections with ornate embellishments are featured in the right hand. (C minor, level 9)

2. *Adagio* [♪ = ca. 68]

The orchestral introduction sets the stage for a poignant musical statement from the soloist. Challenges include control of pulse and melodic inflection. The performer may choose to add additional ornamentation. (E-flat major, level 9)

3. *Allegro* [♩. = ca. 120]

This *Allegro's* robust gigue character will require a focus on balance and clarity of voices to highlight the interactions within the texture featuring compact, idiomatic hand shapes. Orchestral *tuttis* and compositional structure of solo sections recall the music of Vivaldi. (C minor, level 9)

Concerto in F Major

(Harpsichord and orchestra, full score, A-R Editions, Inc.)

1. *Allegro* [♩ = ca. 120]

In concerto grosso form, this movement has four orchestral ritornellos that alternate with three solo sections in the keyboard. Extended trill passages in the right hand and rapid 16th-note patterns in the left-hand accompaniment challenge the performer. It features chromatic coloring, particularly through anticipations and passing tones. (F major, level 8)

2. *Adagio* [♪ = ca. 69]

The *Adagio* is an excellent example of Platti's gift for singing melody, a legacy of his Italian training. Imaginative use of phrase extension avoids harmonic resolutions. The composer has carefully specified embellishments in the score. Diverse rhythms augment this work's complexity. (D minor, level 9)

3. *Presto* [♩ = ca. 132]

Compact hand shapes and a quick tempo create an effective, motivating finger piece. Lengthy solo sections in between orchestral ritornellos contribute to its difficulty, although sequence and repetition are prominently used. The movement is marked by an infectious rhythmic pulse. (F major, level 9)

POLUNIN, Yuri (1913–1982) Russia

Concertino in A Minor

(Piano and string orchestra, two piano reduction, Vitta Music Library for Children)

Allegro (♩ = ca. 108)

Written in one movement, this immediately appealing work sounds more difficult than it is to play. Effective use of rhythm generates excitement and momentum. Sophisticated harmonies and rich sonorities are created through single-note textures. The cadenza offers a dramatic arch in a contrasting slower tempo. Fingerings are provided in the score. (A minor, level 8)

PUCCINI, Domenico Vincenzo Maria (1772–1815) Italy

Domenico Puccini, the grandfather of opera composer Giacomo Puccini, was the third of five generations of distinguished composers in the Puccini family. He was a contemporary of Muzio Clementi and Johann Nepomuk Hummel.

Concerto in B-flat Major

This sparkling work captures the delightful character and brilliant passagework encountered in Viennese concertos from the same period. The three movements are meant to be played continuously, but they can be studied and performed effectively on their own.

(Piano and chamber orchestra, full score, G. Ricordi & C. Editori)

1. *Allegretto* (♩ = 132)

The *Allegretto* movement is a perfect alternative to a Classical sonatina movement for the poised pianist with firm fingers and clear tone. The texture is reminiscent of more difficult sonatinas, with running scalar patterns and delicate figurations in the right hand and Alberti bass accompaniments in the left hand. An engaging and stylistic cadenza is provided by the editor, Marcello Abbado. (B-flat major, level 10)

2. *Adagio* (♪ = 69)

Tender and heartfelt with an honest sentiment, the slow movement is not always completely graceful in compositional execution. The cantabile lines spin long, effortless phrases. A possible realization of the cadenza, based on Puccini's harmonic structure, is provided. (E-flat major, level 9)

3. *Allegretto non presto* (♩. = 100)

This galloping rondo moves along easily without any surprises. The writing is extremely pianistic, and rapid passages that appear in both hands will help to develop evenness, control, and facility. The advancing pianist will not find significant technical challenges here, although tempo is an important factor. (B-flat major, level 9)

RAPHLING, Sam (1910–1988) USA

Concerto No. 1

(Piano and orchestra, two piano reduction, Belwin-Mills Music)

1. *Lively* [♩ = ca. 74]

Contemporary and quirky, this movement has frequent chromatic alterations that pose a challenge to learn and memorize. The articulations of recurrent rhythm and note patterns are unclear. A lengthy cadenza is comprised of basic note values. (C major, level 7)

2. *Somewhat slow* [♩ = ca. 69]

This tender movement includes simple, gently swaying harmonies. The texture gradually thickens as layers are added to the solo piano introduction. It features ascending scale figures and melody with accompaniment patterns in the right hand. (C major, level 6)

3. *Fast* [♩ = ca. 124]

A motivating passagework piece, this lively movement is comprised chiefly of triads and groups of five-finger patterns. The short, rapid patterns should be played with charisma and bravura. The consistent harmonic planing, slight bitonality, and quartal (4th) harmonies maintain the swift pace of the piece, and meter changes help to establish its off-kilter character. (D modal, level 7)

RILEY, Dennis (1943–1999) USA

Concertino for Piano and Orchestra

According to the score, this piece is intended for an advanced high school student and requires a light, transparent approach.

(Piano and small orchestra, full score, CMP Library Edition)

1. *Prelude—Adagio* (♩ = ca. 60)

The first movement is tonal, with alluring textures and sounds. Phrasing is indicated through frequent meter changes. A short, expressive introduction leads directly into the *Toccata*. (A major, level 7)

2. *Toccata—Allegro giusto* (♩ = 116–120)

Jubiliant with an appealing syncopated and harmonic character, this movement is highly patterned, with natural shapes for the keyboard in both solo and accompanimental roles. It is a fine work for a student with a strong rhythmic pulse. (D major, level 9)

ROCHEROLLE, Eugénie R. (b. 1936) USA

Blues Concerto

(Two pianos, Alfred Music)

Maestoso—Allegro Moderato (♩ = 52, 152)

This engaging one-movement piece effectively captures the essence of Gershwin's *Rhapsody in Blue* with memorable themes in a variety of jazz styles in the blues idiom. The solo texture of Piano I creates showy, entertaining patterns that sound more difficult than they are to execute. The piece flows seamlessly through multiple sections, each with an individual tempo and character. The cadenza is substantial in length with primarily triadic textures, and the finale is grandiose. This work is ideal for a student who wants to play a popular jazz concerto. (C major, level 8)

ROLLIN, Catherine (b. 1952) USA

Concerto in C Major

Rollin's effective writing imitates the Classical style in a convincing manner. Detailed pedal markings provided throughout are appropriate and effective.

(Two pianos, Alfred Music)

1. *Allegro con spirito* (♩ = ca. 120)

Spirited motives consist of dotted rhythms and 16th-note five-finger patterns with Alberti bass accompaniments. Alternating hands and a cadenza provide virtuosic flair. (C major, level 5)

2. *Adagio con moto* (♩ = ca. 45)

An expressive and concise movement, this *Adagio* is similar to the easier slow movements of a sonatina. The haunting melody is almost entirely contained within a five-finger pattern. The piece begins with a solo presentation of the theme and broken triads, which are then repeated with gently ascending and descending arpeggios in Piano II. (A minor, level 4)

3. *Rondo—Allegro assai* (♩ = ca. 80)

A lively combination of technical patterns results in a jovial Classical rondo, including scalar passages, doubled 3rds and 6ths, five-finger patterns, and two-note slurs. (C major, level 5)

Concerto Romantique

The model of a Romantic concerto is reflected in the substantial length of these three movements, as well as in the work's broad themes, harmonic treatment, and interaction between soloist and piano accompaniment. Frequent repetition and highly patterned writing are useful in learning this piece. There is extensive use of pedal throughout.

(Two pianos, Alfred Music)

1. *Allegro* (♩ = ca. 80)

This expansive sonata-allegro movement includes an introduction, "orchestral" interludes, a flashy cadenza, and a dramatic coda. A variety of triadic accompaniment patterns in the left hand provide stylistic and textural interest, as well as a considerable amount of the movement's challenges. (A minor, level 7)

2. *Romance: Andante—molto cantabile e espressivo* (♩ = ca. 84)

An appealing work in ABA form, the second movement offers the young student an excellent opportunity for personal expression and interpretation. It serves admirably as a stand-alone piece. Thematic material is doubled at the octave throughout, while Piano II creates rich sonorities underneath. (C major, level 6)

3. *Tarantella: Allegro molto e scherzando* (♩. = ca. 86)

This rollicking finale in $\frac{6}{8}$ is reminiscent of the Grieg *Concerto in A Minor*. The lyrical middle section is in A major. Frequent use of first and second endings requires careful preparation. The cadenza sounds more difficult than it is, and attention to pacing and mood will result in an effective presentation. (A minor, level 7)

ROSCO, B. J. (b. 1932) USA

Miniature Concerto

(Two pianos, Alfred Music)

1. *Allegro con spiritoso* (♩ = ca. 160)

This compact movement in sonata form presents themes and sections without transition. Finger patterns in simple textures and matched articulations between the hands are utilized. The second piano part is slightly more difficult, though still suitable for a student. (F major, level 4)

2. *Adagio espressivo* (♩ = ca. 80)

This movement includes three distinct cantabile themes, each with attractive accompaniment patterns in the second piano. (C major, level 2)

3. *Scherzando* (♩. = ca. 112–120)

A toccata-like piece, this movement features strong fingers in repetitive, showy figurations for an impressive finale. (F major, level 4)

Youth Concerto "A Festival"

(Piano and orchestra, two piano reduction, Alfred Music)

Maestoso—Scherzando—Espressivo (♩ = ca. 112, 116–120, 92)

According to the score, this is a one-movement concerto "especially written for a junior high pianist and youth symphony, high school, community, or college orchestra." The accompaniment is scored for full orchestra, although the textures are primarily pianistic. The piece includes three sections with distinct characters and themes: a grand, dramatic *Maestoso*, a slightly more animated *Scherzando* in ♪, and a slower *Espressivo* section. The work features primarily linear writing in the solo part with some cluster-chord textures. The harmonic color features the frequent use of added notes such as 7ths and 9ths for an attractive popular flavor. A cadenza of arpeggiated figures and a wide dynamic range provide the opportunity for a dramatic presentation. (C major, level 8)

ROSSI, Wynn-Anne (b. 1956) USA

Concertino in Latin Styles

(Two pianos, Alfred Music)

1. *Breath of Bossa Nova—Breezy* (♩ = ca. 120)

Sounding more musically mature than its difficulty level might suggest, this first movement manages to stay within an extended five-finger range while adventuring beyond expected C major harmonies. The opening and ending sections in the solo piano are doubled at the octave, while an eight-measure contrasting middle section moves into accompanimental chord outlines involving flats and division between the hands. Rossi suggests covering a one-octave arpeggiated figure with a cross-hand motion, which may be helpful for less experienced players. (C major, level 2)

2. *Tango by Moonlight—Mysterious* (♩ = 84)

The solo piano serves in a support role through most of this tango, breaking through the texture with a melody doubled between the hands in the middle section. Extended 7th-chord harmonies in the solo piano are divided into 3rds in the hands, and later into a thicker texture of triads. Syncopated pedal is important in creating a legato sound in the midst of chordal motion. This movement would be a good choice for a student who enjoys the sound of jazz harmonies. (D aeolian, level 2)

3. *Clave in Tandem—Fast!* (♩ = 140)

The main challenge of this spirited movement is consistent metric fluctuation between ♪ and ♪, save a four-measure ♪ transition in the middle. Most of the solo part is written in bass clef for both hands. Frequent hand-position changes are required in this movement, but consistent patterning eases the difficulty for the soloist. This is an exciting choice for a rhythmically savvy student. (A modal, level 2)

ROWLEY, Alec (1892–1958) England

Concerto in D Major, Op. 49

(Piano, strings, and percussion, two piano reduction, Hinrichsen Edition)

1. *Allegro ritmico* [♩ = ca. 132]

An intriguing blend of Romantic, Contemporary, and jazz styles is found in this energetic and dynamic movement. The work is intelligently written for the piano by a composer who created many instructional pieces for the instrument. The sound is full without using thick textures, due in part to the scoring in the orchestra. The pace is rapid, and the performer should possess the ability to move quickly around the keyboard. It is a novel, dramatic piece. (D major, level 10)

2. *Andante naïf* [♪ = ca. 124]

This gently rocking lullaby presents fragments of the themes, which feature quartal (4th) and quintal (5th) harmonies. The orchestra makes the first full statement of the theme in the key of A major, and the piano later states the theme in G major near the movement's end. The piece is highly patterned. (G major, level 8)

3. *Allegro alla burlesco* [♩ = ca. 140]

The opening from the first movement is restated here before launching into new material. Dazzling keyboard figurations stand out from the orchestra. A variety of ideas, pianistic textures, and dramatic tempo changes will keep the student and the audience fully engaged. (D major, level 10)

Miniature Concerto

Rowley's work is a sophisticated, well-crafted concerto. The solo piano part, which includes fingerings and pedal markings, balances thematic statements and virtuosic passages that are effective for this level. The engaging second piano part is an orchestral reduction, and the instrumentation is indicated in the score.

(Piano and orchestra, two piano reduction, Boosey & Hawkes)

1. *Andante maestoso—Allegro* (♩ = 72, 132)

The various themes are accompanied by changes of tempo and key modulations. Technical components include scalar passages, broken four-note chords, and triads with a limited variety of articulation. (G major, level 7)

2. *Menuetto—Moderato* (♩ = 104)

The thematic material of this minuet evokes the sound of a folk song, primarily stated in the orchestra while the solo piano experiments with tone color and textures. The harmonies are interesting, but the chord voicings are not always pianistic. A brief B section contains three key modulations. (D major, level 5)

3. *Rondo—Con moto* (♩. = 116)

A "hunting horn" character permeates this movement. The multi-sectional piece has one more section than the typical rondo form, with each section in a different key, making the work a challenge to memorize. Effective articulations and characters are found throughout. The short cadenza is rhythmically and harmonically satisfying. (G major, level 7)

ROZIN, Albert (1906–1987) USA, born in Russia

Little Concerto

This is an excellent introduction to the concerto and two-piano genres as all parts play simultaneously throughout. The second piano could be played by a slightly more advanced student.

(Two pianos, Brodt Music Company)

1. *Allegro moderato* (♩ = 108)

Arpeggiated triads and running triplet figures contrast with quarter-note scalar melodies doubled at the 6th. The piece provides strong reinforcement of the tonic and dominant relationship, as well as the parallel minor. Knowledge of triad inversions is necessary. Stable pulse is provided in the accompaniment. The sustain pedal is indicated for arpeggios, with some hand and finger crossings present throughout. (C major, level 2)

2. *Slow, but not draggy* [♩. = ca. 54]

An attractive accompaniment establishes a simple five-finger pattern melody doubled at the octave with rhythms in §. The B section presents challenges in the left-hand broken-triad accompaniment pattern and the rhythmic interaction between the hands. (A minor, level 2)

3. *Lively* [♩ = ca. 64]

Comprised of three short and varied motives, this study in parallel and contrary motion uses patterns designed for a small hand. Dynamics alternate between *forte* and *pianissimo*. Playful interactions occur with the second piano. (C major, level 2)

RUTINI, Giovanni Marco (1723–1797) Italy

Concerto in D Major

(Harpsichord and string orchestra, full score, Edizioni De Santis)

1. *Allegro* [♩ = ca. 100]

This showy work blends Baroque and Classical elements with a variety of figurations in the keyboard and orchestral parts. The sparkling sextuplet rhythms are prominent—composed of familiar patterns and hand shapes that allow for adept execution—but their constant presence will require a relaxed technique. Simple linear textures are found in the keyboard part, although the *tutti* passages have a slightly awkward feel. Redistributing some notes into the left hand will ease the demands on the right hand. A cadenza is provided. (D major, level 7)

2. *Andante* [♪ = ca. 80]

Cantabile lines flow smoothly, and melodic and rhythmic embellishments add to the charm. The left hand assumes the role of a continuo bass line, requiring attention to avoid monotony. This beautiful music contains many featured solo passages. (B-flat major, level 8)

3. *Allegro* [♩ = ca. 120]

The last movement is a minuet in a modified binary form. *Tutti* passages are short and infrequent; the keyboard solos are often paired with one or both violins, either as a melodic duet or as supportive harmonies. The left hand is simple, similar in style to J. C. Bach's keyboard writing. (D major, level 7)

RYBICKI, Feliks (1899–1978) Poland

Concerto for Small Hands, Op. 53

This piece contains no harmonic intervals larger than a 7th, and the composer has found ingenious ways to create a full texture between the hands. Excellent fingerings, clear articulations, and pedal markings are provided in the score.

(Piano and orchestra, two piano reduction, Polskie Wydamnictwo Muzyczne)

1. *Allegro moderato* [♩ = ca. 116]

Dramatic flourishes, left-hand melody lines, and toccata-like passages in contracted hand shapes encompass the technical demands of this movement. Frequent tempo and character changes provide effective writing for the piano with an attractive, contemporary flair. (F minor, level 9)

2. *Andantino semplice* [♩ = ca. 80]

This theme and variations is based on a popular Polish folk song. Transitional material in the orchestra links each of the seven variations. The tempo and character change in each variation, and the piano becomes increasingly active. The sixth variation is marked *quasi cadenza* for the soloist. (B-flat major, level 9)

3. *Allegro non troppo* [♩ = ca. 88]

In this Classical-style rondo, simple single-note lines often double at the octave. The middle section is in the style of a *krakowiak,* a fast, syncopated Polish dance that imitates horse steps. (F major, level 8)

RZAYEV, Azer Guseinovich (b. 1930) Azerbaijan

Piano Concertino

This work contains exotic harmonies with a Shostakovich influence.

(Two pianos, Associated Music Publishers)

1. Allegretto (♩ = 92)

Simple melodic lines, doubled at the octave, are interspersed with technical passages that utilize unfamiliar patterns. The patterns take some practice but include much repetition. An extensive cadenza concludes this substantial movement. (C major, level 10)

2. Andante (♩ = 66)

A calm statement of expression, the *Andante* has a transparent texture. The melody is doubled at the octave throughout with the exception of an outburst reminiscent of Rachmaninoff at the climax. It includes frequent changes of tonal center and much chromaticism. (A minor, level 8)

3. Allegretto (♩ = 108)

Highly contrasting characters of this *Allegretto* include a rolling 6/8 meter and a lopsided waltz in 3/4. The left hand assumes an accompanimental rather than melodic role. Lively, punctuated, and syncopated rhythms require agility. (C major, level 10)

SAINT-SAËNS, Camille (1835–1921), France

Camille Saint-Saëns was a precocious musician, starting piano lessons at age two-and-a-half, composing his first work at age three, and giving his concert debut at age ten. He studied at the Paris Conservatoire and later worked as a church organist in Paris. Saint-Saëns became a highly respected composer, pianist, and organist, winning recognition and admiration from such masters as Gioachino Rossini, Hector Berlioz, and Franz Liszt. He wrote in virtually all genres, including opera, symphonies, concertos, songs, choral music, solo piano pieces, and chamber music. His compositions follow in the conventional Classical and Romantic traditions, although he was an enthusiastic supporter of modern music of the day.

Caprice-Valse, Op. 76, "Wedding Cake"

(Piano and strings, two piano reduction, A. Durand)

Vivace e grazioso [♩. = 88]

This charming one-movement piece was composed to celebrate the wedding of the composer's pianist friend Caroline de Serres. Sparkling cascades of notes in the piano contrast with the more expansive theme offered by the strings. The middle section features a cadenza for solo piano, which is then joined by the strings. In the return of the opening section, the piano presents the strings' theme in a robust guise. The piece ends delicately with a wink. A facile technique for arpeggiated figures, alternating and repeated note patterns, and an overall lightness of touch will bring this concise, lilting, and elegant confection to life. (A-flat major, level 10)

Africa, Fantaisie pour piano et orchestre, Op. 89

(Piano and orchestra, two piano reduction, A. Durand)

Molto allegro [♩. = ca. 132]

This dazzling one-movement showpiece with a Tunisian flavor includes virtuosic challenges consisting of doubled octaves, scales, and highly patterned flourishes up and down the keyboard. There are several cadenzas and solo moments throughout the movement that feature the soloist. Tuneful melodies abound, and the well-crafted music is full of drama and lightheartedness, moving seamlessly from one character to another throughout the piece. This is rousing and effective music designed to please. (G minor, level 10)

SALIERI, Antonio (1750–1825) Italy •

Antonio Salieri was a highly regarded composer and conductor, primarily of opera but also of chamber and sacred music. In 1774, he was appointed the director of the Italian Opera by the Habsburg court in Vienna. He would later assume the position of the Austrian Imperial Kapellmeister, a post he held from 1788–1824.

Salieri's two concertos for keyboard (harpsichord or fortepiano) and orchestra were composed in Vienna in 1773. Written for amateur musicians of the aristocracy, these expansive and sparkling works belong stylistically in the early Viennese Classical period, along with composers such as Johann Schobert, Carl Philipp Emanuel Bach, Georg Christoph Wagenseil, and the masters of the Mannheim school. The orchestration of these two concertos—including two horns and two oboes, as well as two bassoons in the *Concerto in B-flat Major*—creates a sound that would become the standard for the Classical concerto.

Concerto in B-flat Major

(Keyboard and orchestra, two piano reduction, Edizioni Suvini Zerboni)

1. *Allegro moderato* [♩ = ca. 76]

This is a substantial work in length and scope with a joyful character. Some may find that the repetitive and predictable solo part lacks originality; however, it is a perfect vehicle as a technical display piece for its intended ability level. Salieri provides three cadenzas throughout the movement, each one progressively longer and more involved than the previous one. (B-flat major, level 9)

2. *Adagio* [♪ = ca. 54]

The ornate melodic line is exquisitely Italian and flows over an almost unceasing accompaniment of broken triads in triplets. The peaceful atmosphere is disrupted by forceful outbursts in the solo to create a sense of operatic drama. Rhythmic execution of the right-hand embellishments presents the player with an expressive challenge. (E-flat major, level 8)

3. *Tempo di Menuetto* [♩ = ca. 116]

The finale offers a graceful theme with showy variations and a coda in binary form. Rapid finger patterns lie easily in the hand to impressive effect. (B-flat major, level 8)

Concerto in C Major

The pacing, drama, and moods conveyed through this concerto demonstrate not only Salieri's compositional command of Italian opera, but also his ability to effectively transfer these traits to the keyboard. This work places him firmly at the threshold of the Golden Age of the keyboard concerto.

(Keyboard and orchestra, two piano reduction, Edizioni Suvini Zerboni)

1. *Allegro maestoso* [♩ = ca. 76]

The opening orchestral *tutti*, full of vitality and charm, is followed by an authoritative statement by the soloist without orchestral accompaniment. Throughout most of the movement, the orchestra plays a minimal role, interjecting support at cadential moments, structural interludes, or in brief call-and-response passages with the soloist. The keyboard part is substantial, with efficient use of repetition and sequence for technical elements. (C major, level 9)

2. *Larghetto* [♩. = ca. 46]

A *siciliana* in a lilting ⑫⁄₈ imbues the slow movement with a haunting pastorale quality. The *parlando*-style of the solo is deeply expressive and poignant. As in the first movement, the orchestra plays a supporting role with passages often played pizzicato or doubling the keyboard. A short cadenza is provided. The third movement is played *attacca* following the second movement. (A minor, level 8)

3. *Andantino* [♩ = ca. 120]

The rondo finale is a lively minuet that evokes the spirit of the hunt. As in the previous movements, the soloist is prominently featured, while the orchestra is reserved for short interludes, although there is some trading of phrases in the A section. The delicate violin filigree in the B section mimics charming "bird calls." The middle section in C minor stands in defiant contrast to the elegant minuet, with running sextuplets in the right hand and *forte* orchestral entries that punctuate the texture. A sudden return to C major and the opening material brings the movement to its close in a similarly abrupt fashion. The technical and musical elements are very straightforward and satisfying. (C major, level 9)

SAMMARTINI, Giuseppe (1695–1750) Italy

Giuseppe Sammartini, the older brother of the renowned composer Giovanni Battista Sammartini, was born in Milan. His exceptional skill as an oboist provided him with several orchestral posts and eventually brought him to London, where he gained celebrity status. In 1736, Sammartini was appointed music teacher in the household of Prince Frederick of Wales, a position he held for the rest of his life. While his chamber music was played and published regularly during his lifetime, many of his concertos and overtures were not published until after his death.

Sammartini was a forward-thinking composer, incorporating elements of the galant style into his compositions, and often expanding his concertos and symphonies into four movements. As one of the first composers to write keyboard concertos in England, he was very influential in his time. Unlike Handel, who expected the soloist to improvise, Sammartini wrote parts out completely, including *ad libitum* sections.

Concerto in A Major, Op. 9, No. 1

(Harpsichord and string orchestra, full score, Bärenreiter)

1. *Andante spiritoso* [♩ = ca. 88]

Beginning a sonata or concerto with a slow movement was one of Sammartini's unique compositional devices. The solo is not featured but is part of the continuo. This movement would be appropriately paired with the second movement in performance. (A major, level 5)

2. *Allegro* [♩ = ca. 120]

Fugal treatment of the subject in the *tutti* and solo passages contrasts with virtuosic, sequential passagework, including rapid arpeggios and alternating-note figures. The repetitions of similar material call for variety in interpretation and articulation. (A major, level 9)

3. *Andante* [♩ = ca. 70]

A solo keyboard statement opens this beautiful, simple movement. It consists of linear melodies with expressive half-step gestures and minimal ornamentation. (E major, level 6)

4. *Allegro assai* [♩. = ca. 60]

A spirited rondo in ⁶⁄₈ , this movement features a solo that presents slight variations of the *tutti* statement. The efficient writing has limited position shifts, making it an appropriate selection for a performer who does not yet move around the keyboard with ease. (A major, level 7)

SAVINO, Domenico (1882–1973) USA, born in Italy

Cuban Concerto

(Piano and orchestra, two piano reduction, Robbins Music Corp.)

Maestoso/Andantino—Allegro moderato [♩ = ca. 84; ♩ = 58]

This one-movement concerto is in the Latin-American style, with guaracha rhythms and Creole influences. A brilliant work, it provides an opportunity for virtuosic display by a charismatic performer. Rich harmonic colors and rhythmic patterns in 6/4 are often doubled at the octave to project over the thick orchestration. An arrangement for a smaller symphonic combination is available. Some potentially unfamiliar hand shapes and sounds will take adjustment. A dazzling ending finishes this irresistible piece. (E major, level 10)

SCHAFFRATH, Christoph (1709–1763) Germany

Schaffrath served as a chamber musician for various courts, including the *Kapelle* of King Frederick II of Prussia and, later, Princess Anna Amalia, Frederick's sister. Although he wrote nearly 40 keyboard concertos, many of them were destroyed during World War II.

Concerto in B-flat Major

Schaffrath employs a "five-ritornello" form in the outer movements, a common characteristic in his keyboard concertos. The thematic unity within and between these movements is notable, as is the contemporary use of the cadenza in the second and third movements.

(Cembalo and strings, full score, A-R Editions, Inc.)

1. Allegro [♩ = ca. 120]

The textures and patterns in this movement are derived from broken-chord figurations in steady rhythms. Imitative, amiable interplay between the soloist and the strings propels the music. The simple two-part texture features the right hand with predictable yet satisfying figurations, while the left hand serves a continuo role. (B-flat major, level 6)

2. Adagio [♩ = ca. 56]

The prominent use of dotted figures and *forte* dynamics, particularly in the *tutti* sections, convey the strong character of this rhythmically punctuated, expressive movement. The two-part counterpoint in the solo effectively utilizes ornamentation and the dissonance of nonchord tones to heighten tension. For the more advanced performer, this edition includes two ornamented versions of this movement that feature elaborate, north German-style melodic embellishment. It is not especially tuneful, but the attractive work highlights the player's musical sensibilities. (G minor, level 7)

3. Allegro assai [♩ = ca. 116]

This final movement contains many similarities to the first movement in form, texture, and thematic unity. However, it has a greater sense of urgency and dramatic flair, building to a cadenza-like climax. The extended passages of 16th notes lie comfortably in the hand. (B-flat major, level 7)

SCHOBERT, Johann (ca. 1735–1767) Germany

Beginning in 1760, Schobert served in the Parisian court of the prominent patron Louis François I de Bourbon. There he met Wolfgang Amadeus Mozart, who had clearly been influenced by Schobert's compositions during his youth, and who later arranged a number of movements from Schobert's sonatas to incorporate into his early piano concertos. Schobert's career was cut short when he (and most of his family) died after eating poisonous mushrooms. Although he composed almost exclusively for the keyboard in solo and chamber contexts, his works display a stylistic connection with the dynamic orchestral music that came from Mannheim at the time. Schobert composed five concertos for harpsichord and orchestra, but the three represented here are the most accessible.

Concerto No. 2 in E-flat Major, Op. 12

(Harpsichord and orchestra, full score, Denkmäler deutscher Tonkunst)

1. *Allegro moderato* [♩ = ca. 112]

A jovial character begins in the dynamic orchestral introduction and continues into the solo. The piece's Classical style is clear, and the addition of two flutes (or oboes) and two horns creates a full sonority, although the orchestra is scored strategically for balance and interest. The keyboard writing contains excitement in the right hand with flashy scalar patterns. (E-flat major, level 9)

2. *Adagio ma non troppo* [♪ = ca. 72]

A substantial movement in ABA form, the piece is written in a stately but flowing ¾ meter. A variety of note values in the figurations heighten the expressive power of the solo line, with a beautiful cadenza providing a climax. This movement could stand alone as a poignant display for the musically expressive student. (B-flat major, level 8)

3. *Tempo di Menuetto* [♩ = ca. 108]

This light, easygoing minuet serves as a fitting conclusion to the work. It has a straightforward texture with familiar patterns, although some French-style ornaments may pose a challenge. (E-flat major, level 8)

Concerto No. 3 in G Major, Op. 13

(Harpsichord and orchestra, full score, Denkmäler deutscher Tonkunst)

1. *Allegro non troppo* [♩ = ca. 68]

A cheery and carefree piece, this first movement has active Classical-style figurations of broken chords in energetic harmonic sequences that inventively use Alberti bass. The ritornello form highlights the prominent solos that elaborate on the orchestral *tutti* material. Some passages feature rapid arpeggios divided between the hands and hand crossings that require attention to choreography. A short cadenza is provided, although the performer may choose to improvise additional material. (G major, level 9)

2. *Andante* [♪ = ca. 80]

An emotionally intense and weighty movement, this *Andante* demonstrates the expressive potential of keyboard music that Schobert developed through his compositions. A pronounced orchestral introduction, scored for strings only, opens the work. The keyboard writing exhibits typical French charm and exceptionally florid decoration that adds significantly to the expressive vitality and difficulty of the work, both in technique and attitude. A cadenza must be supplied by the performer. (E minor, level 10+)

3. *Allegro* [♩. = ca. 48]

This final movement restores the lightness of the first movement through a binary-form dance in ⅜ with simple, predictable gestures. Agile fingers will serve the music with the right sense of elegance. (G major, level 9)

Concerto No. 4 in C Major, Op. 15

(Harpsichord and orchestra, full score, CMBV Edition)

1. *Allegro assai* [♩ = ca. 70]

Innovative stylistic features are present in the sonata-allegro form. A brilliant, rich sonority is found in the keyboard and a playful character is featured in the orchestra, scored for strings and horns. Facility and even tone in passagework is a necessity, particularly in the right hand, but the left hand also has sections of doubling. The movement is in the key of C major, but the minor mode makes appearances in this clever, witty, and well-crafted work. (C major, level 10)

2. *Adagio* [♪ = ca. 98]

This movement is filled with expressive extremes. The orchestra opens with a dark, foreboding theme of half steps and continues with a linear theme in C major. The solo entrance displays a decorated version of the orchestral statement using French-style embellishments. Attention to pacing and character will create a moving performance of this poignant work. (A minor, level 10)

3. *Allegro assai* [♩. = ca. 52]

The introduction seems to suggest a typical Classical-style rondo movement, but the solo sounds Baroque in its figuration and harmonic sequencing. Two notable features are the slight diversion into binary form before the C section and the absence of a cadenza (here or in any of the movements). An abundance of running passages divided between the hands and crisp ornaments make a strong, favorable impression. (C major, level 10)

SCHROETER, Johann Samuel (ca. 1752–1788) Germany

The son of a musician, Schroeter made his 1722 London debut in the famous Bach-Abel subscription concerts. Schroeter's entry from the *New Grove Dictionary* offers the following stylistic quote: "He became one of the neatest and most expressive players of his time, and his style of composition, highly polished, resembles that of Abel more than any other. It was graceful and in good taste, but so chaste as sometimes to seem deficient in fire and invention."[15]

Wolfgang Amadeus Mozart, an admirer of Schroeter's writing, composed five cadenzas for Schroeter's Op. 3 concertos. They are included in the A-R Editions publication, along with a number of anonymous cadenzas. All six of Schroeter's Op. 3 concertos are accompanied by a small ensemble of two violins and bass. Despite the score appearing only in full format, the three string lines are easily reduced to create a simple second piano accompaniment. They are similar in compositional style and level to the Abel Op. 11 concertos.

Keyboard Concerto in F Major, Op. 3, No. 1

(Keyboard and chamber strings, full score, A-R Editions)

1. *Allegro* [♩ = ca. 120]

Full of Classical energy, this *Allegro* inserts distinctive figurations and gestures into a stately framework. The pianistic writing fits smaller hands well and challenges the soloist's right-hand facility. An anonymously composed short cadenza is included in the appendix. This work is a suitable option for a student's first Classical concerto movement. (F major, level 8)

2. *Rondo Tempo di minuetto* [♩ = ca. 120]

An unpretentious solo keyboard statement launches this dignified movement, immediately followed by a restatement of the opening theme in the strings. In an interesting juxtaposition to the eighth-note motion of the A motive, the B theme constantly flows in a gentle triplet gesture, supported by minimal strings. A minor modal theme and a fun crosshand segment infuse interest into what could have otherwise been a perfunctory movement. (F major, level 7)

---

[15] John Alexander Fuller Maitland, "Schroeter, Christoph Gottlieb," in *The New Grove Dictionary of Music and Musicians,* eds. Stanley Sadie and J. Tyrrell (London: Macmillan, 2001), Vol. 4: 278.

Keyboard Concerto in B-flat Major, Op. 3, No. 2

(Keyboard and chamber strings, full score, A-R Editions)

1. *Allegro* [♩ = ca. 120–132]

Vivacious and charming, this movement would be a prime choice for a student with facile fingerwork and a smaller hand span. Classical devices—including broken left-hand chord patterns, rapid passages that outline stationary chordal structures, and cadential trills—are hallmarks of this movement. The limited number of musical ideas add to a student's ease in learning the piece, despite the work's $\frac{2}{4}$ time signature that necessitates frequent 32nd notes in the score. (B-flat major, level 7)

2. *Rondo: Grazioso* [♩. = ca. 80–84]

Sprightly and fun, this appealing *Rondo* (in ABACABA form) includes a lyrical opening melody that interchanges with contrasting themes including double 3rds and running scales. Expected chordal progressions dominate the keyboard bass texture, and the frequently recurring A theme serves as a landmark and may aid memorization. It is a predictable yet delightful movement. (B-flat major, level 7)

Keyboard Concerto in C Major, Op. 3, No. 3

(Keyboard and chamber strings, full score, A-R Editions)

1. *Allegro* [♩ = ca. 136]

An extended orchestral introduction of 43 measures ushers in a matter-of-fact statement of the first theme. This movement combines the accessible key of C major with predictable scalar runs and repeated figurations that fit well within the hands. Possible cadenzas—three from anonymous composers and one from Mozart—are provided in the accompanying appendix. (C major, level 7)

2. *Grazioso* [♪ = ca. 80]

This short yet sweet movement is trickier to read than it is to execute, as Schroeter again writes in $\frac{2}{4}$. The prevalence of 32nd notes may initially appear daunting, but the effortless feel of the tempo and the support of constant broken-chord patterns in the bass will assuage concerns. An amplified sense of drama may be achieved by adding either of the supplied cadenzas. Mozart crafted a particularly fine one. (G major, level 7)

3. *Rondeau* [♩ = ca. 126–132]

This entrancing movement, perhaps initially saccharine sounding, has a stirring minor theme that will showcase quick technique and dramatic flair. Quick hand-position changes occur more frequently than in Schroeter's previous concerto movements of Op. 3. Four cadence points may be elaborated with provided "cadenzas" of only one or two measures. (C major, level 8)

Keyboard Concerto in D Major, Op. 3, No. 4

(Keyboard and chamber strings, full score, A-R Editions)

1. *Allegro* [♩ = ca. 132]

Schroeter hints at a Mozartian flair in the introduction to this concerto and follows through in the keyboard line with double 3rds, triplet against eighth-note motion between the hands, and frequent use of dominant harmonies. Rhythms venture into the more complex, and proper Classical execution of the numerous appoggiaturas is necessary. Punctuating the final string *tutti* is a cadenza. Mozart's example is left unfinished, offering the opportunity for a student to complete it. Two additional cadenzas offer truncated but nonetheless interesting options. (D major, level 8)

2. *Grazioso* [♪ = ca. 66–72]

Coordination challenges dominate this poignant work. While the keyboard bass provides a constantly flowing triplet pattern, the right-hand melody weaves in and out of two-, three-, four-, and even five-note groupings.

Two short forays into A minor bring added depth to the line, which demands an appropriate sense of rubato. A maturely beautiful movement, it is appropriate for an intermediate student with an advanced sense of musicality. (A major, level 8)

3. *Rondeau* [♩ = ca. 126]

This final concerto movement deserves to be heard more often. The memorably galant opening theme, full of Classical charm, is stated first in the keyboard and echoed each time after in the strings. Alternating rondeau themes vary, first sticking closely to the opening style and then venturing further into D minor, with hints of the harmonic form dotting the melody. A small hand span requirement adds this to the list of works suitable for younger players. (D major, level 7)

Keyboard Concerto in G Major, Op. 3, No. 5

(Keyboard and chamber strings, full score, A-R Editions)

1. *Allegro* [♩ = ca. 116]

Brimming with energy, this opening movement of Schroeter's fifth concerto from Op. 3 fits easily into smaller hands, yet contains moments of sparkling figuration, flowing scalar passages, and a few double-3rd motives, made more difficult by their rapid neighbor motion. A middle segment with 16th-note arpeggiations divided between the hands may present the greatest technical challenge. (G major, level 7)

2. *Rondo: Grazioso* [♪ = ca. 108]

An attractive, tuneful keyboard theme supported by Alberti bass figures starts this rondo and alternates with a B theme similar in spirit. A highly contrasting C theme in G minor, constructed of right-hand double 3rds and supported by left-hand octaves, punctuates the movement with solemnity and frequent, dramatic dynamic changes from *piano* to *forte*. The excitement of this drama, however, is soon erased with the return of G Major and the opening motives. With only 36 measures of unique material that recurs throughout the rondo form, this movement may be a good option for students overly challenged by memorizing a longer, more involved concerto. (G major, level 7)

Keyboard Concerto in E-flat Major, Op. 3, No. 6

(Keyboard and chamber strings, full score, A-R Editions)

1. *Allegro spiritoso* [♩ = ca. 138–144]

Perhaps the most mature of this opus's first movements, the *Allegro spiritoso* brims with vivacity. Despite frequently occurring familiar Classical figurations, several potentially awkward positions stretch the right hand making the movement less appropriate than Schroeter's previous Op. 3 concertos for a student with limited reach. Running scalar passages in the keyboard melody showcase quick technique. There are three opportunities for cadenzas, with examples from Mozart as well as other anonymous composers. (E-flat major, level 8)

2. *Larghetto* [♩ = ca. 48–52]

The main challenge of this lovely slow movement is the presence of double-3rd motion in the right hand, although the *Larghetto* tempo mitigates its challenge to a large degree. After some initial practice, the unusual accompanying keyboard bass, in broken chords with repeated top notes, falls easily in the hand. Three supplied cadenzas range from predictable to more harmonically and technically adventurous. This beautiful work effectively disperses the energy of the preceding opening movement. (B-flat major, level 7)

3. *Rondo: Presto* [♩ = ca. 100]

A delightful romp closes Schroeter's final offering from the Op. 3 concertos. The 16th-note writing in $\frac{2}{4}$ drives along and the recurring A theme sparkles with each presentation. Contrasting themes including a hunting horn call under a right-hand trill and a brief foray into C minor comprise the remaining rondo elements. (E-flat major, level 8)

SEIXAS, Carlos de (1704–1742) Portugal

Seixas is considered the most famous Portuguese composer of the Baroque era. He was a prolific composer, but tragically the majority of his compositions were destroyed in the devastating Lisbon earthquake of 1755.

Concerto in A Major

This piece exhibits character and style throughout three concise movements and serves as an excellent study in Baroque keyboard style.

(Harpsichord and string orchestra, full score, Portugaliae Musica)

1. *Allegro* (♩ = ca. 104)

In the style of Vivaldi or Corelli, this movement has a sprightly character in concerto grosso form. Florid figuration and running 16th notes require agility from the performer, although the patterns tend to lie naturally in the hand. (A major, level 8)

2. *Adagio* (♩ = ca . 60)

A pensive and expressive movement that demands musical maturity, this work has a da capo repeat that provides the soloist with the opportunity to embellish and ornament the line. It features beautiful harmonic tensions and sequences. (F-sharp minor, level 7)

3. *Allegro* (♩. = ca. 72)

This final movement is a compact and well-written gigue, with flowing eighth-note lines found in the right hand only. Effective interaction occurs between the soloist and orchestra, with an engaging call and response in the B section. (A major, level 8)

SEUEL-HOLST, Marie (1877–1965) USA

In Elfland, Op. 26

Conceived as "a miniature program concerto," this musical fairy tale includes various themes that relate a charming storyline. Accompanying poems are provided at the beginning of each movement. In all three movements, the sustain pedal is utilized appropriately for the young student. Articulations are matched between the hands. This well-written piece may be played as a solo or with second piano accompaniment.

(Two pianos, Summy-Birchard)

1. *"Elfin Prince and Princess"—Allegro con spirito* [♩ = ca. 128]

The movement is cast in sonata-allegro form and includes an introduction, a coda, and a "cadenzetta." The sections are clearly indicated in the score. Frequent repeated patterns, fingerings, and hand crossings serve the needs of small hands. It explores register and articulation to create a light, "elf-like" character. (F major, level 2)

2. *"Elfin Barcarolle"—Andantino* [♩. = ca. 56]

This simple statement in ABA form emphasizes harmonic and melodic intervals in both florid and chorale textures. The dynamic range extends from *pianissimo* to *fortissimo*, with extensive use of the sustain pedal. (B-flat major, level 1)

3. *"Elfin Festival"—Allegretto vivace* [♩ = ca. 112]

A scherzo-like movement creates excitement through oscillating 16th notes and staccato passages. The interplay between soloist and accompaniment will require a good sense of pulse, particularly during rests. Many details in dynamics and tempo fluctuation are essential to effectively capture the character. (F major, level 2)

SHEVTSOVA, Tanya (b. 1952) Canada, born in Russia

Concerto-Variations, Op. 3

(Piano and string orchestra, two piano reduction, Vitta Music Library)

Theme—Allegro moderato (♩ = 104)

A simple theme is followed by eight variations in different genres and characters, with a cadenza and an impressive coda. Pedagogically sophisticated writing develops varied articulations, rapid finger execution, tone production, hand crossings, rubato, ensemble precision, and a sense of dramatic urgency. Excellent fingerings and clear pedal markings are provided in the score. The two-piano arrangement is effective because the more difficult passagework is presented in the accompaniment for an overall dazzling result. Orchestral score and parts are available from the publisher. This work is a true showpiece. (E minor, level 8)

SHOSTAKOVICH, Dmitri (1906–1975) Russia

Concertino, Op. 94

(Two pianos, DSCH, International)

Adagio—Allegretto [♩ = ca. 64, ♩ = ca. 64]

A dynamic one-movement concerto in sonata form, this work was composed for Shostakovich's gifted son, Maxim. It is full of youthful exuberance with technical requirements well-suited for the advanced student. The opening introduction is reminiscent of the slow movement of Beethoven's *Fourth Piano Concerto.* The writing is unique and agile, and strong fingers are required for rapid passagework doubled at the octave and chords that alternate between the hands. The two pianos alternate between solo and accompaniment roles; the solo part is prominent at all times and significantly more difficult. It is a highly energetic work. (A minor, level 10)

Concerto No. 2 in F Major, Op. 102

This uncharacteristically cheery piece was composed for Shostakovich's son Maxim's 19th birthday, and the premiere was at his graduation from the Moscow Conservatory. Although somewhat more simplistic than some of Shostakovich's other works, it remains a deservedly popular piece.

(Piano and orchestra, two piano reduction, International, DSCH, Sikorski, MCA)

1. Allegro (♩ = 160)

A transparent opening statement breaks into a vigorous, rhythmic march with a flurry of dazzling motives. The hands are doubled at the octave almost exclusively, but this thinly textured sonority can create passages of intensity and introspection with equal effectiveness. A full display of pianistic techniques that explore the range of the keyboard will test the performer's skill. *Fortissimo* octaves in both hands need an appropriate balance of power and grace, and chromatic scales and arpeggiated chords add to the excitement. The radical change to a fugal style in the cadenza presents some challenges. It is an appealing piece for the performer with an athletic style of pianism and a sense of flair. (F major, level 10)

2. Andante (♩ = 76)

A restless and wandering Romantic piece with an impassioned sense of phrasing, the *Andante* is highlighted by a simple harmonic flow. The consistent triplet figure in the piano is utilized as an expressive device, pushing and pulling against the stoic orchestra. (C minor, level 9)

3. *Allegro* (♩ = 176)

The final movement is incisive and crackling with youthful excitement. Precise articulations and octave doubling from the first movement return in a lively dance in duple time and as a fast folk dance in an irregular ⅞ meter. The orchestra provides excellent accompaniment. Shostakovich includes a witty musical joke by quoting the Hanon finger exercises at breakneck speed. (F major, level 10+)

SILVANSKI, Nikolai (1915–1985) Russia

Petit Piano Concerto

An attractive piece for a younger intermediate student, this concerto presents wonderful interaction between student and teacher parts. Agile fingers are required in passages that extend slightly beyond a five-finger pattern range, and the piece involves frequent use of parallel rhythms and chord construction between the hands. This work is from a series of pedagogical piano concertos by Soviet composers, written to provide the student with the special opportunity of performing with one's teacher.

(Two pianos, Associated Music Publishers)

1. *Allegretto* [♩ = ca. 80]

A playful children's song establishes the character of this opening immediately. Some awkward fingerings are provided to accommodate the single-line melody, divided between the hands, and also the second theme in parallel octaves. It moves through multiple keys, including a modulation to B-flat major that coincides with the cadenza's contrapuntal texture. (G major, level 5)

2. *Andante* [♩ = ca. 80]

An expressive, haunting theme in D natural minor is presented by Piano II and then joined by Piano I in a gradual, consistent build of rhythmic activity and harmonic intensity. (D minor, level 4)

3. *Allegro ma non troppo* [♩ = ca. 124]

An energetic rondo, this movement features distinct folk elements. The ensemble requires careful, precise rhythmic execution. Compelling writing is found in the middle section, as the parts exchange themes in a game of "cat and mouse." (G major, level 5)

STAMITZ, Johann (1717–1757) Germany

Stamitz was an important composer of the early Classical period. His influence in the symphony's development includes the expansion into four movements, the use of sonata form for the first movement, and the inclusion of a minuet and trio as the third movement. Stamitz is most notable as the conductor of the Mannheim Court orchestra, one of the finest orchestras in Europe, and as the leader of the Mannheim School, a highly respected group of composers of that time.

Concerto in D Major, Op. 10, No. 1

(Piano and orchestra, full score, Schott)

1. *Allegro* [♩ = ca. 120]

The movement opens with an ascending theme that dramatically announces the piece, a gesture similar to the famous "Mannheim Rocket." Elements of Classical sonata form are featured, though not fully developed or immediately apparent. The harmony is exclusively tonic and dominant, and the overall sense of the movement, while appealing in character, is repetitive and predictable. Florid lines lie naturally in the hand, except for some isolated figures and ornamental displays. (D major, level 9)

2. *Andante poco Adagio* [♩ = ca. 45]

A variety of rhythmic values are used in the right hand to create an elegant character, while the left hand is a continuo-style accompaniment of regular eighth notes. Based on familiar keyboard patterns rather than a bel canto style, the melodic content is expressive with many Baroque-style gestures. (D major, level 8)

3. *Allegro assai* [♩ = ca. 126]

This closing movement's robust, poised character is highly engaging. The keyboard writing shimmers, and the sonata form is clear. Its charming excitement captures the essence of the early Classical concerto style. (D major, level 8)

STANLEY, John (1712–1786) Great Britain

Blind from age two, John Stanley had a prominent career in London as composer, violinist, and organist. He stands out among his contemporaries as a composer of "grand concertos," modeling them after Handel's Op. 6 concertos of 1739. His *Six Concertos in Seven Parts, Op. 2*, first appeared in 1742 "for Strings and Continuo, or Keyboard and Continuo." In the Baroque style, each work is short, varied, tuneful, and contrapuntal. This edition by Gerald Finzi presents versions both for strings and continuo as well as solo keyboard with string accompaniment.

Concerto in D Major, Op. 2, No. 1

Each of these concise, compact movements would serve nicely as an individual piece.

(Keyboard and string orchestra, full score, Boosey & Hawkes)

1. *Largo* [♩ = ca. 60]

The first movement is built on a lilting dotted figure reminiscent of a French Overture. To be performed in true legato, parallel 6ths require finger substitution. It could be effective as a short solo work that employs some ornamentation. (D major, level 4)

2. *Allegro* [♩ = ca. 120, 66]

Lively dance sections alternate with a chorale *Adagio* in $\frac{3}{4}$. The three-voice solo is contrapuntal but not fugal. (D major, level 5)

3. *Allegro* [♩ = ca. 126]

The most demanding and substantial movement of the concerto, this quickly moving *Allegro* features fugal treatment of the three-voice texture. The full sonority and the rewarding musical material display fine Baroque craftsmanship. (D major, level 8)

4. *Adagio* [♪ = ca. 72]

A beautiful intertwining of melodic lines in the right hand creates an attractive duet that requires independence and control to balance the voices. (B minor, level 6)

5. *Allegro* [♩. = ca. 60]

A buoyant dance in $\frac{3}{8}$, the simple solo part features two voices. Short runs, musical gestures, and embellishment are on display in the right hand. (D major, level 6)

Concerto in B Minor, Op. 2, No. 2

(Harpsichord and string orchestra, full score, Boosey & Hawkes)

1. *Largo—Adagio* [♩ = ca. 60, 66]

The *Largo* section is a stunning announcement of the piece in $\frac{3}{4}$ time with the entire ensemble in unison rhythms. The *Adagio* continues *attacca* in slow-moving counterpoint, requiring a developed sense of line to keep the right hand phrasing intact. The student needs strong finger independence to play the two lines legato in the right hand. (B minor, level 6)

2. *Allegro* [♩ = ca. 132]

A modified binary-form dance, this *Allegro* has two voices and new material for the second half of the movement. Melodic focus is on the right hand, while the left hand plays continuo downbeats. This movement is effective as a stand-alone piece without accompaniment. (B minor, level 6)

3. *Adagio—Allegro moderato* [♩ = ca. 54, ♩ = ca. 112]

The centerpiece of the concerto, this unique movement alternates between recitative slow sections that provide the soloist with the freedom to improvise and aria-like fast sections. The writing for the keyboard is occasionally angular with a *basso continuo* left-hand part that lacks appeal. The final sections of *Allegro moderato* and *Adagio* feature involved interaction between the hands with effective keyboard writing. (D major, level 8)

4. *Allegro* [♩ = ca. 138]

A lengthy but straightforward three-voice fugue, this movement showcases attractive and engaging writing in a well-designed form. The solo sections feel natural in the hands. This independent movement can be satisfying with or without accompaniment. (B minor, level 9)

5. *Allegro* [♩ = ca. 84]

This light, spirited alla breve work is in binary form. An excellent work, it features a strong Baroque dance style in a two-voice texture with distinctive writing. (B minor, level 7)

Concerto in G Major, Op. 2, No. 3

Stanley's most unique concerto for the keyboard, the *Concerto in G Major* uses imaginative textures and sonorities.

(Keyboard and string orchestra, full score, Boosey & Hawkes)

1. *Adagio* [♩ = ca. 84]

The movement begins with a keyboard solo followed by exchanges between the solo and *tutti* in the style of a Baroque aria. It provides an opportunity for improvised ornamentation in an expressive context. (G major, level 7)

2. *Allegro* [♩ = ca. 132]

This buoyant and spirited movement also serves as an effective solo piece. Varied patterns and figurations appear throughout in two- and three-voice contrapuntal textures. (G major, level 10)

3. *Andante* [♩ = ca. 52]

Expressive dissonances are featured within linear, sequential writing. Trills are used extensively. (E minor, level 9)

4. *Allegro* [♩. = ca. 52]

Written as a concerto grosso movement, this work features a keyboard solo that introduces the main theme, leading to a climactic *tutti* through the gradual addition of instruments. The multiple solo passages and repeats demand embellishment to create interest. The doubling of the keyboard and violin creates an appealing timbre. (G major, level 10)

Concerto in D Minor, Op. 2, No. 4

(Keyboard and string orchestra, full score, Boosey & Hawkes)

1. *Adagio* [♪ = ca. 80]

This is a stately allemande that requires skilled voicing. (D minor, level 8)

2. *Allegro* [♩ = ca. 116]

This dance in binary form includes triplet passages alternating with chordal textures in dotted rhythms. Short, quick trills appear throughout. (D minor, level 8)

3. *Andante* [♩ = ca. 69]

This concise, expressive movement is written in a processional style and features clever modulations. (B-flat major, level 6)

4. *Allegro* [♪ = ca. 138]

Sequences occur frequently in this quick, lively ritornello movement. This accessible work requires an independent left hand. (D minor, level 8)

Concerto in A Minor/A Major, Op. 2, No. 5

(Harpsichord and string orchestra, full score, Boosey & Hawkes)

1. *Largo* [♩ = ca. 60]

A repeat makes this a substantial movement, with multiple opportunities for the performer to add embellishments to the given part. Chordal textures are found throughout. (A minor, level 6)

2. *Allegro* [♩ = ca. 112]

Effective as a solo piece, this is a cheerful three-voice fugue. Fast passagework with sections of exposed solos leave room for a cadenza that is to be provided by the performer. (A minor, level 9)

3. *Adagio* [♩ = ca. 60]

This is a simple piece technically, with room for extensive improvisation. Although not indicated, the soloist should roll the chords in *tutti* passages. The left hand assumes a continuo role throughout. (F major, level 5)

4. *Allegro* [♩ = ca. 96]

The solo is featured primarily in extended passages with sequential treatment of material, and also in alternating passages with the orchestra as an "echo." Repeated-note figures in the *tutti* passages can be played as non-repeated held notes. The movement captures the Baroque style in a simple two-voice texture. Overall, it is appealing and jaunty. (A major, level 8)

5. *Allegro moderato* [♩ = ca. 126]

A graceful minuet in binary form, this movement has variations of the accompaniment pattern that require left-hand independence and agility in each main section. Simple and linear melodic content contribute to its effectiveness as a solo piece as well. (A major, level 6)

Concerto in B-flat Major, Op. 2, No. 6

Stanley published a version of this concerto in his Op. 10 organ concertos in 1775. This edition features more extended solo passages and a three-part string quartet accompaniment (without viola). The *Largo* movement is also omitted.

(Keyboard and string orchestra, full score, Boosey & Hawkes)

1. *Adagio* [♩ = ca. 60]

The opening allemande in three voices requires control and skilled voicing. (B-flat major, level 7)

2. *Allegro* [♩ = ca. 104]

This *Allegro* is written in ritornello form, with the main theme receiving a fugal treatment. Solo passages with figuration are crafted comfortably on the keyboard and in the hand, but the three-voice contrapuntal textures need careful fingering. (B-flat major, level 9)

3. *Largo* [♩ = ca. 66]

A pleading quality permeates this movement, with sighing slurs and remorseful rests reminiscent of Handel. The texture becomes more involved with independent lines in each hand. (G minor, level 8)

4. *Allegro* [♩ = ca. 138]

This engaging work is a delightful bourrée in ritornello form. The two-voice texture requires distinctive articulation of descending two-note slurs and ascending dotted figures. (B-flat major, level 8)

STEFFAN, Joseph Anton (1726–1797) Bohemia

Steffan studied harpsichord and composition with the eminent Georg Christoph Wagenseil in Vienna, where he established his reputation as teacher and composer for the aristocracy. He was eventually appointed Klaviermeister to the imperial court and contributed significantly to the development of the keyboard sonata and concerto genres. His *Lieder* were the first German art songs with independent fortepiano accompaniment to be published in Vienna. Steffan's music serves as a link between the early Classical Viennese concerto school and the fully realized Classical style of Mozart.

Piano Concerto in B-flat Major

(Fortepiano and strings, full score, A-R Editions)

1. *Adagio non molto—Allegro* [♩ = ca. 40, 60]

Steffan's *Adagio* introduction in the key of D minor extends the form and deepens the emotional impact of the first movement. The *Allegro* defies expectations of the Classical concerto movement, including its scoring, form, key, and thematic presentation. An attractive solo part is very active and prominent, displaying a wide array of technical patterns and rhythm groupings in contrast to a relatively sparse orchestral accompaniment. The solo instrument is integral to each *tutti* statement, a highly unusual feature for a concerto of this period. (B-flat major, level 9)

2. *Andante non molto* [♩ = ca. 60]

A stylish movement cast in sonata form, this *Andante* has a quasi-improvisatory, highly embellished solo part. The expressive cantabile themes present contrasting moods and characters that are both elegant and emotionally intense. This movement features the soloist throughout the entire work, a rare characteristic for a concerto from this period. It is an excellent piece full of style and quality, appropriate for the mature, expressive player. (E-flat major, level 9)

3. *Allegro* [♩ = ca. 80]

The broad themes, dazzling runs and figurations, and opposition and alliance of soloist and orchestra in this vibrant sonata-rondo are characteristic of the fully realized Classical-period concerto. This most satisfying movement is reminiscent of Mozart's energy and spirit. (B-flat major, level 9)

STERKEL, Johann Franz Xaver (1750–1817) Germany

First Concerto (Concertino) in C Major, Op. 20

According to the preface, "This soloistically as well as orchestrally rewarding work will be evaluated as a revealing contribution to the development of the piano concerto in the end of the 18th century." Sterkel's stylistic mannerisms became influential to the young Beethoven.

(Piano with oboe, horn, and strings, full score, Schott Music)

1. *Allegro con spirit*o [♩ = ca. 130]

A sunny, upbeat character permeates this movement. A full orchestral presentation of the thematic material precedes the piano entrance. Rapid-fire broken chords and rising scalar passages predominate. The brief, yet flashy, cadenzas occur in both solo and accompanied textures in this thoroughly engaging movement. (C major, level 7)

2. *Andante* [♩ = ca. 55]

This is a poignant, fully realized, slow Classical concerto movement in ABA form with an extended coda. Technical demands and textural considerations of the prominently featured solo part are similar to the more advanced sonatinas from the period. A fermata is provided so that the performer can insert a cadenza *ad libitum*. (F major, level 8).

3. *Rondeau: Allegro* [♩ = ca. 80]

An energetic rondo movement in $\frac{2}{4}$, this work begins with an enthusiastic statement from the piano. The tutti orchestra follows and captures the essence of a hunting party on horseback. A recurrent 16th-note triplet figure will require agile fingerwork despite the carefully planned layout of the notes. The extended middle section begins in C minor with a quasi-cadenza before heading into E-flat major. It then returns to C minor to finish the section with another cadenza. The return of the opening section in C major provides a rousing close to the hunt. (C major, level 8)

SUGÁR, Rezső (1919–1988) Hungary

Sugár studied composition with Zoltán Kodály at the Franz Liszt Academy of Music and later taught at that institution. His music reflects the folk-inspired style of Hungarian culture.

Rondo

(Piano and youth string orchestra, two piano reduction, Editio Musica Budapest)

Adagio—Allegretto [♩ = ca. 58, 126]

An excellent piece for a young pianist's first concerto experience, this work explores the fresh and captivating sounds of modes and folk-like themes. It includes pedagogical material designed to develop a strong tone. The *Adagio* introduction captures the introspective mood with arpeggiated, pentatonic figures. An *accelerando* leads directly into the rondo in a lean, neoclassic style reminiscent of Bartók. The dry articulation of the A section fits into five-finger patterns with doubling at the octave, and the legato B section contrasts with light polyphony. A slower middle section features a simple homophonic texture with appealing harmonies. (G modal, level 6)

THOMAS, Richard Pearson (b. 1957) USA

Concerto in "C-E-G"

(Piano and orchestra, full score, two piano reduction, Portage Press Publishing)

1. *Andante brilliante, con spirito* (♩ = 108)

The colorful opening *Andante* includes playful interaction between the piano and orchestra in a waltz reminiscent of Prokofiev. The integration of contemporary pianistic techniques—white-key chord clusters, glissandos, and a blend of popular and dissonant harmony—is original and striking. Rhythmic energy derives from mixed meters and changing accents within them. Fleet passagework is pianistically conceived. Soaring themes and a clear sense of climax and structure make this an engaging movement. (C major, level 10)

2. *Adagio tenuto, espressivo* (♩ = 46)

The second movement, played *attacca* after the soloist sustains the final *fortississimo* chord of the previous movement, features a tender, pensive piano introduction. The use of nonchord tones throughout evokes the dissonance of Impressionism, which is further demonstrated in rapid figurations. This sophisticated music is appropriate for an expressive player. (E major, level 10)

3. *Allegro cantabile—Presto* (♩. = 126; ♩ = 152)

A *dolce* opening in the solo piano, accompanied by muted strings, establishes a bridge to the *Presto*—a vigorous, jovial finale with prominent brass and jazzy harmony that recalls the Ravel *Concerto in G*. At the contrasting-theme section, a gorgeous texture occurs with a sustained melody in the winds and a 16th-note pattern in the piano. Effective colors in the solo part are achieved through atypical patterns that will pose a sufficient technical challenge, coupled with musically challenging and subtle shifts in meter, tempo, and rhythmic groupings. The overall result is worth the effort. (G major, level 10+)

THOMPSON, John (1889–1963) USA

Concertina (Little Concerto)

(Two pianos, The Willis Music Co.)

Moderato assai (♩ = 168)

This one-movement work includes several tempo changes and a wide range of dynamics. Rhythmic values consist mainly of quarter and half notes, but the piece may provide a challenge with its frequency and varied lengths of rests for Piano I. Dramatic opening chords in Piano II display the *maestoso* character. Piano I doubles at the octave throughout, except during the second theme, which is divided between the hands. Detailed fingerings are provided to facilitate the variety of articulations marked. Four-note chord patterns are prominent in legato and staccato articulations. (E minor, level 2)

Concerto Americana

Accessible writing and familiar themes encourage musicality. The predominant texture features melodies distributed between the hands, while passages played hands together are written an octave apart. Piano I is mostly written with both hands in the treble clef. The sonority created with the combined parts is full and rewarding. The piece provides an opportunity for a student ensemble with a slightly more experienced player on Piano II. The score provides excellent fingerings, clear pedal markings, and appropriate articulations. According to Thompson, "The object of this work is to acquaint the young piano student with the form of a concerto, even though the material used is definitely not in concerto character."

(Two pianos, The Willis Music Co.)

1. *Down South—Andante moderato e molto maestoso* (♩ = 104)

The opening measure imitates the Tchaikovsky *Piano Concerto No. 1 in B-flat Minor*. The "Down South" character is achieved by a lively "Dixie" theme in cut time, followed by a slower version of "Arkansas Traveler." Tempo and character changes are frequent. A dramatic coda concludes the movement. (C major, level 3)

2. *Out West—Andante moderato* (♩ = 120)

The simple, expressive presentation of "Home on the Range" and "Goodbye, Old Paint" effectively create an ABA form. Arpeggiated accompaniment figures in Piano I provide color and contrast to the melody in Piano II. (G major, level 3)

3. *Back East—Molto allegro* (♩. = 104)

The time signature change from 𝄴 in the "Battle Hymn of the Republic" to the 𝄴 meter of the "Yale Boola Song" is achieved with a clever transition in Piano II involving triplets and an introduction of the new rhythmic motive. Lively interaction occurs between the two pianos, with frequent changing of melodic and accompaniment roles. (C major, level 3)

Concerto in D Minor

According to Thompson, "This Concerto is designed for pupils of average high school age and is intended to serve as preparation for the study of the easier concertos of the masters." The majority of the piece consists of patterns familiar to pianists at this level. The first movement is considerably longer and more appealing than the other two movements, which seem terse in comparison. The band accompaniment is at a junior high school difficulty level. A complete set of band parts and the conductor's score are available from the publisher.

(Piano and band, two piano reduction, The Willis Music Co.)

1. *Allegro con brio* (♩ = 144)

The length and technique required to play this movement contribute to its difficulty. The grand chordal gestures and elaborate passagework are created through familiar shapes and subtle changes in harmony. There are hints of Rachmaninoff, Gershwin, and Beethoven throughout the movement. The cadenza is flashy but not overly demanding, leading into an energetic coda and a *presto* ending. (D minor, level 8)

2. *Andantino* (♪ = 138)

The pentatonic scale and dotted rhythms in a lilting 𝄴 meter lend a folk character to this movement. (B-flat major, level 7)

3. *Allegro furioso* (♩ = 104)

A Scottish influence is evident in the accompaniment's bagpipe sounds and the theme's march rhythm. The overall effect is somewhat limited due to repetitive harmonies and melodies and the constancy of the marching rhythm. (D minor, level 8)

TURRINI, Ferdinando (1745–1829) Italy

Turrini was one of the leading Italian composers in the late Classical era, notable especially for his promotion of sonata form.

Concerto in G Minor

Written in one continuous movement with string accompaniment, this work features the form of a Classical concerto, including long orchestral introductions and fully developed cadenzas. This work is an excellent substitute for one of the easier Mozart concertos.

(Harpsichord and string orchestra, full score, Edizioni G. Zanibon)

1. *Allegro moderato ma con molto spirito* [♩ = ca. 116]

Dramatic in character, this substantial work frequently features the soloist through flashy figurations without accompaniment. It is not consistently difficult throughout, but some passages do pose a challenge. (G minor, level 7)

2. *Andante* [♩ = ca. 56]

Ornamentations, chromatic harmonies, and intricate 32nd-note rhythms are some of the distinguishing expressive features of this movement. Some wide spans in the left hand and a vertical, layered approach to texture require skilled voicing and careful attention to lyrical playing. (G major, level 7)

3. *Non molto allegro* [♩. = ca. 88]

This rondo movement with Romantic harmonies and gestures also displays some folk characteristics. The primarily two-voice texture requires careful attention to fingering. Frequent grace notes should be light and provide momentum to the lines. Left-hand independence is crucial to success. (G minor, level 7)

TSYTOVICH, Vladimir (1931–2012) Russia

Piano Concerto

Tzytovich specialized in the music of Bartók, and this influence is reflected in his music in an academic way.

(Two pianos, Associated Music Publishers, Hal Leonard)

1. *Andante con moto* [♩ = ca. 80]

A concise movement, this work sounds similar to the early books of Bartók's *Mikrokosmos.* The hands are an octave apart within a very limited melodic span. Syncopation presents some challenges, particularly because the accompaniment provides little support. Exact repetition of musical material requires careful interpretation to sustain interest and direction. (E minor, level 4)

2. *Allegro* [♩ = ca. 104]

An excellent introduction to irregular meters ($\frac{10}{8}$, $\frac{7}{8}$, and $\frac{5}{8}$), the *Allegro* achieves a distinct Bulgarian feel. A single-note texture generally occurs throughout and requires clear articulation. Using quartal (4th) and quintal (5th) harmonies, this movement has substantial musical ideas and technical requirements. (C major, level 7)

VANDALL, Robert D. (1944–2017) USA

Concertino in C Major

Vandall's *Concertino* contains highly patterned textures that fit the hand beautifully. The harmony is simple and appealing, with half-step harmonic shifts that are characteristic of this composer. A wide range of the keyboard is utilized. Equally matched parts feature lively interaction, and all three movements use fast tempos.

(Two pianos, Alfred Music)

1. *Allegro moderato* (♩ = 72–88)

This energetic piece alternates between cantabile lines and crisp textures. Technical focus is on five-finger patterns and blocked and broken triads. The cadenza moves through various tempos and thematic elements, providing an opportunity for expressive interpretation. The coda pushes toward a showy finish. (C major, level 3)

2. *Scherzo: Allegretto* (♩. = 66–80)

A quick movement, this *Scherzo* is similar to an étude with its repetitive rising and falling five-finger patterns and blocked triads alternating between the hands. The piece does an excellent job of exploring the rhythmic variety of $\frac{6}{8}$ meter. (F major, level 2)

3. *Vivace* (♩ = 120–138)

In compact rondo form, this movement has distinct themes and contrasting textures. The middle section uses both sustain and una corda pedals. Fingerings and key patterns beyond five-finger positions are explored. Rhythmic syncopation and quickly changing thematic material and characters are the two main considerations. (C major, level 3)

Concerto in G Major

Vandall's inventive use of triads and scalar figures fit the hand naturally, resulting in a plethora of enjoyable pianistic figurations for the soloist, primarily in treble clef for both hands. Vandall effectively writes a strong alla breve character in all movements. A full orchestral score and set of parts are available.

(Two pianos, Alfred Music)

1. *Moderato* (♩ = ca. 96)

Highly patterned writing features toccata textures between the hands, with clever use of rhythm and unexpected harmonic shifts. The parts are closely matched in difficulty, and performers should take care to produce a steady pulse with even eighth notes between the two pianos. (G major, level 5)

2. *Allegretto* (♩ = ca. 96)

A melancholy mood with long singing lines makes this an effective piece. Expressive, ascending intervallic passages are easier than they seem. (E minor, level 5)

3. *Vivace* (♩ = ca. 144)

A feeling of perpetual motion and dazzling cross-hand toccata patterns are hallmarks of this movement. Accents clearly denote a left-hand melody within the texture. The multiple repetitions in this rhythmic work call for variety in interpretation to establish an energetic and full sound. (G major, level 5)

VANHAL, Johann Baptist (1739–1813) Bohemia

Keyboard Concerto in F Major

(Keyboard and string orchestra with oboe and horn, full score, IMSLP)

1. *Allegro moderato* [♩ = ca. 126]

Immediately appealing themes in a Classical style make this an effective choice as a first introduction to concerto playing. Left-hand accompaniment figurations are typical for the level and style, and right-hand patterns lie easily in the hand. The orchestral scoring supports and actively interplays with the soloist. Students may wish to provide a cadenza *ad libitum*. Harmonic progressions are predictable, with few surprises along the way. (F major, level 6)

2. *Adagio* [♩ = ca. 56]

The thematic material of this slow movement lacks the inspiration of the outer movements. Although its layout at the keyboard is well conceived, the halting rhythmic nature and meandering patterns of the right hand impact linear flow. The student will need to create a cadenza. (C major, level 6)

3. *Allegro Finale* [♩ = ca. 116]

Very light orchestral scoring puts the focus on the soloist in this rondo movement. The general effect is buoyant, but the thematic motives are not highly imaginative. Much of the interest relies upon the left-hand accompaniment patterns. This lighthearted Classical work includes passages of quick technical display. (F major, level 6)

Piano Concerto in C Major

(Piano and string orchestra, two piano reduction, Editio Musica Budapest)

1. *Allegro moderato* [♩ = ca. 66–70]

Stately in nature, this opening movement requires limited technical forces from both the piano and orchestral reduction. Pianistic demands focus on two-note slurs in 6ths and 3rds, ornamental turns, and broken-octave motion in the bass. Careful attention to articulation is paramount to convey a convincing sense of style. This movement would be a perfect educational tool for studying concerto-sonata form, and it would work beautifully for a student with a limited hand span. (C major, level 5)

2. *Adagio* [♩ = ca. 60]

A short gem of a movement in clearly defined ABA form, this work requires ornamented figuration and the ability to control the shape of a long melodic line. A steady underlying pulse is vital to an effective performance. This piece requires mature sensibility and developed musicality. (F major, level 5)

3. *Finale: Allegro assai* [♩ = ca. 148]

Continuing with the opening movement's focus on melodic 6ths and 3rds, the *Finale*'s appealing main theme alternates with a B section in the key of F major. A short codetta concludes the sprightly work. Terraced dynamic markings allow the student to explore a full range of sound, while also requiring subtle treatment appropriate for a Classical composition. The frequent broken-octave bass line, an energetic tempo, and recurring themes contribute to an impressive overall effect. (C major, level 5)

VERHAALEN, Marion (b. 1930) USA

Concertino

This unique score has the solo part written on a single staff. Both hands are involved at all times, with stem directions indicating which hand plays the notes. The second piano accompaniment provides most of the interest and appeal, aside from the novelty of the notation.

(Two pianos, Lee Roberts Music Publications)

1. *Joyfully* (♩ = 96)

This work's themes are distinct in character and texture. The primary theme, comprised of root-position triads with a recurring rhythm in the right hand, forgoes a creative melody for the sake of convenient hand positions. The secondary theme is attractive, based on a five-finger pattern, with a gently rocking left-hand accompaniment. (F major, level 3)

2. *Gently swaying with feeling* (♪ = 108)

Verhaalen's one-page movement in Dorian mode presents a folk melody that unfolds in both hands, separated by two octaves in the solo part. An evocative second piano ebbs and flows. (G dorian, level 1)

3. *Energetically* (♩ = 104)

The use of difficult-sounding repeated triads in rapidly alternating blocked and broken patterns will appeal to many students. It is an effective technical study for triads and five-finger patterns with some awkward cross-hand positions. (A minor, level 3)

VOGLER, Georg Joseph (1749–1814) Germany

Concerto in C Major

From notes provided in the revised score by the editor, Dr. Alejandro Garri: "On the title page out of print, it is listed as being for either pianoforte or for harpsichord, but it is not likely to have been written for the harpsichord, owing to this instrument's inability to balance the pair of winds in the orchestra." With that said, the composer rarely has the keyboard play against the full orchestra. Cadenzas were composed for the 2007 edition.

(Keyboard and orchestra, full score, Garri Editions)

1. *Allegro* [♩ = ca. 126]

Bold themes in repetitive keyboard figurations are not entirely unique or consistent in difficulty, particularly in the left hand. The movement is in sonata-allegro form with an obligatory cadenza point. Orchestral textures are sparse during solo passages, but the *tutti* sections are buoyant and charming. (C major, level 8)

2. *Andantino* [♩ = ca. 80]

In binary form, the thematic material and harmonic direction can become monotonous without a clear sense of phrasing. It is scored for keyboard and strings only. (F major, level 7)

3. *Allegro* [♩ = ca. 108]

Although labeled a "Rondeau" in the original publication by Sieber, this movement is a charming minuet theme and variations. The composer effectively incorporates technique into musical lines. The third variation is through-composed, leading to a cadenza and a subdued final cadence. (C major, level 8)

WAGENSEIL, Georg Christoph (1715–1777) Austria

The Viennese pre-Classical composer Georg Christoph Wagenseil was equally famous throughout Europe as a harpsichord virtuoso. As the court composer to the Empress Maria Theresa, Wagenseil served as the "court clavier master" to her children. In return, she promoted him as an artist and pedagogue, and rewarded him in an extraordinarily generous manner. In the mid-1750s, he was given broad privilege to publish music, resulting in a huge dissemination of his works in Paris, London, Amsterdam, Germany, and Vienna. Although he wrote 103 concertos, 93 of which are for one or more keyboard instruments, they are generally solo works for an amateur to play with chamber accompaniment by friends.

Concerto per Pianoforte

The diverse orchestration consists of two flutes, two oboes, two horns, and strings with divided violas.

(Pianoforte and orchestra, two piano reduction, Universal Edition)

1. *Vivace* [♩ = ca. 68]

An extended 54-measure opening ritornello features a succession of thematic ideas, with the full orchestra in a variety of instrument pairings. The soloist enters with a statement of the opening theme and then quickly launches into flashy keyboard figurations that sound more difficult than they are to play. The soloist has very few actual thematic lines, and the orchestra provides support without competing with the piano. This substantial movement demonstrates the developing role of the keyboard soloist in a symphonic setting. (E-flat major, level 8)

2. *Andante* [♪ = ca. 69]

The movement opens with a lengthy introduction in the muted strings of the orchestra. The florid keyboard part weaves a delicate contour with ever-changing rhythmic patterns for heightened expressivity, the interpretation of which presents the greatest challenge to the performer. (C minor, level 9)

3. *Allegro molto* [♩. = ca. 92]

In rounded binary form, this vigorous and celebratory *Allegro* in 𝄴 replaces the typical courtly minuet. The constant 16th-note figurations in the right hand are patterned, while the left hand marks the pulse. This is a dazzling keyboard work of considerable difficulty for its period. (E-flat major, level 9)

Concerto in G Major, WV 53

Originally published as *Divertimenti, Op. 2* for unaccompanied harpsichord, this composition has outer movements that are concise and cheerful while the middle movement serves as the emotional centerpiece. Orchestra parts are merely supportive and not integral to the overall effect.

(Keyboard and string orchestra, full score, Doblinger Musikverlag)

1. *Allegro* [♩ = ca. 110]

This bright work features fun-to-play repetitive patterns that fit the hands well. Octave stretches in the left hand may challenge students with smaller hand spans. This piece is a good choice for a first concerto experience. (G major, level 5)

2. *Andante* [♩ = ca. 68]

The key of G minor creates a somber mood that contrasts starkly with the rest of the concerto. Frequent melodic leaps, coupled with expressive rhythmic gestures, intensify the feeling of melancholy. The smooth integration of ornaments into the cantabile line will require even touch and tone. This poignant movement could stand alone to showcase the thoughtful performer. (G minor, level 7)

3. *Tempo di Minuetto* [♩ = ca. 108]

A waltz in ABA form, this final movement reasserts the joviality found in the first movement with highly patterned and repetitive figurations in a two-voice texture. (G major, level 4)

Concerto in D Major, WV 278

(Keyboard and strings, full score, Breitkopf & Härtel)

1. *Allegro* [♩ = ca. 120]

An attractive thematic statement is followed by enjoyable toccata-like passages. An agile left hand will be needed for fluent scales and other nimble patterns. This movement is full of stylistic character and charm. (D major, level 8)

2. *Andante* [♩ = ca. 52]

The piece is elegant and poised in the dramatic key of D minor. The orchestral opening is briefly restated in the solo part, which then becomes embellished with falling triplets and rapid, rising figures. Ornamentation will require control. Exchanges between soloist and orchestra create a beautiful dialogue. (D minor, level 9)

3. *Allegro* [♩. = ca. 64]

A proud dance in ⅜ provides a fitting finale to this work. The dynamics, particularly in the orchestra, underscore the lilting quality of the musical gestures and the "one beat per measure" pulse. (D major, level 8)

Concerto in B Major, WV 335

(Keyboard and string orchestra, full score, Doblinger Musikverlag)

1. *A tempo giusto* [♩ = ca. 82]

The strict tempo and recurrent dotted rhythms create the strong character of this music. A modulation to G minor occurs in the B section, and rapid, ascending 16th-note triplets generate energy throughout the harmonic progression, leading to a *tutti* restatement of the A section. For artistic execution, the prominent embellishments require rhythmic control and sophistication. The piece includes some doubled notes, but is primarily a two-voice texture. (B-flat major, level 9)

2. *Andante moderato* [♩ = ca. 58]

Attractive themes with expressive lines and rhythmic variety are highlighted through sparse orchestration. This movement maintains motivic unity with the first movement through the use of rising dotted figures. (E-flat major, level 7)

3. *Allegro* [♪ = ca. 136]

In a lighthearted rounded binary, this movement has dotted rhythms that evoke a stately dance. The highly patterned, two-voice lines present no significant technical or musical challenges. (B-flat major, level 6)

WAGNER, Joseph Frederick (1900–1974) USA

Concertino in G Minor

According to the score, "*Concertino* was written expressly for pianists with limited technical attainments with an orchestral accompaniment kept within similar technical limitations." The work is intended to be Classical in form and Romantic in style. The work was written in 1919, then revised and premiered in 1925 by the Boston Public Schools Symphony Orchestra with composer Leonard Bernstein as soloist and conductor.

(Piano and orchestra, two piano reduction, Seesaw Music)

1. *Allegro moderato* (♩ = 120)

This sophisticated composition for a young soloist and orchestra features frequent tempo and character changes. The writing is highly patterned with doubling between the hands. An extensive and musically demanding cadenza is included. The musical demands and tempo affect the difficulty level of this movement. (G minor, level 6)

2. *Andante tranquillo* (♩ = 72)

An orchestral prelude introduces the piano entrance. The work is full of repetitive rhythmic figurations in linear patterns and triadic accompaniments, all of which lie easily in the hands. (A-flat major, level 5)

3. *Allegro moderato* (♩ = 107–112)

A virtuosic effect is achieved with lines divided between the hands or doubled at the octave, but the shortest rhythmic values are eighth notes. The orchestral support is attractive and expertly crafted. (G minor, level 6)

WALTER, Fried (1907–1996) Germany

Walter was one of the most versatile and prolific composers of German "upscale entertainment music," a genre created for radio orchestras in the 1920s. The genre is characterized by simple harmonies with complex instrumentation and the inclusion of jazz and folk themes.

Concertino

(Piano and chamber orchestra, two piano reduction, Ahn & Simrock)

1. *Allegro* (♩ = 176)

A lilting $\frac{3}{4}$ meter requires a strong feeling of one beat per measure. A tonal harmonic sense with Impressionistic colors and a mild, easy-listening jazz influence provide an attractive and accessible work. The blending of $\frac{6}{8}$ and $\frac{3}{4}$ meters requires rhythmic independence between the hands. (G major, level 8)

2. *Andante* (♪ = 132, ♩ = 66)

Exotic modal themes and evocative instrumentation make this movement reminiscent of a movie soundtrack. Aside from the pensive introduction and conclusion, and the flamboyant cadenza, the piano provides a contrasting timbre to the orchestra. (E minor, level 8)

3. *Allegro con spirito* (♩ = 120)

An energetic samba, this movement is similar to the last movement of Milhaud's *Scaramouche*. Rapid repeated chords may be technically challenging. An array of patterns throughout combines technical and harmonic shapes that are exhilarating to play. The music includes many twists and musical jokes in its playful spirit. An extensive cadenza showcases the performer's abilities. (G major, level 9)

WAXMAN, Donald (b. 1925) USA

Variations on "Ah, Vous Dirai-je Maman"

(Piano and orchestra, two piano reduction, Galaxy Music)

Andante [♩ = ca. 64]

According to notes provided in the score by Waxman, "In arranging the *'Ah, Dirai-Je Maman'* variations for piano and orchestra, I have wanted to provide students, particularly young ones, with a miniature Mozart concerto with cadenza." The appealing Mozart original for solo piano is presented mostly intact, with the orchestra adding color and harmony. Two of the variations occur in the orchestra, and the other variations feature spirited interaction between soloist and orchestra. A stylistic cadenza has been added following the fermata chord in the *Adagio* variation, offering an opportunity for expressive virtuosity. Waxman's composition is a clever, motivating arrangement of Mozart's work. (C major, level 8)

WERNER, Gregor Joseph (1693–1766) Austria

Werner served as Kapellmeister at the Esterházy court in Eisenstadt from 1728 until his death in 1766. It was a post assumed by the Vice-Kapellmeister, Franz Joseph Haydn. Werner followed the traditions of his age, and his works are brief, clearly constructed, and often inclusive of folk elements.

Concerto in B-flat Major

1. *Allegro* [♩ = ca. 96]

Quick and highly embellished, the movement progresses predictably through G minor and F major before returning to the home key. Active string parts match the energy of the solo. (B-flat major, level 8)

2. *Largo* [♪ = ca. 66]

The compact structure of this *Largo* makes the harmonic progressions feel rushed, despite their expressive intent. The simple melodic movement contains ideas with florid rhythms and ornamentation. (G minor, level 6)

3. *Tempo di menuet* [♩. = ca. 48]

Straightforward textures are featured in the brief solo moments, with the Baroque minuet style evident through the articulation. (B-flat major, level 6)

WESLEY, Charles (1757–1834) Great Britain

Concerto No. 4 in C Major, Op. 2

The *Six Concertos for the Organ or Harpsichord, Op. 2*, from Wesley's early years are his most remarkable works. These concertos are firmly grounded in the "galant" school, and although the influence of the previous generation is apparent, they have more in common with the Classical style. This worthwhile and satisfying piece is scored for strings and two oboes.

(Keyboard and string orchestra, full score, Hinrichsen, C. F. Peters)

1. *Allegro* [♩ = ca. 108]

An enticing alternative for an early Classical work, this movement showcases a prominent keyboard part, with orchestral support throughout. Contrapuntal textures and patterns with frequent changes of direction require finger independence. Passagework is right-hand dominant and reminiscent of the Classical era. A cadenza is provided. (C major, level 9)

2. *Largo* [♩ = ca. 63]

A dignified character is established through the key of C minor and the prevalent dotted rhythmic figure. Wesley was sparing and inconsistent in ornamentation, although the use of trills is encouraged. (C minor, level 7)

3. *Allegro moderato* [♩ = ca. 80]

The rondo form of this lively showpiece presents several opportunities for extended trills and brief virtuosic displays at the cadences prior to each new section. Hand crossing in the B section is effective in sound and appearance. Agile passagework is relegated to a limited keyboard range. (C major, level 9)

WHEELER, Gayneyl (1916–2000) USA

Concerto for Piano and Orchestra

"Traditional with a twist" in sounds and shapes, this piece may captivate students who think they do not like contemporary music. Fingerings require care, as many of the patterns are not always expected. All movements are concise, and no conventional cadenzas are indicated, although extended passages in each movement feature the piano alone.

(Piano and orchestra, two piano reduction, Carl Fischer)

1. *Maestoso—Più mosso* (♩ = 126)

A dramatic *ad libitum* opening in the solo piano is followed by a jaunty theme that employs folk elements. Extensive use of harmonies in 4ths and 5ths creates some unfamiliar hand positions. The melody is doubled frequently at the octave. (D minor, level 7)

2. *Andantino* (♩ = 76)

A calm, flowing piano part dialogues with the orchestra in this *Andantino* in ¾ meter; the two parts only play together briefly in the B section. Slow note values and repetition in the melodic material require a sense of forward motion for a convincing performance. (C major, level 7)

3. *Vivace* (♩. = 52)

This rondo movement features folk music in the style of Bartók, with a quick ⅝ meter and the melody doubled at the octave. Shifting accents and non-legato articulation create excitement. The middle section in ⅝ provides a *dolce* left-hand melody with rolled chordal accompaniment in the right hand. The rousing coda has a *fortissimo* ending. (D major, level 7)

WIGHAM, Margaret (1904–1972) USA

Concerto for Two Pianos

The *Concerto for Two Pianos* is written with equal difficulty in both parts, although Piano I has a slightly more prominent solo role. The piece can be presented by a student performing either the Piano I or Piano II part, or by two students performing the full work.

(Two pianos, R. D. Row Music)

1. *Spirited* [♩ = ca. 120]

A bold opening in octaves from both pianos introduces the piece. The musical material possesses a feeling of urgency that should not be rushed, and frequent character shifts between slower and faster sections require a strong pulse from the ensemble. This engaging work blends pedagogical goals with serious musical intentions. Helpful fingering suggestions are given throughout. Powerful octaves and four-note chords make this appropriate for a performer with large hands. (C major, level 7)

2. *Andante—thoughtfully* [♩ = ca. 82]

An ABA movement in C-sharp minor, this *Andante* is reminiscent of the Rachmaninoff *Preludes* in formal design. The piece begins with a brooding melody played by both pianos and supported by a foreboding accompaniment. Attentive phrasing is important to maintain the direction of the line. The middle section is a very spirited dance in D major with a tempo double that of the opening section, requiring a little more mobility from the fingers. The ability to create a full sound is necessary for the *fortissimo* climax, which reverts back to the opening material with one final outburst in the coda. The sustain pedal is used frequently throughout. (C-sharp minor, level 7)

3. *Allegro* [♩ = ca. 120]

This showpiece for Piano I, with cascading 32nd-note arpeggios, is designed for easy execution at the keyboard. Multiple key changes correlate to thematic material. An array of articulations between the two pianos results in a complex, impressive sonority. This *Allegro* is a commanding piece with dynamic writing that makes it sound difficult. (F major, level 7)

WILLIAMS, Jean (1876–1965) USA, born in England

Jean Williams was born in England and moved to Toronto, Canada. She studied at The Royal Conservatory of Music and the University of Toronto, where she later taught voice and piano. She also taught in Cleveland and St. Louis before moving to Portland, Oregon, in 1932. Her compositions are attractive, pianistic, and pedagogical.

Concerto in A Minor

This popular piece includes many elements of the Romantic style. Written as consecutive *attacca* movements, the piece can be played easily and effectively as three separate movements.

(Piano and orchestra, two piano reduction, Schroeder & Gunther)

1. *Allegro con brio* (♩ = 116)

Grand dramatic gestures in scalar patterns, broken triads, and four-note chords create a virtuosic impression. Single-note textures and doubled octaves prevail, with a four-part chorale for the second theme that presents an opportunity for voicing. Pedal markings and fingerings are provided in the score. The cadenza is dazzling. (A minor, level 8)

2. *Largo—molto cantabile* (♪ = 52)

A simple statement in AABA form provides the soloist with a delicate showpiece featuring an embellished descant line that floats above the orchestra. The work presents an excellent opportunity to develop facile fingers, rhythmic flexibility, and expressivity. (F major, level 8)

3. *Allegro impetuoso—a la Tarantella* (♩. = 144–160)

A short interlude connects the *Largo* and the *Tarantella*. Efficient patterns in the right hand enable fleet execution, and various accompaniment patterns offer support in the left hand. The form follows an ABC pattern. A key change to A major in the B section remains through the rest of the movement. Consecutive harmonic octaves in the right hand may be difficult for smaller hands. (A minor, level 8)

Concerto in F Major

The continuous *attacca* movements can be effectively performed separately. Gestures, themes, textures, and a large orchestra pay homage to the Romantic concerto genre, creating a motivating piece for a late intermediate student.

(Piano and orchestra, two piano reduction, Schroeder & Gunther)

1. *Allegro marziale* (♩ = 108)

The movement is a modified sonata form, divided into distinct sections with multiple themes and two featured cadenzas. It is an excellent piece to work on a diverse array of pianistic techniques, including chord voicing, arpeggios divided between the hands, rapid grace notes, and octave passages. (F major, level 8)

2. *Andante cantabile* (♩ = 66)

A gentle, expressive character is found in this ABA form. The piano is responsible for the overall line and direction of the movement. The texture in the B section requires attention to balance. The orchestra provides light support and a contrasting timbre throughout. (B-flat major, level 7)

3. *Tempo di polka* (♩ = 96)

A rollicking rondo, the movement features lively interaction between the piano and orchestra. Reminiscent of Grieg's *Concerto in A Minor*, it is very patterned between the hands. A climactic ending includes a grandiose coda. (F major, level 8)

Concerto in G Major

This concerto is written as an introduction to the Classical style. The elements of scales, broken chords, and solid harmony are utilized simply, without elaboration, and are suited for small hands.

(Two pianos, Schroeder & Gunther)

1. (♩ = 96)

The composer gives no tempo marking for this movement, only a metronome marking. The style of Haydn and Mozart is captured in the charming cantabile themes and brilliant passagework. An extended measured trill is written out for the performer. Exchanges of melody, countermelody, and accompaniment figures in both pianos create a lively two-piano work that features frequent fluctuation of mode from major to parallel minor. The cadenza begins in A minor and works its way back to G major. (G major, level 6)

2. *Adagio* (♩ = 52)

A concise movement, the *Adagio* features chordal textures and descant lines doubled at the octave. Careful fingering choices are necessary, for the left hand in particular. The harmonic progressions are not always as expected. (G minor, level 6)

3. *Allegro vivace* (♪ = 86)

This galloping rondo has a recurring harmonic progression. Use of double 3rds is appropriate to capture the Classical style. A modulation to B major fits the hands naturally. Fingerings must be considered throughout to achieve the legato articulations indicated by the composer. (G major, level 6)

Fourth Piano Concerto in C Major

(Two pianos, Associated Music Publishers, Hal Leonard)

1. *Adagio—Alla marcia* (♩ = 120)

This movement features dramatic intention and attitude, particularly as the key shifts to C minor in the up-tempo *Alla marcia* section. The attractive cadenza sounds more difficult than it is to play. Effective integration of wide-ranging technical patterns includes frequent octaves and four-note chord shapes in this appealing piece. (C major, level 8)

2. *Scherzo* (♩. = 84)

The *Scherzo* is a galloping romp in ABA form with highly repetitive figurations. Leaps in the A section cover a wide range of the keyboard, and octaves in both hands are required in the B section. (A minor, level 7)

3. *Andante maestoso* (♩ = 80)

This substantial but accessible work is appropriate for an early advanced performer with developed technique.

Meter changes following the cadenza drive the excitement to the end. It is a great piece to practice choreography of motion. (C minor, level 9)

YOUNG, Percy M. (1912–2004) England

Fugal Concerto in G Minor (1951)

(Piano and string orchestra, two piano reduction, Hinrichsen, Peters Edition)

A three-movement work, this concerto derives its chief interest from the effective and sometimes amusing dialogue between the solo instrument and the orchestra. Melodic variety abounds, and players will enjoy the combination of rhythmic vitality, contrapuntal ingenuity, and contemporary harmonic adventure.

Allegro molto (♩ = 176)

The solo character is bold and daring with octave passages and strong rhythmic motives, yet it also provides harmonic color and foundation when the orchestra takes the lead. Quick passages and four-note chord textures are present throughout the movement. (G minor, level 10)

Adagio (♩ = 56)

Beginning with a haunting opening with a modal flavor, the *Adagio* uses expressive chromaticism that avoids the comfort of a tonal center while subtle meter changes keep the rhythmic pulse ungrounded. The B section of the ABA form arrives in D-flat major with Romantic gestures and intent. The return of the A section features a varied orchestral accompaniment and a simple texture. Effective interplay between the solo and orchestra is found throughout. The ending segues *attacca* to the final movement. (D minor, level 9)

Vivace (♩ = 132)

This jaunty rondo movement is a wonderful showpiece for the facile performer. Technical challenges abound, including a wide variety of articulations and frequent thematic motives in both hands that require secure hand independence. Fingerings are not provided in the score but will be imperative for the execution of some tricky passages. The finale showcases an engaging fugue between the solo and the orchestra. (G minor, level 10)

ZACH, Jan (1699–1773) Bohemia

Concerto in C Minor

The *Concerto in C Minor* was one of the few pieces published during the composer's lifetime. Each movement provides a concise venture into the popular styles of that period.

(Harpsichord and string orchestra, full score, Nagels Verlag Kassel, Bärenreiter)

1. Allegro spiritoso [♩ = ca. 116]

This attractive movement reflects the transition from the Baroque style to the emergence of Classical ideals. Sequential patterns fit smaller hands well. (C minor, level 8)

2. Andante [♪ = ca. 70]

This movement features an exotic theme with unexpected harmonic inflections and turns of phrase, probably originating from Czech folk music. A simple but expressive second theme provides contrast. Motives recur throughout. (G minor, level 8)

3. Tempo di Minuetto [♩. = ca. 72]

A showcase piece for technical dexterity, this movement has a strong rhythmic character. Written in concerto grosso form, the piece is highly connected to Baroque style. Some elements of the texture indicate that the piece was intended for a two-manual harpsichord. (C minor, level 9)

ZWILICH, Ellen Taaffe (b. 1939) USA

Written for Carnegie Hall's family concert series by Pulitzer Prize-winning composer Ellen Zwilich, these six short musical portraits are inspired by Charles Schulz's beloved *Peanuts* characters. The piano is used sparingly, often for color, but is a notable feature. Despite the varying difficulty of each piece, hand size is an important consideration, with octaves occuring in every movement. The orchestral reduction for piano is substantially more difficult than the solo part. Orchestral score and parts are available for rent.

Peanuts® Gallery for Piano and Orchestra

(Piano and orchestra, two piano reduction, Theodore Presser)

1. *Schroeder's Beethoven Fantasy* (♩ = ca. 112)

Motives from Beethoven's *Hammerklavier Sonata* and *Ninth Symphony* are combined to create the perfect tribute to the piano-loving Schroeder. Large chords and octaves are the primary technical difficulties, although musical challenges center around capturing the essence of Beethoven's style. (B-flat major, level 8)

2. *Lullaby for Linus* (♩ = ca. 88)

A lullaby represents Linus with his security blanket. The dream-like mood is established by constantly shifting the pulse within $\frac{3}{4}$. The piano plays bell-like motives in the high register with right-hand octaves, while the accompaniment creates a gorgeous undercurrent. (A major, level 4)

3. *Snoopy Does the Samba* (♩ = ca. 114–120)

Zwilich chose the samba to represent Snoopy because "it is both 'hot' and 'cool,' sophisticated and 'a lot of fun.'" The Brazilian flavor is captured through a featured drum part, infectious syncopated rhythms, and soaring violin lines. Pianistic challenges include white-key glissandos, rapid octaves, and capturing the rhythmic feel. (E major, level 8)

4. *Charlie Brown's Lament* (♪ = ca. 104)

According to Zwilich, "This lament is an acknowledgment of times when we want to say 'good grief.'" The piano is featured in the middle section. The work is plaintive but optimistic. (G major, level 6)

5. *Lucy Freaks Out* (♩ = 104)

The "sweet and innocent" opening suddenly turns dark and Hitchcockian with a driving, ominous ostinato in the strings. Rhythmic punctuations in the bass are picked up by the solo piano, which lead to a crash and an extended silence. A short return to the opening mood gives way to a reprise of the "fast and furious" section. The solo piano has a minimal role in this movement. (D major, level 5)

6. *Peppermint Patty & Marcie Lead the Parade—Jaunty* (♩ = 132)

A musical procession of the characters is led by Marcie and Peppermint Patty, with each character arriving in order: Schroeder, Linus, Snoopy, and Charlie Brown (who is abruptly silenced by Lucy). The opening $\frac{2}{4}$ march alternates with $\frac{3}{4}$ (in a $\frac{6}{8}$ feel) to create an off-kilter yet infectious groove. Percussive moments in the accompaniment require a creative touch, much like the opening of Ravel's *Concerto in G Major*. The engaging two-piano work is a fine selection for a rhythmic and energetic player. (B-flat major, level 9)

APPENDIX A
Composers by Historical Period

Baroque (1600–1750)

Arne, Thomas Augustine
Bach, Johann Sebastian
Chilcot, Thomas
Corrette, Michel
Nichelmann, Christoph
Platti, Giovanni Benedetto
Sammartini, Giuseppe
Seixas, Carlos de
Stanley, John
Wagenseil, Georg Christoph
Werner, Gregor Joseph
Zach, Jan

Classical (1750–1825)

Abel, Carl Friedrich
Bach, Carl Philipp Emanuel
Bach, Johann Christian
Bach, Wilhelm Friedemann
Beethoven, Ludwig van
Burgess Jr., Henry
Cambini, Giuseppe Maria
Clementi, Muzio
Dussek, Jan Ladislav
Eberl, Anton
Felici, Alessandro
Galuppi, Baldassare
Graun, Johann Gottlieb
Haydn, Franz Joseph
Hertel, Johann Wilhelm
Hoffmeister, Franz Anton
Hook, James
Hummel, Johann Nepomuk
Kirnberger, Johann Philipp
Koželuch, Leopold
Kuhlau, Friedrich
Linek, Jiří Ignác
Martini, Giovanni Battista
Mayr, Johann Simon
Mozart, Wolfgang Amadeus
Mysliveček, Josef
Paisiello, Giovanni
Pfeiffer, Johann Michael
Puccini, Domenico Vincenzo Maria
Rutini, Giovanni Marco
Salieri, Antonio
Schaffrath, Christoph
Schobert, Johann
Schroeter, Johann Samuel
Stamitz, Johann
Steffan, Joseph Anton

Sterkel, Johann Franz Xaver
Turrini, Ferdinando
Vanhal, Johann Baptist
Vogler, Georg Joseph
Wesley, Charles

Romantic (1825–1900)

Hiller, Ferdinand von
Saint-Saëns, Camille

20th Century/Contemporary (1900–)

Alexander, Dennis
Anderson, Garland
Anderson, Leroy
Anson, George
Asch, Anna
Avery, Stanley
Bauer, Marion Eugénie
Beard, Katherine
Bennett, Richard Rodney
Berkovich, Isaak
Bernstein, Seymour
Blacher, Boris
Bober, Melody
Boutry, Roger
Boykin, Helen
Bozza, Eugène
Bush, Geoffrey
Cannon, Philip
Carré, John F.
Davis, Peter
Diamond, David
Eckstein, Maxwell
Edwards, Matthew
Erdmann, Dietrich
Faith, Richard
Farjeon, Harry
Françaix, Jean
Frank, Marcel G.
Goolkasian Rahbee, Dianne
Gregor, Čestmír
Halloran, Stephen
Hattori, Koh-Ichi
Jacob, Gordon
Jirko, Ivan
Jung, Helge
Kabalevsky, Dmitry
Kasschau, Howard
Kassern, Tadeusz Zygfryd
Kimes, Kenneth Francis

Kraehenbuehl, David
Lancen, Serge
Lantier, Pierre
Larsson, Lars-Erik
Manen, Christian
Margola, Franco
Meunier, Gérard
Mier, Martha
Milford, Robin
Miller, Beatrice A.
Nelhybel, Vaclav
Niemann, Walter
Noona, Walter and Carol
Olson, Lynn Freeman
Olson, Kevin R.
Pasquet, Jean Emerson
Pehkonen, Elis
Peskanov, Alexander
Pitfield, Thomas Baron
Polunin, Yuri
Raphling, Sam
Riley, Dennis
Rocherolle, Eugénie R.
Rollin, Catherine
Rosco, B. J.
Rossi, Wynn-Anne
Rowley, Alec
Rozin, Albert
Rybicki, Feliks
Rzayev, Azer Guseinovich
Savino, Domenico
Seuel-Holst, Marie
Shevtsova, Tanya
Shostakovich, Dmitri
Silvanski, Nikolai
Sugár, Rezső
Thomas, Richard Pearson
Thompson, John
Tsytovich, Vladimir
Vandall, Robert D.
Verhaalen, Marion
Wagner, Joseph Frederick
Walter, Fried
Waxman, Donald
Wheeler, Gayneyl
Wigham, Margaret
Williams, Jean
Young, Percy M.
Zwilich, Ellen Taaffe

APPENDIX B
Concertos by Level

Level 1

Bober, Melody, *Concertino in Dance Styles*, mvt. 1
Françaix, Jean, *Concertino for Piano and Orchestra in G Major, mvt. 2*
Manen, Christian, *Concertino*, mvt. 1
Noona, Walter and Carol, *Little Concertino in C Major*, all mvts.
Seuel-Holst, Marie, *In Elfland*, Op. 26, mvt. 2
Verhaalen, Marion, *Concertino*, mvt. 2

Level 2

Anson, George, *Kid Koncerto*, all mvts.
Anson, George, *Miniature Concerto in C Major*, all mvts.
Bober, Melody, *Concertino in Dance Styles*, mvts. 2 & 3
Bozza, Eugène, *Sicilienne et Rondo*, mvt. 1
Haydn, Franz Joseph, *Concertino in C Major (Divertimento)*, Hob. XIV:3, mvt. 2
Manen, Christian, *Concertino*, mvt. 2
Mier, Martha, *Concertino in Jazz Styles*, mvts. 1 & 3
Noona, Walter and Carol, *Concertino in D Minor*, all mvts.
Olson, Lynn Freeman, *Celebration! A Youth Concerto*, mvt. 2
Rosco, B. J., *Miniature Concerto*, mvt. 2
Rossi, Wynn-Anne, *Concerto in Latin Styles*, all mvts.
Rozin, Albert, *Little Concerto*, all mvts.
Seuel-Holst, Marie, *In Elfland*, Op. 26, mvts. 2 & 3
Thompson, John, *Concertina (Little Concerto)*
Vandall, Robert, *Concertino in C Major*, mvt. 2

Level 3

Avery, Stanley, *Concertino on Familiar Tunes for Young Players in F Major*, mvts. 2 & 3
Boutry, Roger, *Berceuse & Rondo, Pour Piano et Orchestre in A Minor*, mvt. 1
Françaix, Jean, *Concertino for Piano and Orchestra in G Major*, mvt. 3
Haydn, Franz Joseph, *Concertino in C Major (Divertimento)*, Hob. XIV:3, mvts. 1 & 3
Kraehenbuehl, David, *Rhapsody in Rock: A Concerto in One Movement for Piano*, section 1
Meunier, Gérard, *Concertino "Charlotte,"* all mvts.
Mier, Martha, *Concertino in Jazz Styles*, mvt. 2
Olson, Lynn Freeman, *Celebration! A Youth Concerto*, mvts. 1 & 3
Peskanov, Alexander, *Concerto No. 3, "Maryland Concerto,"* all mvts.
Peskanov, Alexander, *Concerto No. 4*, mvts. 1 & 2
Peskanov, Alexander, *Concerto No. 6, "Royal Concerto,"* all mvts.
Peskanov, Alexander, *Concerto No. 9, "Boston Concerto,"* mvt. 1
Peskanov, Alexander, *Concerto No. 10, "Italian Concerto,"* all mvts.
Pfeiffer, Johann Michael, *Concerto in G Major*, mvt. 2
Thompson, John, *Concerto Americana*, all mvts.

Vandall, Robert, *Concertino in C Major*, mvts. 1 & 3
Verhaalen, Marion, *Concertino*, mvts. 1 & 3

Level 4

Alexander, Dennis, *Imperial Concertante*, mvts. 2 & 3
Anderson, Garland, *Concertino for Piano and Orchestra in F Major*, mvt. 2
Asch, Anna, *Concertino No. 2*
Asch, Anna, *Concertino No. 9, Dana's Delight*
Avery, Stanley, *Concertino on Familiar Tunes for Young Players in F Major*, mvt. 1
Berkovich, Isaak, *Piano Concerto*, Op. 44, mvts. 2 & 3
Boutry, Roger, *Berceuse & Rondo, Pour Piano et Orchestre in A Minor*, mvt. 2
Boykin, Helen, *Concerto in F Major*, mvt. 2
Bozza, Eugène, *Sicilienne et Rondo*, mvt. 2
Edwards, Matthew, *Concerto for Young Pianists*, mvts. 1 & 2
Goolkasian Rahbee, Dianne, *Concertino No. 2, Op. 113, for Piano, Strings, and Percussion*, mvt. 2
Haydn, Franz Joseph, *Concerto in C Major, Hob. XIV:4*, mvts. 2 & 3
Kassern, Tadeusz Zygfryd, *Teenage Concerto*, mvt. 2
Lantier, Pierre, *Concertinetto*
Noona, Walter and Carol, *A First Concerto in D Minor*, all mvts.
Peskanov, Alexander, *Concerto No. 4*, mvt. 3
Peskanov, Alexander, *Concerto No. 9, "Boston Concerto,"* mvts. 2 & 3
Peskanov, Alexander, *Concerto No. 12, "Gypsy Concerto,"* mvt. 2
Pfeiffer, Johann Michael, *Concerto in G Major*, mvt. 3
Rollin, Catherine, *Concerto in C Major*, mvt. 2
Rosco, B. J., *Miniature Concerto*, mvts. 1 & 3
Silvanski, Nikolai, *Petit Piano Concerto*, mvt. 2
Stanley, John, *Concerto in D Major, Op. 2, No. 1*, mvt. 1
Tsytovich, Vladimir, *Piano Concerto*, mvt. 1
Wagenseil, Georg Christoph, *Concerto in G Major, WV 53*, mvt. 3
Zwilich, Ellen Taafe, *Peanuts® Gallery for Piano and Orchestra*, mvt. 2

Level 5

Alexander, Dennis, *Imperial Concertante*, mvt. 1
Anderson, Garland, *Concertino for Piano and Orchestra in F Major*, mvts. 1 & 3
Asch, Anna, *Concertino No. 3*
Asch, *Concertino No. 6, Aquila Variations*
Beard, Katherine, *Concerto in D Minor*
Bennett, Richard Rodney, *Party Piece for Young Players*
Berkovich, Isaak, *Piano Concerto*, Op. 44, mvt. 1
Boykin, Helen, *Concerto in F Major*, mvts. 1 & 3
Burgess Jr., Henry, *Concerto No. V in G Minor*, mvt. 2
Bush, Geoffrey, *A Little Concerto on Themes by Thomas Arne in D Minor*, mvt. 3
Carré, John F., *Concertino in C Major*, mvt. 1

Corrette, Michel, *Concerto in D Minor, Op. 26, No. 6,* mvt. 2

Edwards, Matthew, *Concerto for Young Pianists,* mvt. 3

Edwards, Matthew, *Piano Concerto No. 2 in G Major,* mvts. 1 & 2

Faith, Richard, *Concerto for Two Pianos,* mvts. 1 & 2

Frank, Marcel G., *Piano Concerto in E-Flat Major,* "Youth Concerto," mvt. 2

Goolkasian Rahbee, Dianne, *Concertino No. 2, Op. 113, for Piano, Strings, and Percussion,* mvt. 3

Goolkasian Rahbee, Dianne, *Concertino No. 3, Op. 145*

Haydn, Franz Joseph, *Concerto in C Major, Hob. XIV:4,* mvt. 1

Haydn, Franz Joseph, *Concerto in F Major, Hob. XVIII:7,* all mvts.

Haydn, Franz Joseph, *Concerto in F Major, Hob. XVIII:F1,* mvt. 2

Kasschau, Howard, *Country Concerto for Young Pianists in C Major,* all mvts.

Kassern, Tadeusz Zygfryd, *Teenage Concerto,* mvt. 1

Kraehenbuehl, David, *Rhapsody in Rock: A Concerto in One Movement for Piano,* section 3

Martini, Giovanni, *Concerto in D Major,* mvt. 2

Mier, Martha, *Concerto in Classical Style,* mvts. 2 & 3

Mysliveček, Josef, *Concerto No. 2 in F Major,* mvt. 3

Peskanov, Alexander, *Concerto No. 1 for Piano and Strings,* all mvts.

Peskanov, Alexander, *Concerto No. 8, "Spring Concerto,"* all mvts.

Peskanov, Alexander, *Concert Fantasy,* mvt. 2

Pfeiffer, Johann Michael, *Concerto in G Major,* mvt. 1

Rollin, Catherine, *Concerto in C Major,* mvts. 1 & 3

Rowley, Alec, *Miniature Concerto,* mvt. 2

Sammartini, Giuseppi, *Concerto in A Major, Op. 9, No. 1,* mvt. 1

Silvanski, Nikolai, *Petit Piano Concerto,* mvts. 1 & 3

Stanley, John, *Concerto in D Major, Op. 2, No. 1,* mvt. 2

Stanley, John, *Concerto in A Minor/A Major, Op. 2, No. 5,* mvt. 3

Vandall, Robert, *Concerto in G Major,* all mvts.

Vanhal, Johann Baptist, *Piano Concerto in C Major,* all mvts.

Wagenseil, Georg Christoph, *Concerto in G Major, WV 53,* mvt. 1

Wagner, Joseph Frederick, *Concertino in G Minor,* mvt. 2

Zwilich, Ellen Taafe, *Peanuts® Gallery for Piano and Orchestra,* mvt. 5

Level 6

Alexander, Dennis, *Concertino in D Major*

Arne, Thomas Augustine, *Concerto No. 4 in B-flat Major,* mvts. 1 & 2

Asch, *Concertino No. 4*

Asch, *Concertino No. 6, Aquila Variations*

Bach, Carl Philipp Emanuel, *Keyboard Concerto in E-flat Major, Wq. 43, No. 3 (H. 473),* mvt. 2

Bach, Carl Philipp Emanuel, *Keyboard Concerto in C Minor, Wq. 43, No. 4 (H. 474),* mvt. 2

Carré, John F., *Concertino in C Major,* mvts. 2 & 3

Corrette, Michel, *Concerto in A Major, Op. 26, No. 2,* mvt. 2

Corrette, Michel, *Concerto in D Minor, Op. 26, No. 6,* mvt. 1

Davis, Peter, *Spring Fantasy: A Youth Concerto*

Eckstein, Maxwell, *Concerto for Young Americans in C Major,* mvt. 3

Edwards, Matthew, *Piano Concerto No. 2 in G Major,* mvt. 3

Felici, Alessandro, *Concerto per Cimbalo in F Major,* mvts. 2 & 3

Frank, Marcel G., *Piano Concerto in E-Flat Major, "Youth Concerto,"* mvt. 3

Goolkasian Rahbee, Dianne, *Concertino No. 1, "Peasant Folk Dance," Op. 82*

Graun, Johann Gottlieb, *Cembalo Concerto in C Minor,* mvt. 2

Hattori, Koh-Ichi, *Concertino for Small Hands,* mvt. 2

Hook, James, *Keyboard Concerto, Op. 20, No. 2 in C Major,* mvt. 2

Kasschau, Howard, *Concerto Americana, for Piano Solo and Band and Singing/Humming Audience in C Major,* mvt. 1

Kasschau, Howard, *Concerto in C Major,* all mvts.

Kimes, Kenneth Francis, *Rainbow Concerto,* mvts. 1 & 2

Martini, Giovanni Battista, *Concerto in C Major,* mvts. 2 & 4

Martini, Giovanni Battista, *Concerto in F Major,* mvt. 2

Martini, Giovanni Battista, *Concerto in D Major,* mvt. 3

Mier, Martha, *Concerto in Classical Style,* mvt. 1

Miller, Beatrice, *Concerto No. 1 in A Minor,* mvts. 1 & 2

Paisiello, Giovanni, *Concerto No. 5 in D Major,* mvt. 2

Peskanov, Alexander, *Concerto No. 2, "Ukrainian Concerto,"* mvts. 1 & 2

Peskanov, Alexander, *Concert Fantasy,* mvts. 1 & 3

Raphling, Sam, *Concerto No. 1,* mvt. 2

Rollin, Catherine, *Concerto Romantique,* mvt. 2

Sammartini, Giuseppe, *Concerto in A major, Op. 9, No. 1,* mvt. 3

Schaffrath, Christoph, *Concerto in B-flat Major,* mvt. 1

Stanley, John, *Concerto in D Major, Op. 2, No. 1,* mvts. 4 & 5

Stanley, John, *Concerto in B Minor, Op. 2, No. 2,* mvts. 1 & 2

Stanley, John, *Concerto in D Minor, Op. 2, No. 4,* mvt. 3

Stanley, John, *Concerto in A Minor/A Major, Op. 2, No. 5,* mvts. 1 & 5

Sugár, Resző, *Rondo*

Vanhal, Johann Baptist, *Keyboard Concerto in F Major,* all mvts.

Wagenseil, Georg Christoph, *Concerto in B Major, WV 335,* mvt. 3

Wagner, Joseph Frederick, *Concertino in G Minor,* mvts. 1 & 3

Werner, Gregor Joseph, *Concerto in B-flat Major,* mvts. 2 & 3

Williams, Jean, *Concerto in G Major,* all mvts.

Zwilich, Ellen Taafe, *Peanuts® Gallery for Piano and Orchestra,* mvt. 4

Level 7

Abel, Carl Friedrich, *Concerto in F Major, Op. 11, No. 1,* all mvts.

Abel, Carl Friedrich, *Concerto in B-flat Major, Op. 11, No. 2,* all mvts.

Alexander, Dennis, *Concertante in G Major*, mvt. 2

Arne, Thomas, *Concerto No. 4 in B-flat Major*, mvt. 3

Asch, Anna, *Concertino No. 1*

Asch, Anna, *Concertino No. 5, "Festive March"*

Asch, Anna, *Concertino No. 11*

Bach, Carl Philipp Emanuel, *Keyboard Concerto in D Minor, Wq. 23 (H. 427)*, mvt. 2

Bach, Carl Philipp Emanuel, *Keyboard Concerto in C Minor, Wq. 43, No. 4 (H. 474)*, mvt. 1

Bach, Carl Philipp Emanuel, *Keyboard Concerto in G Major, Wq. 43, No. 5 (H. 475)*, mvt. 2

Bauer, Marion Eugénie, *American Youth Concerto in G Minor*, mvt. 2

Bernstein, Seymour, *Concerto ("For Our Time")*, mvt. 2

Bush, Geoffrey, *A Little Concerto on Themes by Thomas Arne in D Minor*, mvts. 1 & 2

Cannon, Philip, *Concertino for Piano and Strings*, mvt. 2

Chilcot, Thomas, *Keyboard Concerto in A Major, Op. 2, No. 2*, mvts. 2 & 3

Corrette, Michel, *Concerto in A Major, Op. 26, No. 2*, mvts. 1 & 3

Corrette, Michel, *Concerto in D Minor, Op. 26, No. 6*, mvt. 3

Erdmann, Dietrich, *Concertino for Piano and Chamber Orchestra*, mvt. 3

Faith, Richard, *Concerto for Two Pianos*, mvt. 3

Felici, Alessandro, *Concerto per Cimbalo in F Major*, mvt. 1

Frank, Marcel G., *Piano Concerto in E-Flat Major, "Youth Concerto,"* mvt. 1

Graun, Johann Gottlieb, *Cembalo Concerto in C Minor*, mvts. 1 & 3

Halloran, Stephen, *Piano Concertino*

Hattori, Koh-Ichi, *Concertino for Small Hands*, mvts. 1 & 3

Haydn, Franz Joseph, *Concerto in G Major, Hob. XVIII:4*, mvt. 2

Hertel, Johann Wilhelm, *Keyboard Concerto in E-Flat Major*, mvt. 2

Hertel, Johann Wilhelm, *Keyboard Concerto in F Minor*, mvt. 2

Hook, James, *Keyboard Concerto, Op. 20, No. 2 in C Major*, mvt. 3

Hummel, Johann Nepomuk, *Concertino for Piano and Orchestra, Op. 73, in G Major*, mvt. 2

Jung, Helge, *Konzert für Klavier und Kammerorchester, Op. 11 in F*, mvts. 1 & 2

Kassern, Tadeusz Zygfryd, *Teenage Concerto*, mvt. 3

Kimes, Kenneth Francis, *Rainbow Concerto*, mvt. 3

Kirnberger, Johann Philipp, *Concerto in C Minor*, mvt. 2

Kraehenbuehl, David, *Rhapsody in Rock: A Concerto in One Movement for Piano*, sections 2 & 4

Kraehenbuehl, David, *Marches Concertantes: A Short Piano Concerto for Young People*, all mvts.

Martini, Giovanni Battista, *Concerto in F Major*, mvts. 3 & 4

Martini, Giovanni Battista, *Concerto in D Major*, mvt. 1

Mayr, Johann Simon, *Concerto No. 1 in C Major*, mvt. 2

Miller, Beatrice, *Concerto No. 1 in A Minor*, mvt. 3

Mozart, Wolfgang Amadeus, *Concerto in B-flat Major, K. 39*, mvt. 2

Mozart, Wolfgang Amadeus, *Concerto in D Major, K. 107, No. 1*, mvt. 3

Mysliveček, Josef, *Concerto No. 2 in F Major*, mvts. 1 & 2

Nelhybel, Vaclav, *Passacaglia*

Paisiello, Giovanni, *Concerto No. 2 in F Major*, mvts. 1 & 2

Paisiello, Giovanni, *Concerto No. 5 in D Major*, mvt. 3

Peskanov, Alexander, *Concerto No. 2, "Ukrainian Concerto,"* mvt. 3

Peskanov, Alexander, *Concerto No. 5*, mvts. 2 & 3

Peskanov, Alexander, *Concerto No. 12, "Gypsy Concerto,"* mvt. 1

Platti, Giovanni Benedetto, *Concerto in A Major*, mvt. 2

Raphling, Sam, *Concerto No. 1*, mvts. 1 & 3

Riley, Dennis, *Concertino for Piano and Orchestra*, mvt. 1

Rollin, Catherine, *Concerto Romantique*, mvts. 1 & 3

Rowley, Alec, *Miniature Concerto*, mvts. 1 & 3

Rutini, Giovanni Marco, *Concerto in D Major*, mvts. 1 & 3

Sammartini, Giuseppe, *Concerto in A Major, Op. 9, No. 1*, mvt. 4

Schaffrath, Christopher, *Concerto in B-flat Major*, mvts. 2 & 3

Schroeter, Johann Samuel, *Keyboard Concerto in F Major, Op. 3, No. 1*, mvt. 2

Schroeter, Johann Samuel, *Keyboard Concerto in B-flat Major, Op. 3, No. 2*, all mvts.

Schroeter, Johann Samuel, *Keyboard Concerto in C Major, Op. 3, No. 3*, mvts. 1 & 2

Schroeter, Johann Samuel, *Keyboard Concerto in D Major, Op. 3, No. 4*, mvt. 3

Schroeter, Johann Samuel, *Keyboard Concerto in G Major, Op. 3, No. 5*, all mvts.

Schroeter, Johann Samuel, *Keyboard Concerto in E-flat Major, Op. 3, No. 6*, mvt. 2

Seixas, Carlos de, *Concerto in A Major*, mvt. 2

Stanley, John, *Concerto in B Minor, Op. 2, No. 2*, mvt. 5

Stanley, John, *Concerto in G Major, Op. 2, No. 3*, mvt. 1

Stanley, John, *Concerto in B-flat Major, Op. 2, No. 6*, mvt. 1

Sterkel, Johann Franz Xaver, *First Concerto (Concertino) in C Major, Op. 20*, mvt. 1

Thompson, John, *Concerto in D Minor*, mvt. 2

Tsytovich, Vladimir, *Piano Concerto*, mvt. 2

Turrini, Ferdinando, *Concerto in G Minor*, all mvts.

Vogler, Georg Joseph, *Concerto in C Major*, mvt. 2

Wagenseil, Georg Christoph, *Concerto in G Major, WV 53*, mvt. 2

Wagenseil, Georg Christoph, *Concerto in B Major, WV 335*, mvt. 2

Wesley, Charles, *Concerto No. 4 in C Major, Op. 2*, mvt. 2

Wheeler, Gayneyl, *Concerto for Piano and Orchestra*, all mvts.

Wigham, Margaret, *Concerto for Two Pianos*, all mvts.

Williams, Jean, *Concerto in F Major*, mvt. 2

Williams, Jean, *Fourth Piano Concerto in C Major*, mvt. 2

Level 8

Abel, Carl Friedrich, *Concerto in E-flat Major, Op. 11, No. 3*, mvt. 2

Abel, Carl Friedrich, *Concerto in D Major, Op. 11, No. 4*, all mvts.

Abel, Carl Friedrich, *Concerto in G Major, Op. 11, No. 5*, mvt. 2

Abel, Carl Friedrich, *Concerto in C Major, Op. 11, No. 6*, all mvts.

Alexander, Dennis, *Concertante in G Major*, mvt. 1

Asch, Anna, *Concertino No. 7, "Taratina"*

Asch, Anna, *Concertino No. 8, "Jubilation!"*

Asch, Anna, *Concertino No. 10*

Asch, Anna, *Concertino No. 12*

Bach, Carl Philipp Emanuel, *Keyboard Concerto in F Major, Wq. 43, No. 1 (H. 471)*, mvt. 2

Bach, Carl Philipp Emanuel, *Keyboard Concerto in E-flat Major, Wq. 43, No. 3 (H. 473)*, mvt. 1

Bach, Carl Philipp Emanuel, *Keyboard Concerto in C Major, Wq. 43, No. 6 (H. 476)*, mvt. 2

Bach, Johann Christian, *Keyboard Concerto in D Major, Op. 7, No. 3*, mvt. 2

Bach, Johann Christian, *Keyboard Concerto in D Major, Op. 13, No. 2*, mvt. 3

Bach, Johann Sebastian, *Keyboard Concerto No. 5 in F Minor, BWV 1056*, mvt. 2

Bach, Wilhelm Friedemann, *Keyboard Concerto in D Major, F. 41*, mvt. 2

Bauer, Marion Eugénie, *American Youth Concerto in G Minor*, mvts. 1 & 3

Bernstein, Seymour, *Concerto ("For Our Time")*, mvt. 1

Burgess Jr., Henry, *Concerto No. V in G Minor*, mvts. 1 & 3

Bush, Geoffrey, *A Little Concerto on Themes by Thomas Arne in D Minor*, mvt. 4

Cannon, Philip, *Concertino for Piano and Strings*, mvts. 1 & 3

Erdmann, Dietrich, *Concertino for Piano and Chamber Orchestra*, mvts. 1 & 2

Françaix, Jean, *Concertino for Piano and Orchestra in G Major*, mvts. 1 & 4

Haydn, Franz Joseph, *Concerto in F Major, Kleines Konzert, Hob. XVIII:3*, mvts. 1 & 2

Haydn, Franz Joseph, *Concerto in G Major, Hob. XVIII:4*, mvt. 1

Haydn, Franz Joseph, *Concerto in G Major, Hob. XVIII:9*, mvt. 3

Haydn, Franz Joseph, *Concerto in F Major, Hob. XVIII:F1*, mvts. 1 & 3

Hertel, Johann Wilhelm, *Keyboard Concerto in F Minor*, mvt. 3

Hoffmeister, Franz Anton, *Concerto in D Major, Op. 24*, mvt. 2

Hook, James, *Keyboard Concerto, Op. 20, No. 2 in C Major*, mvt. 1

Hummel, Johann Nepomuk, *Concertino for Piano and Orchestra, Op. 73, in G Major*, mvt. 3

Jung, Helge, *Konzert für Klavier und Kammerorchester, Op. 11 in F*, mvt. 3

Kabalevsky, Dmitry, *Piano Concerto No. 3 ("Youth"), Op. 50, in D Major*, mvt. 2

Kabalevsky, Dmitry, *Piano Concerto No. 4 ("Prague"), Op. 99, in C Minor*, mvt. 2

Kasschau, Howard, *Concerto Americana, for Piano Solo and Band and Singing/Humming Audience in C Major*, mvts. 2 & 3

Kasschau, Howard, *The Legend of Sleepy Hollow (A Program Concerto)*, mvt. 1

Linek, Jiří Ignác, *Concerto in F Major*, mvts. 2 & 3

Martini, Giovanni, *Concerto in C Major*, mvts. 1 & 3

Martini, Giovanni, *Concerto in F Major*, mvt. 1

Mozart, Wolfgang Amadeus, *Concerto in F Major, K. 37*, mvts. 1 & 2

Mozart, Wolfgang Amadeus, *Concerto in D Major, K. 107, No. 1*, mvts. 1 & 2

Mozart, Wolfgang Amadeus, *Concerto in G Major, K. 107, No. 2*, mvts. 1 & 2

Mozart, Wolfgang Amadeus, *Concerto in E-flat Major, K. 107, No. 3*, mvt. 2

Mozart, Wolfgang Amadeus, *Concerto in D Major, K. 175*, mvt. 2

Olson, Kevin R., *Concerto Bravo*, all mvts.

Paisiello, Giovanni, *Concerto No. 2 in F Major*, mvt. 3

Paisiello, Giovanni, *Concerto No. 5 in D Major*, mvt. 1

Pasquet, Jean Emerson, *Concertino in G Minor*

Peskanov, Alexander, *Concerto No. 5*, mvt. 1

Peskanov, Alexander, *Concerto No. 12, "Gypsy Concerto,"* mvt. 3

Pitfield, Thomas Baron, *Concerto No. 2, "The Student,"* mvts. 1 & 2

Platti, Giovanni Benedetto, *Concerto in F Major*, mvt. 1

Polunin, Yuri, *Concertino in A Minor*

Rocherolle, Eugénie, *Blues Concerto*

Rosco, B. J., *Youth Concerto, "A Festival"*

Rowley, Alec, *Concerto in D Major, Op. 49*, mvt. 2

Rutini, Giovanni Marco, *Concerto in D Major*, mvt. 2

Rybicki, Feliks, *Concerto for Small Hands, Op. 53*, mvt. 3

Rzayev, Azer Guseinovich, *Piano Concertino*, mvt. 2

Salieri, Antonio, *Concerto in B-flat Major*, mvts. 2 & 3

Salieri, Antonio, *Concerto in C Major*, mvt. 2

Schobert, Johann, *Concerto No. 2 in E-Flat Major, Op. 12*, mvts. 2 & 3

Schroeter, Johann Samuel, *Keyboard Concerto in F Major, Op. 3, No. 1*, mvt. 1

Schroeter, Johann Samuel, *Keyboard Concerto in C Major, Op. 3, No. 3*, mvt. 3

Schroeter, Johann Samuel, *Keyboard Concerto in D Major, Op. 3, No. 4*, mvts. 1 & 2

Schroeter, Johann Samuel, *Keyboard Concerto in E-flat Major, Op. 3, No. 6*, mvts. 1 & 3

Seixas, Carlos de, *Concerto in A Major*, mvts. 1 & 3

Shevtsova, Tanya, *Concerto-Variations, Op. 3*

Stamitz, Johann, *Concerto in D Major, Op. 10, No. 1*, mvts. 2 & 3

Stanley, John, *Concerto in D Major, Op. 2, No. 1*, mvt. 3

Stanley, John, *Concerto in B Minor, Op. 2, No. 2*, mvt. 3

Stanley, John, *Concerto in D Minor, Op. 2, No. 4*, mvts. 1, 2 & 4

Stanley, John, *Concerto in A Minor/A Major, Op. 2, No. 5*, mvt. 4

Stanley, John, *Concerto in B-flat Major, Op. 2, No. 6*, mvts. 3 & 4

Sterkel, Johann Francis Xaver, *First Concerto (Concertino) in C Major, Op. 20*, mvts. 2 & 3

Thompson, John, *Concerto in D Minor*, mvts. 1 & 3

Vogler, Georg Joseph, *Concerto in C Major*, mvts. 1 & 3

Wagenseil, Georg Christoph, *Concerto per Pianoforte*, mvt. 1

Wagenseil, Georg Christoph, *Concerto in D Major, WV 278*, mvts. 1 & 3

Walter, Fried, *Concertino*, mvts. 1 & 2

Waxman, Donald, *Variations on "Ah, Vous Dirai-je Maman"*

Werner, Gregor Joseph, *Concerto in B-flat Major*, mvt. 1

Williams, Jean, *Concerto in A Minor*, all mvts.

Williams, Jean, *Concerto in F Major*, mvts. 1 & 3

Williams, Jean, *Fourth Piano Concerto in C Major*, mvt. 1

Zach, Jan, *Concerto in C Minor*, mvts. 1 & 2

Zwilich, Ellen Taaffe, *Peanuts® Gallery for Piano and Orchestra*, mvts. 1 & 3

Level 9

Abel, Carl Friedrich, *Concerto in E-flat Major, Op. 11, No. 3*, mvt. 1

Abel, Carl Friedrich, *Concerto in G Major, Op. 11, No. 5*, mvt. 1

Alexander, Dennis, *Concertante in G Major*, mvt. 3

Anderson, Leroy, *Concerto in C Major*, mvt. 2

Bach, Carl Philipp Emanuel, *Keyboard Concerto in D Minor, Wq. 23 (H. 427)*, mvt. 1

Bach, Carl Philipp Emanuel, *Keyboard Concerto in D Major, Wq. 27 (H. 433)*, all mvts.

Bach, Carl Philipp Emanuel, *Keyboard Concerto in F Major, Wq. 43, No. 1 (H. 471)*, mvt. 1

Bach, Carl Philipp Emanuel, *Keyboard Concerto in D Major, Wq. 43, No. 2 (H. 472)*, mvt. 3

Bach, Carl Philipp Emanuel, *Keyboard Concerto in C Minor, Wq. 43, No. 4 (H. 474)*, mvt. 3

Bach, Carl Philipp Emanuel, *Keyboard Concerto in C Major, Wq. 43, No. 6 (H. 476)*, mvts. 1 & 3

Bach, Johann Christian, *Keyboard Concerto in D Major, Op. 7, No. 3*, mvt. 1

Bach, Johann Christian, *Keyboard Concerto in E-flat Major, Op. 7, No. 5*, mvt. 2

Bach, Johann Christian, *Keyboard Concerto in B-flat Major, Op. 13, No. 4*, mvts. 1 & 2

Bach, Johann Sebastian, *Keyboard Concerto No. 4 in A Major, BWV 1055*, mvt. 2

Bach, Johann Sebastian, *Keyboard Concerto No. 7 in G Minor, BWV 1058*, mvt. 2

Bach, Wilhelm Friedemann, *Keyboard Concerto in D Major, F. 41*, mvt. 3

Bernstein, Seymour, *Concerto ("For Our Time")*, mvt. 3

Blacher, Boris, *Piano Concerto No. 1, Op. 28 in A Minor*, mvt. 2

Cambini, Giuseppe Maria, *Concerto in B-flat Major, Op. 15, No. 1*, mvt. 1

Cambini, Giuseppe Maria, *Concerto in G Major, Op. 15, No. 3*, mvt. 1

Chilcot, Thomas, *Keyboard Concerto in A Major, Op. 2, No. 2*, mvt. 1

Chilcot, Thomas, *Keyboard Concerto in F Major, Op. 2, No. 5*, mvt. 3

Clementi, Muzio, *Piano Concerto in C Major*, mvt. 2

Eberl, Anton, *Concerto for Piano and Orchestra in E-flat Major, Op. 40*, mvts. 2 & 3

Eckstein, Maxwell, *Concerto for Young Americans in C Major*, mvts. 1 & 2

Françaix, Jean, *Concerto for Piano and Orchestra, Op. 19, in D Major*, mvt. 2

Galuppi, Baldassare, *Concerto in F for Harpsichord and Strings*, mvts. 1 & 3

Goolkasian Rahbee, Dianne, *Concertino No. 2, Op. 113, for Piano, Strings, and Percussion*, mvt. 1

Gregor, Cestmir, *Concerto Semplice*, mvt. 2

Haydn, Franz Joseph, *Concerto in F Major, Kleines Konzert, Hob. XVIII:3*, mvt. 3

Haydn, Franz Joseph, *Concerto in G Major, Hob. XVIII:9*, mvts. 1 & 2

Haydn, Franz Joseph, *Concerto in D Major, Hob. XVIII:11*, mvt. 2

Hertel, Johann Wilhelm, *Keyboard Concerto in E-flat Major*, mvts. 1 & 3

Hertel, Johann Wilhelm, *Keyboard Concerto in F Minor*, mvt. 1

Hoffmeister, Franz Anton, *Concerto in D Major, Op. 24*, mvts. 1 & 3

Hummel, Johann Nepomuk, *Concertino for Piano and Orchestra, Op. 73, in G Major*, mvt. 1

Jacob, Gordon, *Concertino for Pianoforte and String Orchestra in D*, all mvts.

Jirko, Ivan, *Piano Concerto No. 3 in G Major*, mvt. 2

Kabalevsky, Dmitry, *Piano Concerto No. 3 ("Youth"), Op. 50, in D Major*, mvts. 1 & 3

Kirnberger, Johann Philipp, *Concerto in C Minor*, mvt. 1

Koželuch, Leopold, *Concerto in D Major, Op. 25*, mvt. 1

Lancen, Serge, *Concertino*, mvts. 1 & 2

Linek, Jiří Ignác, *Concerto in F Major*, mvt. 1

Martini, Giovanni, *Concerto in G Major*, all mvts.

Mayr, Johann Simon, *Concerto No. 1 in C Major*, mvts. 1 & 3

Mayr, Johann Simon, *Concerto No. 2 in C Major*, mvt. 1 & 3

Mozart, Wolfgang Amadeus, *Concerto in F Major, K. 37*, mvt. 3

Mozart, Wolfgang Amadeus, *Concerto in B-flat Major, K. 39*, mvts. 1 & 3

Mozart, Wolfgang Amadeus, *Concerto in D Major, K. 40*, all mvts.

Mozart, Wolfgang Amadeus, *Concerto in G Major, K. 41*, mvt. 2

Mozart, Wolfgang Amadeus, *Concerto in E-flat Major, K. 107, No. 3*, mvt. 1

Mozart, Wolfgang Amadeus, *Concerto in B-flat Major, K. 238*, mvts. 2 & 3

Mozart, Wolfgang Amadeus, *Concerto in C Major, K. 246*, all mvts.

Mozart, Wolfgang Amadeus, *Concerto in F Major, K. 413*, all mvts.

Mozart, Wolfgang Amadeus, *Concerto in A Major, K. 414*, mvts. 2 & 3

Mozart, Wolfgang Amadeus, *Concerto in C Major, K. 415*, mvt. 2

Mozart, Wolfgang Amadeus, *Concerto in E-flat Major, K. 449*, mvts. 1 & 2

Mozart, Wolfgang Amadeus, *Concerto in D Major, K. 451*, mvt. 2

Mozart, Wolfgang Amadeus, *Concerto in B-flat Major, K. 456*, mvts. 1 & 2

Mozart, Wolfgang Amadeus, *Concerto in F Major, K. 459*, mvts. 1 & 2

Mozart, Wolfgang Amadeus, *Concerto in C Major, K. 467*, mvts. 2 & 3

Nichelmann, Christoph, *Concerto in A Major*, mvts. 1 & 2

Nichelmann, Christoph, *Concerto in E Major*, mvt. 2

Niemann, Walter, *Piano Concerto No. 1 in C Major, Op. 153*, mvts. 1 & 3

Paisiello, Giovanni, *Concerto No. 1 in C Major*, mvt. 3

Peskanov, Alexander, *Concerto No. 7, "Anniversary Concerto,"* all mvts.

Pitfield, Thomas Baron, *Concerto No. 2, "The Student,"* mvt. 3

Platti, Giovanni Benedetto, *Concerto in A Major*, mvts. 1 & 3

Platti, Giovanni Benedetto, *Concerto in F Major*, mvts. 2 & 3

Platti, Giovanni Benedetto, *Concerto in C Minor*, all mvts.

Puccini, Domenico Vincenzo Maria, *Concerto in B-flat Major*, mvts. 2 & 3

Riley, Dennis, *Concertino for Piano and Orchestra*, mvt. 2

Rybicki, Feliks, *Concerto for Small Hands, Op. 53*, mvts. 1 & 2

Salieri, Antonio, *Concerto in B-flat Major*, mvt. 1

Salieri, Antonio, *Concerto in C Major*, mvts. 1 & 3

Sammartini, Giuseppe, *Concerto in A Major, Op. 9*, No. 1, mvt. 2

Schobert, Johann, *Concerto No. 2 in E-Flat Major, Op. 12*, mvt. 1

Schobert, Johann, *Concerto No. 3 in G Major, Op. 13*, mvts. 1 & 3

Shostakovich, Dmitri, *Concerto in F Major, Op. 102*, mvt. 2

Stamitz, Johann, *Concerto in D Major, Op. 10, No. 1*, mvt. 1

Stanley, John, *Concerto in B Minor, Op. 2, No. 2*, mvt. 4

Stanley, John, *Concerto in G Major, Op. 2, No. 3*, mvt. 3

Stanley, John, *Concerto in A Minor/A Major, Op. 2, No. 5*, mvt. 2

Stanley, John, *Concerto in B-flat Major, Op. 2, No. 6*, mvt. 2

Steffan, Joseph Anton, *Piano Concerto in B-flat Major*, all mvts.

Wagenseil, Georg Christoph, *Concerto per Pianoforte*, mvts. 2 & 3

Wagenseil, Georg Christoph, *Concerto in D Major, WV 278*, mvt. 2

Wagenseil, Georg Christoph, *Concerto in B Major, WV 335*, mvt. 1

Walter, Fried, *Concertino*, mvt. 3

Wesley, Charles, *Concerto No. 4 in C Major, Op. 2*, mvts. 1 & 3

Williams, Jean, *Fourth Piano Concerto in C Major*, mvt. 3

Young, Percy, *Fugal Concerto in G Minor (1951)*, mvt. 2

Zach, Jan, *Concerto in C Minor*, mvt. 3

Zwilich, Ellen Taaffe, *Peanuts® Gallery for Piano and Orchestra*, mvt. 6

Level 10

Bach, Carl Philipp Emanuel, *Keyboard Concerto in D Major, Wq. 43, No. 2 (H. 472)*, mvt. 2

Bach, Carl Philipp Emanuel, *Keyboard Concerto in G Major, Wq. 43, No. 5 (H. 475)*, mvt. 3

Bach, Johann Christian, *Keyboard Concerto in E-flat Major, Op. 7, No. 5*, mvt. 1

Bach, Johann Christian, *Keyboard Concerto in D Major, Op. 13, No. 2*, mvts. 1 & 2

Bach, Johann Sebastian, *Keyboard Concerto No. 2 in E Major, BWV 1053*, mvt. 2

Bach, Johann Sebastian, *Keyboard Concerto No. 4 in A Major, BWV 1055*, mvts. 1 & 3

Bach, Johann Sebastian, *Keyboard Concerto No. 5 in F Minor, BWV 1056*, mvt. 1

Bach, Wilhelm Friedemann, *Keyboard Concerto in D Major, F. 41*, mvt. 1

Beethoven, Ludwig van, *Concerto in E-flat Major, WoO 4*, mvt. 2

Beethoven, Ludwig van, *Rondo in B-flat Major, WoO 6*

Beethoven, Ludwig van, *Piano Concerto No. 2 in B-flat Major, Op. 19*, mvt. 2

Cambini, Giuseppe Maria, *Concerto in B-flat Major, Op. 15, No. 1*, mvt. 2

Cambini, Giuseppe Maria, *Concerto in G Major, Op. 15, No. 3*, mvt. 2

Chilcot, Thomas, *Keyboard Concerto in F Major, Op. 2, No. 5*, mvts. 1 & 2

Clementi, Muzio, *Piano Concerto in C Major*, mvt. 1

Diamond, David, *Concertino for Piano and Small Orchestra*, mvt. 1

Dussek, Johann Ladislav, *Concerto for Piano and Orchestra, Op. 49, in G Minor*, mvt. 2

Farjeon, Harry, *Phantasy Concerto for Piano and Chamber Orchestra, Op. 64*

Galuppi, Baldassare, *Concerto in F for Harpsichord and Strings*, mvt. 2

Goolkasian Rahbee, Dianne, *Urartu Rhapsodie, Op. 80, for Piano and Orchestra*

Gregor, Čestmír, *Concerto Semplice*, mvt. 1

Haydn, Franz Joseph, *Concerto in G Major, Hob. XVIII:4*, mvt. 3

Haydn, Franz Joseph, *Concerto in D Major, Hob. XVIII:11*, mvt. 1

Hiller, Ferdinand, *Concerto in F-sharp Minor, Op. 69*, mvt. 2

Jacob, Gordon, *Concerto for Piano and Orchestra*, mvt. 2

Jirko, Ivan, *Piano Concerto No. 3 in G Major*, mvts. 1 & 3

Kabalevsky, Dmitry, *Rhapsody on a Theme of the Song "School Years," Op. 75, in G Minor*

Kabalevsky, Dmitry, *Piano Concerto No. 4 ("Prague"), Op. 99, in C Minor*, mvt. 1

Kasschau, Howard, *Candlelight Concerto in F Major*

Kasschau, *The Legend of Sleepy Hollow (A Program Concerto)*, mvt. 2

Kirnberger, Johann Philipp, *Concerto in C Minor*, mvt. 3

Koželuch, Leopold, *Concerto in D Major, Op. 25,* mvts. 2 & 3

Kuhlau, Friedrich, *Piano Concerto in C Major, Op. 7,* all mvts.

Lancen, Serge, *Concertino,* mvt. 3

Larsson, Lars-Erik, *Concertino, Op. 45, No. 12,* all mvts.

Margola, Franco, *Kinderkonzert,* all mvts.

Margola, Franco, *Terzo Concerto,* all mvts.

Mayr, Johann Simon, *Concerto No. 2 in C Major,* mvt. 2

Milford, Robin, *Fishing by Moonlight, Op. 96*

Mozart, Wolfgang Amadeus, *Concerto in G Major, K. 41,* mvts. 1 & 3

Mozart, Wolfgang Amadeus, *Concerto in D Major, K. 175,* mvts. 1 & 3

Mozart, Wolfgang Amadeus, *Concerto in B-flat Major, K. 238,* mvt. 1

Mozart, Wolfgang Amadeus, *Concert Rondo in D Major, K. 382*

Mozart, Wolfgang Amadeus, *Concert Rondo in A Major, K. 386*

Mozart, Wolfgang Amadeus, *Concerto in A Major, K. 414,* mvt. 1

Mozart, Wolfgang Amadeus, *Concerto in C Major, K. 415,* mvt. 1

Mozart, Wolfgang Amadeus, *Concerto in E-flat Major, K. 449,* mvt. 3

Mozart, Wolfgang Amadeus, *Concerto in D Major, K. 451,* mvt. 3

Mozart, Wolfgang Amadeus, *Concerto in B-flat Major, K. 456,* mvt. 3

Mozart, Wolfgang Amadeus, *Concerto in F Major, K. 459,* mvt. 3

Nelhybel, Vaclav, *Cantus et Ludus*

Nichelmann, Christoph, *Concerto in A Major,* mvt. 3

Nichelmann, Christoph, *Concerto in E Major,* mvts. 1 & 3

Niemann, Walter, *Piano Concerto No. 1 in C Major, Op. 153,* mvt. 2

Paisiello, Giovanni, *Concerto No. 1 in C Major,* mvts. 1 & 2

Pehkonen, Elis, *Concerti with Orchestra*

Peskanov, Alexander, *Concerto No. 13, "Azery Rhapsody,"* all mvts.

Puccini, Domenico Vincenzo Maria, *Concerto in B-flat Major,* mvt. 1

Rowley, Alec, *Concerto in D Major, Op. 49,* mvts. 1 & 3

Rzayev, Azer Guseinovich, *Piano Concertino,* mvts. 1 & 3

Saint-Saëns, Camille, *Caprice-Valse, Op. 76, "Wedding Cake"*

Saint-Saëns, Camille, *Africa, Fantaisie pour piano et orchestre, Op. 89*

Savino, Domenico, *Cuban Concerto*

Schobert, Johann, *Concerto No. 4 in C Major, Op. 15,* all mvts.

Shostakovich, Dmitri, *Concertino, Op. 94*

Shostakovich, Dmitri, *Concerto No. 2 in F Major, Op. 102,* mvt. 1

Stanley, John, *Concerto in G Major, Op. 2, No. 3,* mvts. 2 & 4

Thomas, Richard Pearson, *Concerto in "C-E-G,"* mvts. 1 & 2

Young, Percy, *Fugal Concerto in G Minor (1951),* mvts. 1 & 3

Level 10+

Bach, Carl Philipp Emanuel, *Keyboard Concerto in D Minor, Wq. 23 (H. 427),* mvt. 3

Bach, Carl Philipp Emanuel, *Keyboard Concerto in F Major, Wq. 43, No. 1 (H. 471),* mvt. 3

Bach, Carl Philipp Emanuel, *Keyboard Concerto in D Major, Wq. 43, No. 2 (H. 472),* mvt. 1

Bach, Carl Philipp Emanuel, *Keyboard Concerto in E-flat Major, Wq. 43, No. 3 (H. 473),* mvt. 3

Bach, Carl Philipp Emanuel, *Keyboard Concerto in G Major, Wq. 43, No. 5 (H. 475),* mvt. 1

Bach, Johann Christian, *Keyboard Concerto in E-flat Major, Op. 7, No. 5,* mvt. 3

Bach, Johann Christian, *Keyboard Concerto in B-flat Major, Op. 13, No. 4,* mvt. 3

Bach, Johann Sebastian, *Keyboard Concerto No. 2 in E Major, BWV 1053,* mvts. 1 & 3

Bach, Johann Sebastian, *Keyboard Concerto No. 5 in F Minor, BWV 1056,* mvt. 3

Bach, Johann Sebastian, *Keyboard Concerto No. 7 in G Minor, BWV 1058,* mvts. 1 & 3

Beethoven, Ludwig van, *Concerto in E-flat Major, WoO 4,* mvts. 1 & 3

Beethoven, Ludwig van, *Piano Concerto No. 2 in B-flat Major, Op. 19,* mvts. 1 & 3

Blacher, Boris, *Piano Concerto No. 1, Op. 28, in A Minor,* mvts. 1 & 3

Clementi, Muzio, *Piano Concerto in C Major,* mvt. 3

Diamond, David, *Concertino for Piano and Small Orchestra,* mvt. 2

Dussek, Johann Ladislav, *Concerto for Piano and Orchestra, Op. 49 in G Minor,* mvts. 1 & 3

Eberl, Anton, *Concerto for Piano and Orchestra in E-flat Major, Op. 40,* mvt. 1

Gregor, Čestmír, *Concerto Semplice,* mvt. 3

Haydn, Franz Joseph, *Concerto in D Major, Hob. XVIII:11,* mvt. 3

Hiller, Ferdinand von, *Concerto in F-sharp Minor, Op. 69,* mvts. 1 & 3

Jacob, Gordon, *Concerto for Piano and Orchestra,* mvts. 1 & 3

Kabalevsky, Dmitry, *Piano Concerto No. 4 ("Prague"), Op. 99, in C Minor,* mvt. 3

Kasschau, Howard, *The Legend of Sleepy Hollow (A Program Concerto),* mvt. 3

Mozart, Wolfgang Amadeus, *Concerto in C Major, K. 415,* mvt. 3

Mozart, Wolfgang Amadeus, *Concerto in D Major, K. 451,* mvt. 1

Mozart, Wolfgang Amadeus, *Concerto in C Major, K. 467,* mvt. 1

Schobert, Johann, *Concerto in G Major, Op. 13,* mvt. 2

Shostakovich, Dmitri, *Concerto No. 2 in F Major, Op. 102,* mvt. 3

Thomas, Richard Pearson, *Concerto in "C-E-G,"* mvt. 3

INDEX